MILLENNIAL DREAMS IN ACTION

# MILLENNIAL DREAMS
# IN ACTION

*Studies in Revolutionary Religious Movements*

EDITED BY

SYLVIA L. THRUPP

SCHOCKEN BOOKS · NEW YORK

First SCHOCKEN edition 1970

Library of Congress Catalog Card No. 70–107614

*Published by arrangement with the Society for the Comparative Study of Society and History*

Manufactured in the United States of America

# PREFACE

This volume is the outcome of a conference held at the University of Chicago on April 8th and 9th, 1960, under the auspices of the Editorial Committee of the quarterly review, *Comparative Studies in Society and History*. Some of the papers were made available in draft form beforehand but since have been revised; others were not written until after the conference. It follows that all who participated in the discussions have helped to shape the book. Acknowledgments are therefore due to the following, who are not named in the table of contents: H. G. Barnett, Cyril Belshaw, Reinhard Bendix, Edward A. Kracke, Jr., John L. Phelan, J. R. Strayer, and Ernest Tuveson. Special thanks are due also to four members of the Editorial Board of the review who served as chairmen at the conference sessions: G. E. von Grunebaum, M. J. Herskovits, Everett C. Hughes, and Eric R. Wolf.

SYLVIA L. THRUPP
Editor

# CONTENTS

8                **CONTENTS**

# I

# INTRODUCTION

# MILLENNIAL DREAMS IN ACTION:
## A REPORT ON THE CONFERENCE DISCUSSION

### I. THE CONDITIONS OF VALID COMPARATIVE STUDY

The aim of the conference out of which this book has grown was to draw together certain findings of historical work and of recent work by anthropologists and sociologists, on religious movements that have been animated by the idea of a perfect age or a perfect land. The group included men who have worked in many areas of the world and many historical periods, but by no means in all. We dealt with only one country in Latin America and one in Africa. India, Japan, most of the Islamic world, and early modern Europe were passed over, and the resurgence of millennial movements in the 19th and 20th century urban industrial scene received all too slight attention. These limitations were imposed both because our time was limited and in order to keep our group small enough for informal exchange of ideas. Our plan was not so much to test existing generalizations about the nature of millennial movements, but rather to look for similarities among movements, and for differences between them, taking a wider range of cases than any single writer has yet examined carefully in this way. The purpose of this introductory chapter is to show how the various kinds of generalization that emerged in the course of our discussions are related to our evidence and also to modern thought about the general functioning, in a developmental sense, of society and culture.[1]

We found no need to coin new terms. It was necessary for our purpose only to draw some line of demarcation between millennial movements on the one hand and utopian movements and revolutionary socialism on the other. Norman Cohn's opening paper draws this line primarily in terms of the element of salvationism in the former.[2] The movements that his definition allows us to class together as millennial (or, to use the 17th century term that some of our contributors prefer, as millenarian), have frequently a political as well as a religious character. But their political character derives its strength largely if not wholly from millennial inspiration, and some idea of preparation for salvation is always present if not central.

[1] The editor alone is responsible for this report. For views of other members of the conference see Appendix.
[2] See below, p. 31.

To the purist, the millennium can properly refer only to the fixed period of 1000 years that is found in the Judaic-Christian tradition. In our perspective, however, the term may be applied figuratively to any conception of a perfect age to come, or of a perfect land to be made accessible. The picture will vary according as time is fitted into the scheme of the cosmos. The perfect age may come by an act of regeneration, time being bent back, as it were, to recapture some state of harmony in which the world began. It may have some of this quality of early freshness and yet come as time is running out. It will then last for a period that is fixed, variable, or indeterminate, and it may even form part of a cycle of ages.[3] Or it may be an age to last indefinitely, with no doom ahead.

Comparative study of movements of a millennial style has been for the most part either haphazard or else restricted to scenes in which tribal life has been disturbed by Western influence. Although the disturbance of tribal life does not necessarily produce them, the movements have not been reported at first hand in tribal culture except in circumstances of abnormal disturbance that create hardship or make the tribesmen feel deprived because members of the intruding society are better off.[4] In consequence there has been a tendency to interpret them as cultural devices for relieving the painfulness of social changes that degrade or seriously jeopardize the status of a group. Through ritual and the stimulus of new leadership the movement may "revitalize" the tribal culture. At the very least it will rally those who have been uprooted and dispersed into what is for them at first a social vacuum, giving them something to live for until the wider society may offer more satisfactory alternatives. In these interpretations religious thinking figures less importantly than ritual, and ritual is considered mainly as it enables people to work themselves up into states of excitement in which they can either assure themselves of a speedy solution of their problems or ignore them. The observer of the movements attends more to emotional states than to ideas, and these states of mind are held to reflect, more or less directly, a social situation. In short, the method tends to be reductionist.

The conference rejected reductionist interpretations on logical grounds, and because if one attempts comparison on a broader scale the development of ideas has to be taken into account as well as states of emotion. In any culture the thinking in which a millennial dream is embedded has a logic of its own that is not an automatic reflection of social situations. The variety and the development of ideas are a part of our problem.

For valid comparative study we need similar kinds of information about each case. It does not matter if writers differ in their interpretation. But if one movement is described only in terms of social tension, another only in terms of its ideas, and another through a blow by blow account of its conflicts

---

3  See Appendix, p. 218.
4  On theory relating to absolute and relative deprivation see Appendix, pp. 209-14.

with authority, we have nothing to compare. It was agreed that enquiry should ideally cover the nature and history of the ideas involved, the circumstances in which these excited action, the character of leadership and recruiting, and the career of the movement. If investigators would use a common question-naire elaborated along these lines, research would be more fruitful.

Yet because much of the evidence is elusive, even a common questionnaire would not guarantee complete comparability of findings. Field workers in the ex-colonial areas can seldom be sure whether the ideas at issue came first from Christian or Moslem sources, nor can they always untangle the role of indigenous myth from that of outside influence. They cannot identify the first stirring of a movement nor describe its surreptitious phases. One speaker declared that a number of African movements have flourished unobserved under the noses of anthropologists. We lack any figures as to turnover in the membership of movements, and biographical data that would reveal the rea-sons for loyalty or disloyalty to a leader are very scant.

Historians working solely from documentary sources have all these diffi-culties and more. The text of a prophet's orations cannot communicate the nuances that rest on the cadence of speech and on facial expression. When prophecies circulated in writing we do not know who read them nor how readers responded. Liturgical ritual may be well described in writing, but only first-hand observation can discover the part that other forms of ritual or cus-tom may have played in holding a group or a community together. As a check on his own personal impressions, the field worker may be able to question many of the members of a movement and to cross-examine other first-hand witnesses. The historian of a pre-20th century movement can do none of these things.

For these reasons there was at first some doubt as to the feasibility of our plan of comparing the results of field and historical studies. There is however no other way of taking account of the dimension of development. Besides, these two modes of research cannot in practice be separated, for documentary sources are usually indispensable for filling out the background of a contem-porary scene. There is no occasion for a generalized distrust of documents, for training and practice in their use alerts one to the probable directions of bias, deception, and carelessness in their composition. Most direct written evidence about a movement comes from advocates or from hostile witnesses, rarely from a wavering convert and almost never from a quite disinterested onlooker. In one respect the bias of the evidence is valuable, for it is certain to highlight the forms of thought and behavior that are novel or unwelcome to entrenched authority. The colonial official, the missionary, the medieval inquisitor, had special competence in administrative routine, in theology, and in law. They can hardly be trusted in their estimate of the character or mental balance of people of whom they disapproved, but on such neutral points as these people's organization, their occupations or previous social status, and the places from which they came, there is more reason to believe their testimony than to disbelieve it. The confessions of people on trial, however they were extracted, are also likely to be trustworthy on matters that were neither of credit to them nor discredit. As to the general environment from which the membership of a movement is drawn, documentary evidence may be as reliable, so far as it goes, as information gathered on the spot. If basic research in the social and economic conditions of the scene is well advanced, historical evidence may on the whole be fairly comparable with that of field observation.

As it happens, the most serious single deficiency in our knowledge of millennial movements relates to those types that have not produced very clearcut doctrines nor extremist leaders, that is, the movements whose members are content to await the consummation of their hopes quietly. This gap is not due to lack of evidence but rather to a failure to exploit it. The literature is heavily biased towards the more dramatic types of movement, those that alarm civil and religious authorities or openly clash with them.

Despite these handicaps, there are numerous cases in which our information is reasonably comparable. Turning to the cases before it, the conference found that they suggest several kinds of hypotheses or tentative generalizations. The first step, the simplest form of generalization, was to establish a pattern or patterns in the appearance and nature of movements within each culture under consideration. The elements of such patterning consist in the degree of continuity or change in the ideas at work and in the characteristic forms of organization, and in the clustering of movements in space or time. Other elements more difficult to discover lie in the relationships of movements to the structure of the wider society in which they appear.

A second stage of generalization follows, through comparison of the patterns established in different cultures. These may differ in the degree of change that indigenous ideologies undergo, in the relationship of the latter to orthodox religious tradition, and in the degree of syncretism that occurs. Against this ideological pattern one can then compare the social pattern of the movements. Are they invariably an expression of "underdog" unrest? What relation do they bear to other forms of social protest? Or do they provoke unrest independently of other causes? Do they appear continuously, or are there long periods of latency broken by sudden eruptions? Do they tend to cluster in periods of strain occasioned by changes in social structure and in traditional values? Are there similarities in the urban movements that emerge, in different cultures, at such times? In what way are such urban movements related to the spread of education? Perhaps all these questions could be summed up in one: is there a connection between the forms that millennialism takes, in any given circumstances, and the prevailing attitude to change, in that society at that time?

In contrast to the above historical line of generalization, a third line of enquiry sought for limited and precise generalization regarding special characteristics of movements. These are such aspects of their ideas, their ritual, and organization as can be abstracted from cultural tradition.

A necessary supplement to these three lines of enquiry is a fourth and more ambitious approach – that of puzzling over why millennial thought and agitation should occur at all. Inevitably one inclines towards one among several possible approaches to the formulation of general laws that might govern all cases. The conference favored explicit statement of all such preferences, but it made use of them primarily in indicating where further research, as well as further reflection, is needed.

## II. HISTORICAL PATTERNS

### 1. *Brazil*

On the basis of differences in ideology, in the role of leaders, and in social character, René Ribeiro distinguishes five different types of movement in Brazil. These fall into five separate traditions, with a kind of broken continuity between the first two, which are Indian, but only tenuous continuity between the last three, which are predominantly manifestations of "folk" Christianity, having no connection with the Indian traditions. All of the Indian migratory movements that are classed as millennial were inspired by ancient cosmic myth and were tribal in organization. Yet the need to revive both the myth and the organization by deliberate effort after tribal life had been disrupted by conquest and missions marks off the 16th century cases as different in type: the initial ritual rally for a journey in search of the perfect land had now an aspect of social protest, and the first stage of the journey was designed as escape from the Portuguese. One may say therefore that the second type develops out of the first through reaction, as Ribeiro puts it, against forced acculturation.

The millennial aspect of Christianity apparently excited no direct popular action until the early 18th century. It then gave rise to two traditions, both under rural prophets, appearing in widely separate backward areas, and hinging on migratory motifs. The first of these took the form of sporadic dramatization of the Portuguese Sebastian legend in a symbolic crusading march that, in the face of growing pressure for order in Brazilian society, invited clashes with civil authority. It died out within a century. The second rural tradition, which with many local idiosyncrasies represents essentially a resurgence of the hopes of early Christianity, is still at work. To say that it displays a clear pattern of development would be misleading, for the pattern is, rather, one of variation with the ability and the opportunities of prophets to organize. Nevertheless it displays three different stages. For the most part movements have not grown beyond what might be called stage 1. In this stage the prophet seems very much like a joint reincarnation of John the

Baptist and a village Francis of Assisi. He wanders about with a straggle of followers preaching apocalyptic revelations, is credited with miracles, and induces the penitent to build new churches. In a few cases stage 2 is achieved: the prophet leads a multiplied following to a remote centre among hills for the building of a holy "city" where the Second Coming may be awaited with perpetual prayer. But stage 3, the peaceable integration of a new holy city, a centre of millennial faith and tension, with the ordinary life of a populated region, has been reached only in one case, that of Father Cicero's city of Jõazeiro. By a combination of luck and political shrewdness Father Cicero was able to create a movement and a city that stood for mystic withdrawal in anticipation of the millennium, without ever leading a migration. His city was not founded but grew out of the following that he attracted to his village headquarters. Having great local power he was able to make stable political alliances that gave him a free hand. The leaders of migrating bands were never able to consolidate their position in this way. Living by gifts that were often stolen, and being suspected of politically subversive aims, they could keep no firm friends save among lawless frontier figures. In consequence their fate was to be dispersed or killed by government forces, to the last man, woman, and child.

The latest type of movement in Brazil, now spreading in the coastal industrial cities, is continuous with the rural movements in the sense that it brings personal religious help, through charismatic prophets, to people who have not found it elsewhere. Prophecy produces a following, if only an evanescent one, but there is no rupture with the ties of ordinary life, indeed, no sign of withdrawal. The use of printed propaganda however indicates the development of organized proselytization and of appeal to a more educated public.[5]

René Ribeiro did much to invigorate the conference discussion by his emphasis on the *normalcy* of millennial movements, not only in Brazil but wherever they form a tradition. To dismiss them as eccentricities or madness and to fall back on abnormal psychology to explain the behavior of their leaders or adherents simply betrays one's insensitivity to the range of motivations within the culture in question. Actions that may seem pathological from the standpoint of our own values or of our own scientific conception of the universe may be perfectly normal for someone whose values and social experience are derived from a different culture and who may receive his only coherent view of the universe through the medium of a millennial myth. As an anthropologist trained also in psychiatry Ribeiro spoke with persuasive authority on these points; moreover he was the only member of the conference to bring evidence from psychiatric examination of a group of millennial extrem-

---

[5]  George Shepperson writes: "There is an interesting mixture of the traditional Christian Apocalypse and flying saucer millennialism in the Brazilian Dino Kraspedon's *My Contact with Flying Saucers,* translated from the Portuguese by J. B. Wood (London, 1959)."

ists, evidence that shows them to have been ignorant and naive people but in sound mental health.

By the same reasoning it follows that our modern obsession with the themes of anxiety and insecurity should not be projected, without good supporting evidence, into the interpretation of millennial movements. A belief that the end of the world is imminent may cause excitement and call for certain decisive actions, without any spirit of anxiety. It follows also that we need not insist on finding special occasions of insecurity in the social situations in which the movements arise. Such occasions may exist, in a very harsh degree, as in the case of the Brazilian Indians exposed to forced acculturation. But the situations in which the other four types of Brazilian movement arose were no more anxiety-provoking than the general run of conditions in other areas where neither millennialism nor social protest movements occurred. Dr. Ribeiro's explanation of these other four types is a positive contribution to general explanatory theory, and will be considered later.

## 2. *Indonesia*

Historical background to our three 20th century Indonesian case studies was considered in respect of traditional Javanese cosmology, namely, in the light of the persistent strain of stasis-seeking, of emphasis on the need of harmony between man and the universe, that this displays, and of the age-long religious respect for even alien messiah-figures whose role would be to restore a lost harmony.[6] In this perspective it is not surprising that when the Dutch began to upset the balance of local life without offering any intelligible rationale for their policies they encountered some messiah-led resistance.[7] None of the detailed cases presented, however, was primarily a movement of rebellion. All were ritualistic movements looking for a new order through union with the ancestors, or at least, through the agency of the tribe's ancestor, for protection against evil. It is remarkable that the people of each locality, after the movements had subsided, are reported as participating in the money economy, which had at first perturbed them, with abandon. Justus van der Kroef sees the movements as an expression of inner crisis, of anxiety sharpening into desperation as the Dutch attempted to suppress cult practices through which the people had maintained a psychological dependence on the ancestors. He thus interprets the states of ecstasy sought by ritual means as a necessary relief. Van der Kroef does not, it should be noted, project the theme of anxiety into the scene in the unreflecting way that René Ribeiro criticizes. Instead, he deduces it from the Indonesian cultural tradition of regarding any change or event that has once been diagnosed as causing "loss of harmony" as a matter

[6]  See Justus M. van der Kroef, "Javanese Messianic Expectations: their Origin and Cultural Context," *Comparative Studies in Society and History*, I, 4 (1959), pp. 299-323.
[7]  See below, p. 114.

of dire urgency to be righted only by man righting his relations with the cosmic powers.

## 3. Melanesia

The next two papers set movements looking for a new order, a perfect age, through reunion with the ancestors, who in Melanesia are expected to arrive by boat with cargoes of gifts, in a different perspective. Jean Guiart, supplementing his own long experience in the field by critical study of mission reports going back to the 1830's, unites the history of native and Christian religion on these islands in a common frame of social analysis. Mircea Eliade unites them in the still broader perspective afforded by comparative study of ancient religious traditions. Guiart treats in some detail the unrest occasioned in the islands by the peculiarly avaricious traders who gave them their first taste of Western individualism. He describes also the mission policies which gave the islanders the impression that conversion to Christianity would automatically bring them the benefits of economic progress without other effort on their part. The problem is to explain why the pattern of development runs from initial hesitation in the face of both Catholic and Scottish Presbyterian modes of preaching, through waves of mass conversion, to a revival of indigenous religion in the form of the Cargo cults. Why should total acceptance turn into total rejection?

Both analyses explain the total acceptance as due fundamentally to affinity between the missionaries' millennial preaching and native beliefs. Both also explain the later rejections as due to growing disillusionment when conversion failed to bring the millennium. There are differences only in emphasis, Eliade stressing particularly the significance of disappointment over delay in the resurrection of the dead. Guiart's social and political analysis grapples further with the problem of why rejection has occurred only in some areas and not in others.

## 4. Nyasaland

From the wealth of African material only Nyasaland cases were selected. These, as George Shepperson wishes me to emphasize, are by no means necessarily typical; experience has varied from one part of Africa to another, and even in Nyasaland there are several serious gaps in our information that may yet be filled by further research.[8] One of these concerns the exact nature of the appeal that Christian teaching has had. What echoes did it strike in native traditions? There is a logic in African religious thinking, Shepperson insisted: we should try to understand it. Citing from the recently published edition of

[8]  George Shepperson writes: "There are several special factors in the growth of Nyasaland which make its millennial-style movements unrepresentative perhaps, of African millennialism as a whole."

David Livingstone's letters, he pointed to certain parallels between the reception of missionaries in Central Africa and in Melanesia. For example, Livingstone states that the Africans identified the coming of the missionary with the arrival of a cornucopia of material goods.[9] Again, Livingstone himself was credited with power to raise the dead.[10]

Historically, the establishment of the Scottish missions was followed by far-reaching disruption of tribal life through new economic pressures, which in turn prepared the way for the favorable reception of Fundamentalist Baptist missions. This in fact coincided with the first large-scale recruiting of migratory labor by the mines to the south. African millennialism then spreads in the form of the Watch Tower movement. The social character of local branches of this movement, in relation to the disturbance of tribal life, is however not yet fully worked out. Shepperson's paper traces in some detail the influence of American Negro apostles, and of African contact with the latter's training schools, in giving the African Watch Tower movement its fervent racialism. Discussion emphasized also how the spread of the American Negro Baptist view of the millennium as the age of the colored man coincides with the world-wide fall in the white man's prestige at the close of the Russo-Japanese war.

In introducing his paper, Shepperson raised two further points that are important for interpretation of the development of African millennialism. Both concern the primacy of Protestant influence. Is it not true, as has often been remarked, that millennial movements in dependent colonial areas have been engendered chiefly among peoples who have been in contact with Protestant rather than Catholic missionaries? The conference was not however inclined to give this generalization any weight. The significant variables in missionary influence, it was felt, are to be found not in the missionaries' allegiance to Protestantism or Catholicism, but in their modes of preaching and in general mission policies.[11] There was more interest in the second point, which is touched on also in the paper, namely, the seminal influence in Nyasaland of certain elements in the ideology of the Scottish missionaries there. David Livingstone, who came from the same area as the secular millenarian, Robert Owen, carried with him the philosophy of progress of classical Scottish social science.[12] As the saying goes, Scotsmen have always one foot in the future. The continuing influence of Scottish missionaries meant that conversion was not to a religion of personal salvation only but also to a doctrine of the inevitability of moral and social progress. To Shepperson it is highly significant that the Watch Tower movement was built on these foundations.

[9]  *David Livingstone. Family Letters,* ed. Isaac Schapera (London, 1959), II, p. 226.
[10]  *Ibid.,* I, p. 44; also F. S. Arnot, ed., *David Livingstone, Missionary Travels* (London, 1899), p. 437.
[11]  See Jean Guiart's remarks below, p. 127.
[12]  See George Shepperson, "David Livingstone the Scot," *Scottish Historical Review,* October 1960.

## 5. The Medieval West

The early Christian strain of millennialism that has enjoyed so exotic a revival in Brazil and Melanesia had faded out, in Europe, with the ancient world. In the Augustinian world view there was no logical place for it. The Church now represented the Kingdom of God on earth, and its eschatology served simply to sustain awareness of the spiritual purpose of life. Yet between the 11th and the 15th centuries at least three new kinds of millennialism appeared.

The first of these emerged in the early Palestinian Crusades, mainly in the people's expeditions. It is however clearly recognizable only in the symbolist interpretation that has been expounded by the French historian Alphandéry.[13] For example, the belief among the poor that they had a special role to play in the freeing of Palestine from the infidel is seen as symbolic of the role of the elect in the millennium. Norman Cohn follows Alphandéry in tracing such beliefs to "the obscure underworld of popular religion",[14] in which some surviving elements of older Christian millennialism had drawn new life from association with the sybylline prophetic tradition. Prophecy could cast a messianic aura about any figure – king, emperor, or self-appointed leader.

The second type of medieval movement took the form of urban sects appearing first in French and Italian cities in the 12th century and spreading to other urbanized areas. The teaching of the sects has a clear affinity with gnostic tradition, which had possibly survived in the West and was certainly reintroduced from the East in the 12th century. Gnostic influence tended to transmute or transform the millennium into the theme of man's perfectibility. In Joachim of Fiore's thought this theme in turn becomes one of historical development. To the sects the new Age of the Spirit was already arriving as their more zealous members learned to perfect themselves.[15]

A third type of movement may be distinguished as the ideas of these sects spilt over into both rural and urban situations that were breeding revolt. On a symbolist interpretation the Flagellants may be counted as constituting still a fourth type of movement, their violence being intended to assure them of salvation in the face of an anticipated world disaster.[16]

The conference discussion turned on conflicting interpretations of the social character of the sects. In both Norman Cohn's view and that of the Marxian medievalist Ernst Werner,[17] the formation of such movements is preceded by accumulating tension from social and economic causes. Cohn postulates also

[13]  Paul Alphandéry, La Chriétenté et l'idée de Croisade, 2 vols., (Albin Michel, 1959–1960), edited by Alphonse Dupront.

[14]  Norman Cohn, The Pursuit of the Millennium, 2nd. ed. (Harper Torchbooks, New York, 1961), pp. 14–15.

[15]  See Howard Kaminsky's account below, pp. 166-68.

[16]  See Cohn, op. cit., ch. VI.

[17]  See Ernst Werner, "Popular Ideologies in Late Medieval Europe: Taborite Chiliasm and Its Antecedents," Comparative Studies in Society and History, II, 3 (1960), pp. 344–65.

religious fear of universal disaster to come through the unworthiness of the Popes: in Max Weber's terminology, the latter had lost legitimacy. He believes further that a millennial movement takes form only as more or less psychopathic individuals sense that tension is near breaking-point and exploit the situation as leaders. For Werner, tension mounts through a groping perception of the realities of class struggle. The situation itself produces both the movement and the leader.[18]

Both of these views were challenged in respect of their common emphasis on growing social tension. How can one prove that this leads to the formation of a movement? Howard Kaminsky, raising this question, claimed that his own study of the Taborite movement yields evidence only of eschatological tension, that is, of moods of tension which were created by the movement. For him, the class position of adherents is irrelevant, for their behavior is shaped by the totally new relationships into which they enter in the movement.[19]

J. R. Strayer proposed a different approach by way of the actual occasions of anxiety, the prevailing attitudes to change, and the effects of the spread of education. In the towns of the 12th and 13th centuries the cares of prosperity, in the shape of the new responsibilities attendant on social mobility, are more in evidence than those of poverty. Later, as trade contracted and failed to recover, there were new insecurities, as well as new fear from plague. Spiritual anxieties, which one might say that Christianity is in some degree designed to arouse, were always present. All these and other cares may well have converged, as Ernest Tuveson suggested, in the form of heightened fear of death. But what bearing had any form of anxiety on the rise of the sects? This one can hardly tell without very full knowledge of other means of solace and other avenues of hope. Far more research is needed on medieval attitudes to change, in different walks of life and at different periods. In general there was so little conceptualization of historical trends that reception of Joachite ideas was governed probably by localized moods of optimism, pessimism, or desire for glory. In Florence, as Donald Weinstein's paper shows, the Joachite prophecies of an Angelic Pastor to come were welcomed out of civic patriotism and naive tendencies to self-glorification: the new leader was to give Florence her true place in the world.[20]

More is known about the spread of education, which was characteristically shallow in the extreme. The half-educated multiplied. It is in these circumstances that pseudo-intellectuals and pseudo-professionals flourish, acquiring

[18]   The standing argument against a Marxian interpretation of the medieval movements has been the mixed character of their membership. Werner feels this to be evidence only that the peasants' and workers' perception of the class struggle was imperfect. He shows incidentally that many members of the sects were far from totally committed, but drifted in and out again. *Ibid.*, p. 356.

[19]   See Appendix, p. 215.

[20]   See below, pp. 195-202.

status through competition with the orthodox. They thrive in part through inducting followers into the pleasure of debating half-understood ideas. In Italy this entered into the cult of novelty, a byword of the time, which had a strong aesthetic appeal. The habit of discussion may however often have grown serious enough, as Eric Voegelin feels, to lead many people to realize for the first time that Christianity is a difficult religion, and to turn in consequence to the sects as an easier alternative.[21]

## III. THE COMPARISON OF HISTORICAL PATTERNS

The purpose of tracing our theme historically through such dissimilar societies was to be able to compare its place in different cultural traditions. In all of these the idea of a perfect age has certain common aesthetic and magical overtones. It is an element in the aesthetic perception of the cosmos and it demands of the faithful some kind of ordeal that will magically make them worthy – a difficult journey, the building of a city in the hills, the carrying out of ritual and of ascetic purification, or the perpetration of vioience. However, except in Eliade's reconstruction of its role in primitive seasonal fertility rites the aesthetic and magical appeal are not institutionalized in regularly recurrent practices. In the historic societies the chief feature of millennial tradition is the irregularity of its call to action. To explain its power to incite action we have to look beyond the aspect of aesthetic appeal, to circumstances that are not present in the long periods when the tradition is latent or merely talked about.

The facts suggest that the perfect age was more or less consciously brought into action to serve a variety of social purposes. One of these was social protest, either through passive withdrawal or active revolt. But before one can assess the importance of millennial ideas in bringing social protest to a head one needs to know a great deal about non-millennial forms of protest and revolt. In China stasis-seeking philosophy parallel to that which Van der Kroef describes in Indonesia for centuries provided adequate justification for revolt by itself, without requiring any special ritual or messianic belief. Christian millennial thought had no influence before the Taiping movement of the 19th century.[22] Yet in Indonesia, whose culture was persistently eclectic, Hindu, Islamic and Christian messianic traditions were all adopted and served to strengthen justification for revolt. In the medieval West aggressiveness was so pervading that no specific doctrines were needed to trigger protest

---

[21]   Eric Voegelin, *The New Science of Politics* (University of Chicago Press, 1952), p. 123.

[22]   Eugene Boardman writes: "Christian millennial influence is notably excluded from all protest movements save the great Taiping Rebellion and entered there in a very impure form." He adds that to his knowledge there is no record in China of the kind of ritual Van der Kroef describes for Java (see note 6 above).

through violence. In the vast majority of the many hundreds of medieval peasant revolts and urban revolutions on record there is no evidence of any millennial influence.

As has been noted above in reference to Alphandéry's interpretation of the Palestinian Crusades, millennial ideas can serve also to mobilize aggression on the part of one society against another. Spanish and Portuguese colonial conquest in the Americas provides another example. The 20th century alliance between negro Baptist eschatology and African nationalism contributed also to attitudes of aggression.

Its association with aggression should not overshadow the peaceable uses of millennial faith in cooperative African villages and in the "Anglo-American international" of sectarians of which George Shepperson writes. In both of these the aesthetic aspect of the millennium appears to provide some harmonizing influence in the lives of people who do not withdraw from society and who may perhaps not protest against anything save war.

## IV. CROSS-CULTURAL COMPARISON OF SPECIAL ASPECTS OF MOVEMENTS

The special aspects of millennial movements that came up for discussion involving indiscriminate cross-cultural comparison were problems of organization and of ethos. Comparison of the different types of leadership that appear would in itself be a fascinating subject to investigate. We could do no more than block out a few of the questions that would arise in such an investigation. The leader who originally takes the initiative, it was felt, is usually a visionary who acquires more practically-minded lieutenants, or one *alter ego* in particular, who handles the daily problems of building a manageable organization. Even with this help, at a certain stage of success the movement tends to force the leader into a new role that may not be congenial to him. Various exigencies may account for a swing towards new goals not envisaged in the first vague program. In Melanesia the movements have swung in several different directions, some persistently myth-guided, some directed to expectation of the arrival of cargo as the sole end, some having additional political expectations, and some developing a village cooperative movement which may slough off the purely religious aspect of the millennial expectations. All may contrive to work for greater village autonomy. In the process great demands are made on the leader's gifts of combining compromise with maintenance of hopes. He must often be hard pressed to legitimize his position, in Max Weber's sense of the term, by providing his followers with some of the satisfactions for which they look.

There is evidence of a variety of ritual means of identifying the core of loyal followers. Whereas in the Brazilian movement of 1819 followers were admitted through a special confession, the Melanesian movements were in general opposed to any initiation rite. They did however stress the drinking of kava, a beverage the missionaries had banned.

Study of the organizational career is too often cut short in the better documented cases, by the suppressive action of civil and religious authorities. The leader may have shown great shrewdness and adaptability but suddenly have to rely on military lieutenants and, like Fra Dolcino, with failure become a martyr. Why is there so frequently a conflict with authority? One reason proposed was the fact that any such movement is likely to upset kinship roles. This alone might create problems in dealing with local authority and perturb higher authorities, even when no novel economic demands were at issue and no subversive political intents. If in addition the leader has cast himself in the role of a Messiah the vaguest political element in his teaching may bring uneasy authorities down on the movement. Thus prophecy inimical to the Republic made it inevitable that the Brazilian authorities, for fear of losing face, should persevere in wiping out the migrants of 1893. Again, acts of violence may be undertaken as a kind of ritual vindication of the role of the movement. The Picards committed murder and arson to prove that the catastrophes to attend the end of the world were at hand, and in so doing ensured their own speedy extinction. They had not meant to attack civil authority as such, but aimed only to coerce belief in the verity of their doctrines.

When one tries to understand the ethos of leader and followers the criterion of an otherworldly outlook or of reliance on supernatural intervention, which may at first sight seem a necessary condition for delimiting religious movements from miscellaneous political agitation, is of little or no use. To those who believe that a cargo is to arrive the event is a perfectly natural one. Those who believe in any kind of terrestrial millennium cannot really be classed as otherworldly in outlook.

The criterion of a peculiarity in the sense of time may seem more promising but it too is difficult to handle. To the intellectual who reasons that with the arrival of the millennium time will acquire a new property that might be classed as sacred, the matter may at first sight be simple. But what is the difference between the properties of time as it now passes and time as it will be then, in the new age, to the convinced believer? For most people, even in the modern West with its pride in historical consciousness, and for all who live in cultures that have not developed this, it is only memory that can give time any immediacy. Yet memory is treacherous and arbitrary. People find it difficult to believe in their own aging. They live in a kind of pragmatic present. Time is an actual dimension of the universe only to those who can give it body through an intellectual grasp of the succession of events in a given framework or an understanding of the processes that change society. To such people the concept of sacred time may have meaning as the replacement of event and of change by timeless experience of the act of worship.

To the extent that they are mystic, they can escape fleetingly from time into eternity through practices of worship and meditation.

To the non-intellectual, and the non-mystic, it is likely that neither time nor eternity are real enough to be contrasted, and different kinds of time would be inconceivable. But belief in a perfect age may affect the sense of time in one or both of two ways. One would be through a sense of effort, of tension. If the perfect age promises satisfaction of all wants it would stand for relaxation of effort. If the hope is vivid it would justify what many of the movements we have been considering demand of their members, a heightening of effort, a sense of tension. Something of this is present in any salvationist movement and it is evident in some degree in the modern Anglo-American millennialist international. Yet not all of its members find it possible to maintain much tension. Their sense of time may be affected in a second way, through imaginative perception of a condition of life different from life here and now. This would be an aesthetic perception much like that of a theatre-goer's perception of the world of Shakespeare's plays, for example, or of the world on any stage or screen. Popular historical novels owe their appeal to creating such a world. It is not really set in history as the historian views it but is a mere dramatic contrast with the pragmatic present in which the reader lives. To the believer in a millennial movement the perfect age to come has all the attractions of this dramatic contrast plus one tremendous appeal that the theatre, the screen and the novel cannot offer. One can believe in entering the perfect age, in one's own right, through adhering to the movement. The reader and the theatre-goer can enter their dramatic world only by the poor device of identifying themselves with another character. They enter in disguise, not in their own right. Nor does the dramatic world promise them relaxation of effort.

To evoke this kind of sense of time requires, as was stressed, great vision. The idea of the millennium has been one of humanity's great inventions. In a sense every prophet and leader of a movement has reinvented it, but he has leaned, in all our evidence, on a tradition that takes us back into an antiquity where we lose the trail.

## V.  FOUR TYPES OF EXPLANATION

Could an analytical scheme be devised in terms of which a single explanation would account at least for the appearance of all types of millennial movement, if not for their subsequent careers? Several members of the conference were insistent that we produce such a scheme. Yet to do so would have required the preparation beforehand of draft formulations, taking cognizance of our new empirical studies, and the latter were not completed in time for this plan to be feasible. As was indicated above there was strong resistance

to "reductionism", that is, to any assumption that either the ethos of a movement or the turn it gave to the development of myth or of formal reasoning
about the character of the perfect age was necessarily a direct reflection of a
social or political situation. It was felt that better communication has to be
established between those who work on the history of millennial thought and
those who work on the analysis of situations in which this thought has incited
action, before a truly satisfactory scheme of general explanation of millennial
movements can be devised. This improved communication is all the more to
be desired because of the ultimate bearing of millennialism on the evolution
of 20th century forms of socialism, communism, and post-colonial nationalism.

The explanation that was put forward most forcibly was cast in terms of
"deprivation" and can be variously interpreted. In its simplest form it is
exemplified by many cases of the disruption of tribal culture both in its economy and its system of status. This has undoubtedly occurred in the African
setting of movements, as the effect of administrative and economic policies,
and in some of the settings of the Cargo cults in Oceania. Absolute deprivation in the sense of a lowering of subsistence levels and of status would also
be present wherever the less privileged groups in a society increased in numbers without a proportionate increase in opportunities to filter off into new
land or new industries or otherwise find new kinds of opportunity to maintain
or improve their position. Marxian interpretations are one form of this general type of explanation. It has never yet dealt satisfactorily with the problem
that resort to millennialism is only one of many ways of reacting to deprivation. As with Freudian theory, its proponents have to base their case on faith
that if we had perfect information, all of the facts would fall consistently into
place as they wish.

A similar difficulty confronts another type of explanation that was cast in
terms of the universal human propensity to suffer from distress and anxiety,
regardless of objective causes. This theory has also some value as guidance
for research if one adds the qualification that there are many different reactions to distress and that the degree to which one hopes for solace is a factor
modifying the reaction. Presumably then a peculiar kind of tension or anxiety could be induced by the tradition of millennial thought itself, which creates
expectation of perfect solace. We are then thrown back for explanation on
pure historical contingency. We can generalize only as, within situations
where the hope of participating in the millennium can be detached from the
impersonal context of apocalyptic doctrines, certain kinds of circumstances
recur. Each set of circumstances may be unique but there may be certain
kinds of uniqueness. Objective deprivation may occur in some kinds of situation, and not in others.

Explanation based on the powerful aesthetic attraction that millennial
thought and imagery can exercise would have to distinguish between situa-

tions in which the millennial tradition coincides with the official view of the cosmos, as in early Indian Brazil, or is at variance with it. Again, the variance may or may not be suppcrted by dispositions to vary from orthodox norms of belief in other matters. The medieval sects arose in circles already predisposed to the pantheistic trend of gnostic thought which dialectic skill tried to banish from schools of theology. These circles then "accumulated" millennial imagery. This is a quite different situation from that of modern urban sects which have never accepted the scientific view of the cosmos but are not otherwise out of step with the general culture of their environment.

A fourth theory is implicit in the discussion of the medieval evidence as reported above. Although applied there only to an urban scene with a high degree of professionalization it might be equally relevant to any society with specialized roles of religious and intellectual leadership. The social structure is seen, not as necessarily causing deprivation by blocking the entry of any particular groups to new opportunity and reward, but as chronically embodying tension between the formally authorized leaders and a set of rivals. Tension of this kind may always accompany the spread of education and in any but a totalitarian society may be tolerated as reconciling people to authority through a rivalry that is regarded as harmless. This view found some favor as applying to modern urban millennial sects.

The conference closed with these four possible ways of synthesis in mind, and differing combinations of them, as guides to research. Although we did not deal directly with the problem that most of all arouses contemporary interest in the millennial dream – its relation to action leading into totalitarian society, we felt that the lines of enquiry explored were relevant also to this. Finally, in all aspects of our subject we were deeply conscious that the most plausible of conclusions are no more than tentative until there is better understanding of the negative cases, the situations and the cultures in which one might expect millennial excitement to appear but where it did not appear. Comparative study is from this point of view initially not so much a short cut to final conclusions as a means of communication among people who work and think in different fields, hedged off from each other by allegiance to different ways of expression. There is pleasure and stimulus in realizing that we encounter common fundamental problems. It is in this spirit that we offer our papers to a wider public.

SYLVIA L. THRUPP
*University of Michigan*

II

# MEDIEVAL MILLENARISM:
## ITS BEARING ON THE COMPARATIVE STUDY
## OF MILLENARIAN MOVEMENTS

### PRELIMINARY DEFINITIONS

A necessary preliminary is to determine what meaning is to be given to the word "millenarian".

Its original meaning was narrow and precise. It referred to the belief held by some Christians on the authority of Revelation XX 4–6 that after His Second Coming Christ would establish a messianic kingdom on earth and would reign over it for 1000 years before the Last Judgment. According to the Book of Revelation the citizens of that kingdom will be the Christian martyrs, who are to be resurrected for the purpose 1000 years in advance of the general resurrection of the dead. In general Christian millenarians have interpreted that part of the prophecy in a liberal rather than a literal sense: they have equated the martyrs with the suffering faithful – themselves – and have expected the Second Coming in their lifetime.

It is natural that Christian theologians should in general insist upon this traditional sense of the term "millenarian". But we are concerned not with classifying beliefs from the standpoint of any Christian orthodoxy but with analysing certain types of behaviour in a variety of societies, not all of them even nominally Christian. The term "millenarian" is clearly intended to be understood here in that wider sense which in recent years has become customary amongst anthropologists and sociologists and to some extent among historians too. Understood in this sense, "millenarism" becomes simply a convenient label for a particular type of salvationism.

It remains to define that type. At least for the purpose of this introductory paper I propose to regard as "millenarian" any religious movement inspired by the phantasy of a salvation which is to be

(a) collective, in the sense that it is to be enjoyed by the faithful as a group;

(b) terrestrial, in the sense that it is to be realised on this earth and not in some otherworldly heaven;

(c) imminent, in the sense that it is to come both soon and suddenly;

(d) total, in the sense that it is utterly to transform life on earth, so that the new dispensation will be no mere improvement on the present but perfection itself.

(e) accomplished by agencies which are consciously regarded as supernatural.

## HISTORICAL PERSPECTIVES

It is to be expected that a conference which is concerned to further the socio-logical interpretation of millenarian movements will give particular attention to comparatively recent movements, for only these have been studied, in detail and at first hand, by social scientists.  It is nevertheless important to bear in mind that movements such as the Ghost Dance among the Indians of the American Northwest, the Cargo Cults in Melanesia, Sematism in Java, Jehovah's Witnesses in the United States and Europe and Africa, are but new installments of a story which began more than 2000 years ago.

The oldest form of millenarism of which much is known is the messianic hope of the Jews.  Chapter VII of the Book of Daniel, which was composed about 165 B.C. at the height of the Maccabean revolt, is a millenarian manifesto which foretells how Israel will overthrow the Greek empire and thereafter dominate the whole world for all eternity.  Similar fantasies abound in the militant apocalypses composed during the struggles which the Jews waged against the Romans from 63 B.C. to 72 A.D.  Thus the Apocalypse of Baruch tells how the messiah will shortly break the power of Rome, exterminate all nations which have ever ruled over Israel and establish a kingdom which will last to the end of the world.  Then pain, disease, untimely death, violence and strife, want and hunger will be unknown and the earth will yield its fruits ten-thousandfold.  There is evidence that the party of the "zealots" who precipitated and led the wars of 66–72 A.D., and of 131 A.D. was a truly millenarian movement, obsessed by such fantasies as these and convinced of the imminent coming of a supernatural messiah.

Those wars resulted in the destruction of the Temple, the annihilation of political nationality and the final dispersion of the Jews; and the messianic hope changed its form accordingly.  The messiah was no longer expected to lead Israel to military victory or to establish a world-empire under Jewish domination but only to reassemble the scattered communities and reconstitute the national home.  Nevertheless this was still a millenarian belief, for the messianic reign was still thought of as a new Golden Age in which God's plan for the world was to find its consummation.  That Jewry has been able to endure an unparalleled series of catastrophes and still survive has undoubtedly been due in part to the hold exercised by this collective fantasy.  And it is most significant that whereas usually the coming of the messiah was relegated to some vague and distant future, it became a matter of tense, urgent expectancy whenever some major disaster occurred.  It was during the massacres which ran from the eleventh to the fourteenth centuries that European Jewry first produced pretenders to the role of messiah; and each time the result was a wave of millenarian enthusiasm which often expressed itself in a sudden mass migration towards Palestine.  The great expulsion from Spain and Portugal at the close of the fifteenth century was followed by the appearance of several messiahs who attracted large followings. Up to the seventeenth century Polish Jewry, which enjoyed a uniquely favourable position, was immune to messianic excitement; but during that century it was subjected to persecutions which culminated in the massacre of some 300,000 and resulted in permanent ruin – and at once we find Polish Jewry supplying the most enthusiastic followers of the most celebrated of Jewish messiahs, Shabbetai Zvi.

More than any other religion, Jewish religion centers on the expectation of a future Golden Age; and Christianity, developing out of Judaism, inherited that expectation. Moreover in the time of Jesus the Jews were much given to millenarian movements; and for many of its early adherents Christianity was just such a movement. Whatever Jesus himself may have meant when he talked of the imminence of the kingdom of God, it is certain that many Christians from the first to the fourth centuries, including such eminent Fathers of the Church as Papias, Irenaeus and Lactantius, expected a dispensation in which the earth would without cultivation produce unheard-of abundance of wine and corn and milk and in which the heathen would be handed over to servitude under the faithful. Such fantasies are indistinguishable from those in the Jewish apocalypses; even the very notion that the age of bliss will occupy the last thousand years before the End is of Jewish origin. And for Christians as for Jews the messiah was to be an avenger, annihilating the wicked, casting down the mighty, exalting the faithful. The one point of difference was that while the Jews were awaiting the coming of such a deliverer the Christians were awaiting his return.

Millenarism remained powerful in the Christian Church so long as Christians were an unpopular minority threatened with persecution. When in the fourth century Christianity attained a position of supremacy in the Mediterranean world and became the official religion of the Roman empire, the Church set out to eradicate millenarian beliefs. Little is heard of them for many centuries. Then suddenly they reappear, held now in more or less explicit opposition to the teaching of the Church. This new millenarism was far more complex than the old, drawing on a variety of ideological traditions and inspiring a variety of movements. Out of the proliferation of such movements in western Europe during the later middle ages and the Reformation period it is possible to identify a few principal types.

The earliest movements form as it were a Christian counterpart to the mass migrations of Jews towards Jerusalem. To medieval Christians Jerusalem was not only the scene of the passion and resurrection of Christ – it was also a symbol of that heavenly Jerusalem "like unto a stone most precious" which according to the Book of Revelation was to replace it at the end of time. Even the learned referred to it as "the navel of the world, the land fruitful above all others, like another paradise of delight"; and simple folk did not easily distinguish between the celestial and the terrestrial city. This fantasy of a miraculous realm, abounding both in spiritual and in material blessings,

played a large part in many of the crusades which were launched between the
end of the eleventh and the beginning of the fourteenth centuries – not however so much in the official crusades of professional warriors under the auspices of the pope as in the unofficial crusades of the poor. These movements
arose from recurrent waves of popular excitement in which masses of men and
women and young folk would follow some ascetic, miracle-working preacher
on a wild, desperate expedition across unknown lands and seas until they
perished. Ideologically these movements owed much to the works known as
the medieval Sibylline Oracles, with their prophecy of a great emperor who
is to arise before the Second Coming, massacre all Moslems, establish a Gold-
en Age of plenty and make his way to Jerusalem. At least some of the leaders
of the crusades assumed this role; while their hordes, seldom able to reach
the Moslems, massacred Jews instead, and by the thousand.

These crusades of the common people constituted an enterprise which was
carried on for generations in conscious rivalry with the official crusades. The
poor claimed that their very poverty made them God's elect and ensured them
the success which was denied to the knights; and they were apt to be set in
motion by the news either that an official crusade was preparing or else that
it had failed. What is most striking however is the part played in these movements by mass insecurity. The areas which saw the rise of popular crusades
were always those areas north of the Alps that had a relatively dense population including landless peasants; Flanders, northern France, and the Rhine
valley. In these areas many people, because they found themselves in such
an insecure position reacted all the more sharply to any sudden, overwhelm-
ing threat. It is significant that at the time of the First Crusade of 1095 the
areas which were swept by mass enthusiasm had for ten years been afflicted
by famine and drought and for five years by plague; while the crusades of
1146, 1309 and 1320 were all preluded by famines. Nor must it be assumed
that famine was a normal condition. In the long period 1225–1309, for instance, there were only three major famines in the Low Countries and along
the lower Rhine; and each of these was accompanied either by a people's
crusade or by some mass movement of a similar kind.

Flourishing at first in the shadowy margins of orthodox Catholicism, in the
thirteenth century the popular crusades turned against the Church, which they
condemned for its wealth and worldliness. In this they pointed forward to the
next wave of millenarism, the movement known as Joachimism. The twelfth
century had seen a rapid increase in the economic prosperity of western Europe; and this affected the way of life of the higher clergy. Abbots turned their
monasteries into luxurious establishments, while bishops built palaces in which
they could live in the same magnificent style as other great feudal lords. The
greater circulation of money and the revival of trade enabled the papacy to
develop a vast fiscal system, which in turn enabled it to fight political battles,
to hire armies and to maintain a court of the utmost splendour – in fact, to

behave just like a particularly powerful secular monarchy. Joachimism developed as a protest against this state of affairs.

Around the middle of the thirteenth century certain of the so-called "Franciscan Spirituals" – rigorous ascetics who had broken away from the main body of the Franciscan order over the issue of absolute poverty – began to produce their commentaries on the prophetic writings of the Calabrian abbot Joachim of Fiore, who had died half a century earlier. In these works Joachim was made to tell how in 1260 the Spirituals would inaugurate the Third and last Age, the age of the Holy Spirit, which would abrogate the Christian dispensation in the same way as that had abrogated the dispensation of the Old Testament and the Law. This would mark the beginning of the Millennium in which all men – including Jews, Moslems and other heathen, now converted – would be united in prayer, mystical contemplation and voluntary poverty. Other forged prophecies attributed to Joachim foretell how, as preparation for the millennial Church, the existing Church is to be chastised and the clergy massacred by the German emperor. When the year 1260 passed without bringing the awaited transformation the date was postponed again and again. In one form or another the Joachimite faith persisted down to the Reformation and even beyond, and it provided the ideology for various millenarian movements.

Inevitably the Joachimite Spirituals were condemned as heretics and persecuted accordingly; and this in turn increased their fury against the Church. They came to see it as the Whore of Babylon and the Pope as Antichrist and the Beast of the Apocalypse; and at the same time they came to expect a saviour from their own ranks to mount the papal throne as the "Angelic Pope" chosen by God to convert the whole world to a life of voluntary poverty. In the conviction that this was on the point of happening a certain Fra Dolcino collected, about the year 1300, a following of over a thousand armed men. Entrenched in the mountains of Piedmont the band waged ruthless war against the papal armies until, as was bound to happen, it was defeated and massacred. Dolcino was burnt as a heretic, but so great was his prestige that years later followers of his still chose to perish at the stake rather than deny their master.

Marxists have sometimes tried to interpret the millenarism of the Spirituals, and particularly the militant movement around Dolcino, as a protest by poor peasants against a church which was exploiting and oppressing them. This interpretation is certainly mistaken. Research shows that the Spirituals were drawn mainly from the more privileged strata of society, notably from the mixture of noble and merchant families which formed the dominant class in the Italian towns. Far from belonging to the poor peasantry, many of them had renounced great wealth in order to become poorer than any beggar. And when they condemned the wealth and worldliness of papacy and church they were protesting not against economic exploitation but against a defection of spiritual authority – indeed of the one divinely ordained authority which with its prescriptions and demands embraced the life of every Christian and which alone, through its sacraments, could offer him hope of salvation after death. Medieval men, accustomed to see in asceticism the surest sign of grace, naturally questioned the validity of a church which was manifestly unascetic. But uncertainty on so vital a matter was bound to engender intolerable anxieties. It was in response to these anxieties that the Spirituals elaborated their fantasy of the Millennium as one vast, all-embracing, poverty-loving church. And as in all millenarian fantasies, the imperfect existing order was to be replaced not by one less imperfect but by perfection itself. The age of the Holy Spirit was to be an age of supernatural bliss and harmony and its denizens were to enjoy a knowledge of God superior to that of Christ himself.

The Church was the chief agency traditionally charged with the task of regulating relations between men and the powers ruling the cosmos – but it was not the only one, for supernatural authority pertained also to the national monarchy. Medieval kingship was still to a large extent a sacred kingship; however restricted in his political powers, the monarch was a representative of divinity, an incarnation of the moral law and the divine intention, a guarantor of the order and rightness of the world. Joachimism was an international movement, but on the interpretation advanced above its appeal in a given country might reasonably be expected to be in inverse ratio to the prestige of the monarchy. And it would seem that this was indeed the case. Joachimism flourished most vigorously in Italy, where there was no national monarchy and where the Pope was himself a great territorial potentate. In France and England, where the prestige of the monarchy stood high, Joachimism had relatively little influence. In Germany, on the other hand, where there was a monarchy but one which was falling into ever greater impotence and discredit, Joachimism took a peculiar form. There the fantasy of the coming Angelic Pope was sometimes accompanied, sometimes even replaced, by that of the coming supernatural German emperor, a poverty-loving monarch sent by God to institute a world-wide messianic empire.

The Joachimites held that in the Third Age mankind would become a community of perfected beings, rejoicing in divine insight and needing guidance from neither church nor state; and they believed themselves to be inaugurating that dispensation. A very similar fantasy underlay the heterodox mysticism known as the Free Spirit, which flourished from the thirteenth century onwards and inspired a number of millenarian sects. But whereas for the Joachimites perfected beings were *ipso facto* ascetics, for the adepts of the Free Spirit they were *ipso facto* moral anarchists – total amoralists who could do whatever they chose without disquiet of conscience. Typically, a sect of the Free Spirit would be headed by a man claiming to be the Second Adam, engaged in establishing on earth a Third Age which would be at the same time a recreation of Paradise as it existed before the Fall. In theory the members of such a sect were free to commit murder or robbery and indeed every conceivable crime. In practice they seem merely to have practised free love among themselves and occasionally, by way of dramatizing the restoration of primal innocence, performed communal ceremonies in a state of ritual nakedness.

Although the individual sects were small, collectively they formed an underground movement which ramified across vast areas of Europe and preserved a certain ideological continuity over some five centuries. Like other heretical and millenarian doctrines, the Free Spirit was disseminated by wandering prophets who included many former monks and priests – but with this peculiarity, that they disseminated it chiefly amongst unmarried women and widows in the upper strata of urban society. In medieval Europe, with its constant wars and its celibate clergy, the number of women always far exceeded the number of possible husbands; and while spinsters and widows in the lower strata could always work and those in the aristocracy could always become nuns, in the prosperous merchant class they often found themselves both idle and despised. It was common for such women to become experimenters in religious experience, practising extreme mortifications and developing mystical ecstasies; and unlike nuns, they were little supervised by the clergy. It was amongst such women that adepts of the Free Spirit would make their way, in the guise of miracle-working holy men, inspired confessors and preachers. In this manner the adepts built up, in conspiratorial secrecy, their millenarian groups dedicated to the reconquest of total innocence. The Millennium of the Free Spirit was an invisible empire, held together by the emotional bonds – which of course were often erotic bonds – between men and women.

The adepts of the Free Spirit were not social revolutionaries and did not normally seek followers amongst the poor – but as part of their creed of total emancipation they did conserve the one thoroughly revolutionary social doctrine known to the middle ages. That human beings had at first lived as a community of equals holding all things in common and knowing nothing of "Mine" or "Thine" was a commonplace in the ancient world. The Fathers too held that such was the original intention of God, and from them the notion was taken over by the medieval scholastics and canonists. But it was certain adepts of the Free Spirit who, towards the end of the fourteenth century, first tried to call the egalitarian State of Nature out of the depths of the past and to present it as an attainable ideal. In doing so they provided the basis for a new form of millenarism. The Millennium could now be imagined as a recreation of that lost Golden Age which had known nothing of social classes or of private property. During the great social upheavals which accompanied the close of the middle ages various extremist groups were inspired by the conviction that at any moment the egalitarian, communistic Millennium would be established by the direct intervention of God.

It was always in the midst of some great revolt or revolution that the revolutionary millenarian group first emerged into daylight. This is equally the case with John Ball and his followers in the English peasants' revolt of 1381; the extreme Taborites during the early stages of the Hussite revolution in Bohemia, 1419–1421; Thomas Müntzer and his "League of the Elect" in the German peasants' revolt of 1525; and the Radical Anabaptists who, in the midst of a wave of revolts in the capitals of the ecclesiastical states in north-west Germany, established the "New Jerusalem" at Münster in 1534–1535. What is seldom realised – and what Marxist and right-wing historians have united in concealing – is how little these groups had in common with the mass uprisings which they tried to exploit. Yet to appreciate the contrast one has only to consider what kind of objectives the mass movements set themselves. Thus the English peasants, seeing new possibilities opened up by the labour shortage after the Black Death, were concerned to have manorial dues commuted for cash rents and villeinage replaced by wage labour. The Hussites were concerned to expropriate the church in Bohemia (and incidentally the German aliens who governed it) and, in varying degrees, to increase the status and independence of the laity as against the clergy. The German peasants, a prosperous and rising class, were concerned to increase the autonomy of their communities and to defend their traditional rights against encroachments by the new territorial states. In the ecclesiastical states of north-west Germany the powerful and wealthy guilds in the capital cities were concerned to restrict the economic privileges and immunities of the local clergy. These were all limited and realistic aims. On the other hand the aims of the millenarian group in each case corresponded not to the objective social situation and the possibilities it offered but to the salvationist fantasies of a handful of freelance preachers; and they were accordingly boundless.

A millenarian revolt never formed except round a prophet – John Ball in England, Martinek Hauska in Bohemia, Thomas Müntzer in Thuringia, first Jan Matthys and then Jan Bockelson at Münster. Wherever the career of such a prophet can be traced, it turns out that he had been obsessed by apocalyptic fantasies for years before it occurred to him, in the midst of some social upheaval, to address himself to the poor as possible followers. And what he then offered them was not simply a chance to improve their material lot – it was also, and above all, the prospect of carrying out a divinely ordained mission of stupendous, unique importance. On the strength of supernatural revelations, the social conflict of the moment was presented as essentially different from other struggles known to history, a cataclysm from which the world was to emerge totally transformed and redeemed. A movement fighting such a battle under a divinely inspired leader inevitably regarded itself as an elite set infinitely above the rest of mankind, infallible and incapable of sin. Avowedly concerned to purify the world of sin in preparation for the coming of the Millennium, these movements commonly showed themselves very bloodthirsty indeed.

It has sometimes been argued that a revolutionary millenarian group fulfils the function of preparing the way for more realistic social movements. This was not the case with the movements which have just been described, for each of these appeared only when an organised insurrection of a decidedly realistic kind was already under way. The spectacle which presents itself is, rather, of a band of a few hundred dedicated enthusiasts struggling to master, in the interests of its own apocalyptic fantasy, a vast popular movement numbering tens or hundreds of thousands. And if the millenarian group differed vastly from the mass movement around it in aim and outlook and strategy, it differed just as much in social composition. The prophet himself was not normally, any more than in other millenarian movements, a manual worker or even a former manual worker, but an intellectual or half-intellectual. Ball, Hauska and Müntzer were all former priests turned free-lance preachers; while of Müntzer it is known that he was born to modest comfort and became a graduate with a voracious appetite for reading. Of the prophets at Münster Matthys was indeed a master-baker, but Bockelson was the bastard son of a village mayor, literate, and a failed cloth-merchant; while their manifestos were composed for them by Rothmann, another former priest. As for their following – it is significant that all these movements flourished in areas where there existed a population which had no institutionalised means of defending or furthering its interests.

The life of a settled peasant or a skilled artisan in medieval Europe was often a hard one but it did not normally lack a certain basic security. On the land the manorial regime was by no means a system of uncontrolled exploitation. The custom of the manor which bound the peasants also bound their lord; and in the village group peasants possessed an organisation which was highly efficient in defending traditional rights and even on occasion in extending them. The guilds in which the skilled artisans in the towns were organised were formidable bodies, perfectly capable of planning and leading a successful revolt against an obstinate overlord or an extortionate patriciate. But in the most populous and economically advanced areas of Europe there existed numbers of poor folk who had no such organisations behind them: in the countryside landless peasants and farm-hands, in the towns journeymen (who were forbidden to organise), unskilled workers (who had no guilds) and a floating population of beggars and unemployed. It was such people as these that provided the revolutionary prophets with their following.

In social composition not so very different from the popular crusades of earlier centuries, these last millenarian movements of the middle ages took place in a very different context. The society which bred them was a society profoundly disoriented by the defection of the traditional relationships crumbling under the pressure of the new capitalist economy. In more than a purely chronological sense these movements stand at the threshold of the modern world.

## SOCIOLOGICAL COMMENTS AND QUERIES

The future miraculous age of bliss can be imagined in many very different ways. And being themselves so various, millenarian fantasies can appeal to people of the most varied kinds and in the most varied situations. The present survey of medieval millenarism deals with only a few of the immense number of variations revealed by historical, anthropological and sociological research. Even so, it may still prompt some general reflections which are relevant to the comparative study of millenarian movements.

It seems certain, then, that the rise of millenarian movements is favoured by certain specific circumstances – and all the more strongly when two or more of those circumstances are present together. It is possible to identify some of the circumstances which so operated in medieval Europe, and legitimate to enquire whether they have operated elsewhere too.

1. Catastrophe or the fear of catastrophe; e.g. the famines and plagues which preceded several popular crusades and similar movements; the massacres which preceded the mass movements of dispersed Jews towards Jerusalem. Are catastrophe or the fear of catastrophe particularly favourable to millenarian movements of a migratory kind?

Have we a related phenomenon in the recurrent migrations of the Apapo-kuva-Guarani of Brazil in search of the Land without Evil? It appears that such migrations were occurring already before the arrival of the Portuguese and are dictated by sudden panic fears, based on Guarani mythology, of the impending destruction of the whole world save only the Land without Evil. It is significant that by medieval Christians catastrophes were accepted as "signals" for the Second Coming and the Last Judgment; while for the Jews intensified persecution was traditionally expected to herald the coming of the messiah.

2. Supposed defection of the authority traditionally responsible for regulating relations between society and the powers governing the cosmos. Italian Joachimite movements around or in expectation of the last, "Angelic" Pope; German Joachimite movements around or in expectation of the final world-emperor – these have their counterparts in various Russian sects which from the time of the Raskol (1666) regarded the Czar as the Antichrist who had ruined the church as an agency of salvation. Some of these sects were millenarian, e.g. the Skoptsi, who in the nineteenth century numbered tens of thousands scattered all over Russia and including nobles, officials, army officers and rich merchants as well as peasants. The basic rule of the Skoptsi was that within their organisation (a clandestine but highly efficient one) all men must be castrated and all women must lose their breasts. The leader of the Skoptsi, Selivanov, was regarded as a reincarnation of Christ – but also as Czar Peter III, saved from his murderers and now biding his time to mount the imperial throne, hold the Last Judgment and establish a world-wide millennial kingdom of sexless beings. The case has its importance, for here is a

millenarian movement which quite clearly cannot be interpreted in terms of class conflict or indeed of anything except religiously motivated anxiety.

It would be worth while to examine what part the defection of a ruler as cosmocrator may have played in non-Christian millenarian movements, e.g. after the collapse of the Burmese monarchy and the desecration of the Golden Palace at Mandalay. This could perhaps be treated as part of a more general question: Can one not detect in the genesis of a great number of millenarian movements, from medieval Europe to Java and from the Guarani of Brazil to the Taiping rebels in China, the workings of mass anxiety concerning the stability and orderly functioning of the cosmos?

3. Emotional frustration in women of means and leisure but without social function or prestige. Throughout the history of Christianity this circumstance has contributed to the rise of revivalist movements and it still does so today. What ideal such a movement sets itself seems to depend chiefly on personal factors – in the first place on the particular personality of the prophet, which will appeal only to certain types of women. The antinomian and erotic millenarism of the Brethren of the Free Spirit does however indicate one recurrent possibility. Nineteenth-century France, for instance, saw similar sects spring up – e.g. the transformation of the Saint-Simonian movement under Barthélemy-Prosper Enfantin, in 1831–1833, and the clandestine sect around Jean-Antoine Boullan in the 1880's.

Do comparable movements occur in societies where the sexual life is less guilt-ridden than it has usually been in Christendom?

4. The existence, in a society which recognises that the relative power and prosperity of different sections (classes, ethnic groups, etc.) can change, of elements which cannot organise for the purpose of defending and furthering their interests by secular means. This circumstance, which in Europe so greatly assisted revolutionary prophets from Ball to Bockelson, seems also to have provided the stimulus for many of the anti-European millenarian movements which have flourished in Africa and Asia and the Americas during the past century. Central to this form of millenarism is the belief that the oppressors are about to be cast down, even annihilated, with the help of supernatural beings. Where medieval sectarians expected the return of Christ as judge and avenger, many of the "primitive" peoples of today and yesterday have awaited the return of their long-dead ancestors.

It is not, incidentally, only "nativistic" movements which imagine the Millennium as the restoration of a lost Golden Age – medieval millenarians did so too.

Has there ever been a millenarian movement which can confidently be attributed to this circumstance alone, or is this always reinforced by circumstances making for cosmic anxiety, as described above?

It remains to ask whether the above observations help towards a general sociological interpretation of millenarian movements.

They would seem at any rate to invalidate, as inadequate to the complexity of the matter, those current quasi-teleological interpretations (not all of them Marxist) which see millenarian movements as necessarily contributing to cultural evolution. As one's mind ranges from the Skoptsi to the Apapokuva-Guarani one is impelled, rather, to consider the psychic prerequisites for these movements, i.e. the common emotional needs of those who participate in them.

With all due tentativeness I shall now advance, as a possible topic for discussion, a general socio-psychological hypothesis concerning the causation of millenarian movements. Of course, to suggest that all millenarian movements arise in situations which have certain identifiable features in common is not to suggest that wherever such situations exist millenarian movements must infallibly arise. Whatever other value it may or may not have, the following hypothesis has certainly no predictive value at all.

It is suggested, then, that the decisive causative factors are these:

1. Many traditional religious world-views include a promise of a future age of bliss to be enjoyed by the faithful. This traditional promise provides the indispensable basis for a millenarian faith. It seems that in societies – such as that of ancient Greece – where the religious world-view has no place for such a fantasy, millenarism cannot develop. Where on the other hand such a fantasy is familiar it can sometimes be given the immediacy and particularity necessary to convert it into an effective millenarian ideology.

2. It is the prophet who carries out this adaptation of traditional lore and who becomes the bearer of the resulting ideology. If in addition the prophet possesses a suitable personality and is able to convey an impression of absolute conviction, he is likely in certain situations of emotional tension to become the nucleus of a millenarian movement.

3. It is perhaps possible to indicate how such situations of emotional tension arise. It seems that there is in many, perhaps in all, human psyches a latent yearning for total salvation from suffering; and that that yearning is greatly intensified by any frustration or anxiety or humiliation which is unaccustomed and which cannot be tackled either by taking thought or by any institutionalised routine. Where a particular frustration or anxiety or humiliation of this nature is experienced at the same time and in the same area by a number of individuals, the result is a collective emotional agitation which is peculiar not only in its intensity but also in the boundlessness of its aims.

4. Such a situation provides the perfect opportunity for a prophet promising a collective salvation which is to be both immediate and total. It is the discharge of accumulated emotional tension that gives such energy to the resulting millenarian movement.

There remain many problems which the above hypothesis, even if it proved correct, would do nothing to clarify. Why, for instance, has Indian society been almost free from millenarian movements – even though in the prophecy of Vishnu's avatar as Kalki Hinduism has its own millenarian myth? Is it perhaps because a series of reincarnations ending infallibly in Nirvana offers the individual a more convincing prospect of total salvation than does the Christian hope (which must remain most uncertain) of heaven? And in general what are the factors, historical or immediate, which militate against the growth of millenarian movements? Is one such factor, operating in the West today, that strengthening of the ego which is said to be a characteristic modern trend?

Again: What relationship can be established between a given millenarian ideology and the religious world-view which underlies it? Is it true, for instance, that those world-views (such as the Christian, the Jewish and the Moslem) which include the notion of a divine will working through history towards a preordained end provide a better climate for millenarism than world-views which know nothing of a divine purpose and see history as an unending series of cycles? Or is such a climate better only for some kinds of millenarism? In particular, is the fantasy of a "chosen people", divinely appointed to inaugurate and enjoy the Millennium, confined to those movements which are of Christian, Judaic or Moslem origin? Such movements often show signs of collective megalomania; would the same be true of millenarian movements which spring from other types of world-view?

And finally: To what extent can millenarism be self-generating? The Greek and Roman empires, normally so tolerant in matters of religion, persecuted Jews and Christians. Have we here examples of religious communities which, precisely because they regard themselves as agents of the divine will and predestined heirs to the millennial kingdom, call down persecution – and then, in response, develop still more strongly the millenarian aspects of their religions?

These are difficult problems indeed – and if we could solve them all we should no doubt find others as difficult confronting us. But then the aim of this conference is not, presumably, to produce a comprehensive sociology of millenarism but rather, by comparing the various groups of data available to it, to advance a little in that direction.

NORMAN COHN
*King's College*
*University of Durham*

# THE COMPARATIVE STUDY OF MILLENARIAN MOVEMENTS

"... with the Lord one day is as a thousand years,
and a thousand years as one day" (2 Peter, 3, 8; R.S.V.)

Jewish and Christian thinking on the Last Things has influenced millennial-style movements in all parts of the world. Perhaps because of the very extent of this influence, considerable vagueness has crept into the use of concepts from this thought. In particular, many recent writers on these movements in colonial areas have been notoriously lax in their use of terms borrowed from the Jewish-Christian tradition to describe social phenomena for which there are, obviously, considerable terminological difficulties.[1]

Outstanding here is the tendency to use the term "millennium" to refer to the *final* state of society in which all conflicts are resolved and all injustices removed after a preliminary period of purging and transformation. In reality, of course, the traditional concept of the Millennium has a *transitional* rather than a final character.[2] A highly interesting essay in the history of ideas could be written on the way in which the concept of the millennium has tended to acquire a double meaning.

Some of the confusion may be due to the fact that not enough care is taken to distinguish between premillennialism and postmillennialism. Most of the movements which have caught scholarly attention recently are of the premillennial type: that is, they believe that the Second Coming – or an equivalent "deliverer" – will take place before the millennial, transitional period. Such movements usually reflect a pessimism about the efficacy of human agencies and a belief that social transformation can only come about by cataclysmic means. Postmillennialism, on the other hand, holds that the millennium will come first, usually "as the fruit of the present Christian agencies now at work in the world",[3] and that the Second Coming or the delivering agency will oc-

---

[1] For some of these problems, see Marian W. Smith and others, "Towards Classification of Cult Movements", *Man* (London), LIX, January, 1959, pp. 8–12 and February, 1959, pp. 25–28.
[2] John Henry Blunt, *Dictionary of Sects, Heresies ...* (London, 1874), p. 329, claims that the Jewish conception of the Millennium has an element of finality which is lacking in the Christian Millennial concept.
[3] James Black, *New Forms of Old Faith* (London, 1948), p. 232.

cur at the end of this process.[4] Postmillennial movements are usually well within the Jewish-Christian tradition. It would be interesting to discover if movements of a postmillennial character occur with any degree of frequency outside this tradition. And are postmillennial movements outside the Jewish-Christian tradition primary manifestations of millenarianism within their particular societies or do they take place – as has happened frequently in the direct Christian tradition – after the failure of a premillennial movement?

Pre- and postmillennialism correspond, in the secular sphere, to the revolutionary and reformist attitudes to social change. Yet the line between the religious and secular aspects of such movements is a narrow one; many would maintain – and surely rightly – that in "primitive societies" it is an unreal distinction. In so-called "advanced" societies, however, the distinction has become increasingly valid over the last two centuries.

Yet there are secular millennial equivalents within these advanced societies and it is possible that the study of them, side by side with the millennial-type religious manifestations, will throw light on the latter, historically and sociologically. One of the most important secular millennial equivalents is undoubtedly utopianism. There is a vast literature on this subject – in which, incidentally, the term "millennium" is often vaguely and inaccurately used – and from this it appears that utopians may be divided into two broad groups: "passivists", whose interest is purely theoretical, and activists, who make an actual attempt to set up new societies. It may be that what can be learned of the psychology of passivists and activists from the relatively well-documented literature of utopianism will be helpful for the understanding of these types in religious movements of a millennial character. In millennial-style religious movements, however, the focus of interest is more often on the activist than on the passivist.

The connection between utopia and millennium has been described by Martin Buber as the search for perfection within, on the one hand, "perfect space" and, on the other, "perfect time". This is certainly a helpful distinction. But from the point of view of millennialism alone it may be misleading, for space and time are rarely distinguished in millenarian thought and action. Cohn raises the question whether mass anxiety about the working and stability of the cosmos does not always play a part in the genesis of millenarian movements.[5] Certainly from primitive societies, in which cosmos and society are seen as inextricably interwoven, to more advanced societies where, even if there is a more easily observed line between the two, the latest millenarian manifestations have assumed the form of flying saucers, the cosmic element in millennialism seems always present.[6]

[4] One of the few recent works which takes particular care to distinguish between the types of millennialism is Stow Persons, *American Minds* (New York, 1958).

[5] See above, p. 41.

[6] See Mircea Eliade, *Cosmos and History: The Myth of the Eternal Return* (New York, 1959).

In this respect, it seems worth noting that the most important secular millennial equivalent, the Communist Party, makes obligatory for its members training in dialectical materialism, in which its premillennial philosophy of social change – the delivering agent, the Party, comes first – is set within a cosmic perspective.[7]

Norman Cohn has a number of useful references to the Marxist approach to millennialism. Particularly important is his implied criticism of Marxist attempts to interpret millenarian movements as religio-political risings of poor against rich.[8] Nevertheless, it should be pointed out that while this is the Marxist tendency – well exemplified in K. Marx and F. Engels, *On Religion*[9] – other interpretations are possible within this theoretical framework. Trotsky, for example, claimed that "the thought which was drilling through the thick of the working class (in Russia on the eve of the February Revolution) was far bolder, more penetrating, more conscious than those little ideas by which the educated classes live."[10] As an example of those little ideas, he went on to quote "the ideas of those government circles who were inspired by the Apocalypse and believed in the dreams of Rasputin."

Similarly, E. J. Hobsbawm's 1956 Simon Lectures display interesting variations on the traditional Marxist pattern. For example, referring to the Andalusian village anarchists of the period 1870–1936, he asserts that "The anarchists are chiefly interesting in that they show millenarianism wholly divorced from traditional religious form . . ."[11] Should it be argued that this is true of anarchism in general, the response might be that anarchism, as a political philosophy, was nurtured in countries with a very definite Jewish-Christian tradition.

E. J. Hobsbawm assumes that a millenarian movement in modern times can turn into or be absorbed by a revolutionary movement of a non-religious character.[12] Another Marxist writer, Peter Worsley, at the conclusion of his study of Melanesian Cargo cults, suggests that the future of the millenarian movement is to play a passive rather than an active role in contemporary politics.[13] But Norman Cohn states of the millenarian movements that he describes, that "each of these appeared when an organised insurrection of a decidedly realistic kind was already under way." It is worth considering whether this may not be generally true of other periods and outside Europe. Obviously, no clear answer can be given until a much greater variety of mil-

---

[7] Reference to the "Communist Millennium" is of course a contradiction in terms since in the Marxist scheme the transitional period that ushers in Communism is that of Socialism.

[8] See above, p. 35-6.

[9] See 1957 edition, Foreign Languages Publishing House, Moscow.

[10] Ed. F. W. Dupee (New York, 1959), p. 146.

[11] *Primitive Rebels: Studies in Archaic Forms of Social Movements* (Manchester, 1959), p. 65.

[12] *Ibid.*, p. 59.

[13] *The Trumpet Shall Sound* (New York: Schocken Books, 1968), pp. 255-6.

lennial-style movements has been examined. But Cohn's statement should make one pause before accepting any simple schema. It seems that the history of millennial-style movements is not one of a simple observable progression. It is studded with survivals of once militant groups, bravely carrying on the battle or else quietly withdrawing into positions of passive contemplation; of new creations which may become secularized; of memories of movements which have disappeared altogether but which may reappear repeatedly in novel guise.

Any study of millenarianism must also include investigation into the messiah mechanism. I use a mechanical analogy deliberately because there seem to be movements of a millennial type in which a personal messiah does not always play a part and in which the delivering role is taken by some impersonal agency. More work needs to be done on impersonal messianic agencies and why they occur in some millennial-style movements and not in others. Nevertheless, if there is no individual, personal messiah, an invariable part of all millennial-style movements seems to be some "triggering-off" agency, apparently from outside the society or group concerned, in forms as various as invading American soldiers and flying saucers. That great social laboratory of colonial nationalism and culture conflict, Ireland, as always, provides an example. If Giraldus Cambrensis is to be believed, in the twelfth century in Ireland the prophecy ran that "after the English have experienced reverses there and been weakened . . . an unknown king shall come . . . who will . . . drive almost all of them out of Ireland."[14] Examples of "unknown kings" and kindred forces could be multiplied, particularly for colonial societies, all of which serve to raise the question, how far may the messianic agencies, personal or impersonal, of millennial-style movements be conceived as *external* to the society or group whose transformation, it is believed, they will achieve? And how far is this externality apparent only, the messianic agency being, in fact, organically linked to the society concerned? Or are there two forms of messianic agencies to be noted: one which is genuinely external and the other which is external in appearance only, and may not even be external in appearance but an easily observable offshoot of its society? It seems to me that much greater study is needed of both the role and the form of the messianic agency.

A further problem in millennial-style religious movements is the role of women, both as followers and as leaders.[15] Notable among women leaders is Joanna Southcott, the Devonshire farm girl, to whom a "voice" promised,

---

[14] Quoted in Francis Pierrepoint Barnard, *Strongbow's Conquest of Ireland* (London, 1888), p. 125.

[15] On their role as followers see N. Cohn, *The Pursuit of the Millennium* (London, 1957), pp. 165–7, 283, 293. See also Keith Thomas, "Women and the Civil War Sects", *Past and Present* (April, 1958), pp. 42–62; Donald Fraser, "An African Panic", *Southern Workman*, XXVIII, 10, (Hampton, October, 1909), pp. 568–9; *London Times* (June 21, 1960), p. 9, "A Suk tribeswoman . . . managing Dini ya Msambwa."

early in 1814, that, although she was in her sixty-fifth year, she would give birth to the Messiah, whereupon she began to show well-authenticated symptoms of pregnancy.[16] Her amazing career began a millennial movement which still continues in the form of the English Panacea Society of to-day. Mother Ann Lee, founder of the Shakers,[17] is another prominent female leader, for whose blend of pre- and postmillennialism Stow Persons has coined the term "intramillennialism".[18] An important place, too, must be found for the visionary Ellen G. White, mid-nineteenth century founder of the Seventh-day Adventists.[19] As an example of the many women who have played lesser, but still significant roles, in the creation of millennial movements, the figure of Mary Campbell, of Port Glasgow, Scotland, in the 1830s may be cited. This "working-class girl, who instead of being content with the estate into which it had pleased God to call her, suddenly appeared dressed in fair raiment and silks . . . and chose to have her own ideas of what the missionary call meant, based on the newest apocalyptic theories", influenced Edward Irving and the emerging millenarian Catholic Apostolic Church.[20]

Women have also played a prominent part in millennial-style movements in colonial territories. A recent example is the so-called "Alice" movement in the Northern Rhodesia of the 1950s, led by Lenshina Mulenga. Such a figure raises the question, which might also be applied to other similar societies, how far is this a modern expression of the prophetic functions traditionally assumed by women amongst some Central African tribes?[21]

Much more work is needed on the many religious movements of a millennial-type that flourished in Europe and in America between the 18th and the 20th centuries. When such movements have been examined by recent writers, too often they have been looked upon as products of the "religiously neglected poor".[22] Even a cursory glance at the neglected subject of millenarianism in Britain and America in modern times reveals a much more complicated picture.

Although the history of popular and unorthodox religion in Great Britain – with the signal and often distracting exception of Methodism – has been

---

[16] See G. R. Balleine, *Past Finding Out. The Tragic Story of Joanna Southcott and her Successors* (London, 1956).

[17] See Edward Deeming Andrews, *The People Called Shakers* (New York, 1953).

[18] Persons, *op. cit.*, p. 177.

[19] There is a vast Seventh-day Adventist literature. But special mention should be made of Edwin Leroy Froom, *The Prophetic Faith of Our Fathers* (Washington D.C., 1946–54) which, in spite of its denominational bias, is a scholarly if selective guide to millennial writings in general as well as to the Seventh-day Adventists in particular.

[20] P. E. Shaw, *The Catholic Apostolic Church* (New York, 1946), p. 32. See also Gordon Rattray Taylor, *The Angel-Makers: A Study in the Psychological Origins of Historical Change, 1750–1850* (London, 1958).

[21] See Cullen Gouldsbury and Hubert Sheen, *The Great Plateau of Northern Rhodesia* (London, 1911), p. 83.

[22] Elmer T. Clark, *The Small Sects in America* (New York, 1949), pp. 16–17, quoted in Worsley, *op. cit.*, p. 233.

grossly neglected, there seems to be enough evidence to suggest immediately that those "fantasies of impending doom", which Mr. Rattray-Taylor calls a "feature of the middle class behaviour in the early nineteenth century" Britain,[23] affected the middle as much as the poorer classes. It is, of course, true that in the Britain of the period of the American, the French and the Industrial Revolutions, such groups as those which built their hopes on Mother Ann Lee of Manchester, were usually of humble origin and that the poor from the days of Wesley, through the thunderous era of the young Salvation Army, to the present-day frequenters of "Kingdom Halls" have been an important element in the development of British millenarianism. These groups afford many episodes which demand further study, such as the career of John Nichols Tom, the "peasants' Saviour" who was followed into pitched battle with troops by armed Kentish peasants in 1838.[24] Nevertheless, there has also been a distinct middle-class element in the millenarianism of the British Isles in the 19th century, although, in the absence of detailed researches, it is not clear whether this took the form of specifically middle-class millenarian churches or whether it appeared as participation in millennial groups of a primarily working-class origin. That there were specifically British middle-class millennial churches is seen in the rise of the affluent "Irvingite" Catholic Apostolic Church in mid-19th century Britain, to which such men as the father of the African explorer and administrator, Sir Harry Johnston, belonged: he was "the well-to-do secretary of a large insurance company, a shrewd, well-informed, widely travelled man of business, whose work took him regularly all over Western Europe and Scandinavia, and occasionally as far afield as Russia, Asia Minor and South Africa".[25] The leaders of the Catholic Apostolic Church have been described as "upper or middle class . . . men of culture and education . . . of some social importance".[26] There were few, if any, underprivileged elements in this British millennial group.

A variation on this theme, however, is suggested in Sir Edmund Gosse's description, in his autobiography, *Father and Son* (1907) of his millennial-minded parents, members of the Brethren (Plymouth), as "poor gentlefolk". Such people formed an important section of Victorian Britain and it would be interesting to know the types of millennialism which attracted them. Were they drawn to affluent bodies like the Catholic Apostolic Church? Did they sink their differences and make common cause with working-class millenarianism? Or did they find a *modus vivendi* in such groups as the Plymouth Brethren?

The picture is a highly complex one. For example, it is easy – and, in

---

[23]   *Op. cit.,* pp. 265–6.

[24]   Ronald Matthews, *English Messiahs. Studies in Six English Religious Pretenders, 1656–1927* (London, 1936). D. H. Lawrence's *Apocalypse* (New York, 1932) provides a highly personalized commentary on the British poor and the Millennium.

[25]   Roland Oliver, *Sir Harry Johnston and the Scramble for Africa* (London, 1957), p. 1.

[26]   Shaw, *op. cit.,* p. 237.

general, correct – to describe the adherents of Jehovah's Witnesses in Britain as members of traditionally underprivileged groups. And yet, if one looks at the origins of the Witnesses in Britain, when they were part of what was known as the Watchtower movement, and their leader was Pastor Charles Taze Russell, one finds that one of their British founding fathers was Dr. John Edgar, Professor of Midwifery at Anderson's College, Glasgow, who visited Russell in America in 1906.[27] He can hardly be described as a member of the Glasgow proletariat – a significant number of whom were, at this time, deserting religion altogether, for Marxian socialism.

A further complicating feature of British millennialism has been its inter-actions with American movements. The Christadelphians, for example, were started by a British medical man, Dr. John Thomas, who emigrated to Ohio in the early 1830s and built up a movement in Britain and America, drawing on similar sources of support on both sides of the Atlantic.[28] The Atlantic community, as it has often been called, has received increasing attention from scholars since 1945; but, in religious history, particularly revivals and mil-lenarian movements (both, obviously, closely allied) there has been little se-rious work. Yet here is surely a field for comparative study which is potenti-ally rich in interactions, ideological and social.

The pursuit of the Millennium in America itself has, of course, not lacked attention and there are a number of scattered studies of it, historical and so-ciological. Sociologically, however, American millenarianism has been looked upon too often as only one element in the much-examined phenomenon of sectarianism. It has not been given the attention it deserved in its own right. Here, perhaps, by accumulating details of the many United States millennial movements, the historian can play a leading part.[29]

Some general ideas about the pursuit of the Millennium in America are readily apparent: the New World as a free field for all the heresies of Europe; the influence of the American frontier on sectarianism; America as a social laboratory for millennial-style movements among primitive peoples. Above all, there is millenarianism as a form of American "manifest destiny", from colonial times onward, reflecting and fostering many-sided forms of American optimism and belief in progress.[30]

---

[27] Minna Edgar, *Memoirs of Dr. John Edgar* (Britain, n.d.), p. 19.
[28] Their history has been treated with exemplary thoroughness in Bryan A. Wilson's *Social Aspects of Religious Sects: A Study of some Contemporary Groups in Great Britain, with Special Reference to a Midland City* (Ph. D. thesis, London University 1955), probably the only serious sociological investigation of contemporary British millennialism.
[29] It would be enormously helpful to have a synthesis of the various studies that have been made by scholars in various disciplines of American millennial-style movements, Indian, Negro and white, since the appearance of H. Richard Niebuhr's pioneering *The Kingdom of God in America* (New York, 1937).
[30] Compare Rush Welter, "The Idea of Progress in America", *Journal of the History of Ideas*, XVI, 3, (June, 1955), p. 408; Everett Weber's *Escape to Utopia: The Com-munal Movement in America* (New York, 1959) has some useful comparative material.

And yet, paradoxically, this optimistic millennialism coexisted and co-exists – not always peacefully – with the fundamental pessimism of the pre-millennial groups of America, by far the most common form of American millenarianism. This paradox runs throughout the history of the pursuit of the Millennium in America. Stow Persons notes it, in passing, in connection with William Miller's prophecies and the Great Disappointment of 1844:

It is difficult to reconcile premillennialism with the secular interests of the age. Many of the Americans of the early nineteenth century must have remained untouched both by the secularism of the Establishment and by the practical optimism of the believers in progress.[31]

Interesting though this view is, it is insufficient because premillennialism as a counterpoint to American optimism is not limited to the early 19th century.

The example of Jehovah's Witnesses is instructive. One of the great gaps in American biography is a serious study of the founder of the faith, Pastor Charles Taze Russell of Alleghany, Pennsylvania. In Russellism, it seems, many schools of American millennialism converged. Elements in his thought may be found from American millennial groups as apparently different as the Shakers, the Millerites, the Mormons, the Campbellites, the Christadelphians, the Seventh-day Adventists, and others. (Although they would all indignantly repudiate this juxtaposition, they are all products of a common millennial matrix.) Russell's deep distrust of earthly agencies as a manifestation of the basic premillennial pessimism was cogently expressed in his "The Battle of Armageddon", Volume V of his *Studies in the Scriptures* (1897), the ideological foundation of the present-day Jehovah's Witnesses. Its material was largely drawn from the contemporary American press of the Populist era and suggests that orthodox historians of American politics should pay greater attention than they do to such unorthodox works.

Millenarianism has been neglected for too long by historians of American reform movements. The appearance of Timothy L. Smith's *Revivalism and Social Reform in Mid-Nineteenth Century America* (New York, 1957) may indicate that this period of neglect is coming to an end. His observations on this subject are all too brief but they may stimulate research. He is surely correct when he points out that mid-19th century American "revivals and perfectionism became socially volatile only when combined with the doctrine of Christ's imminent conquest of the earth" (p. 225); when he emphasizes how the reaction against Millerism after the Great Disappointment of 1844 "speeded the adoption of a fervent postmillennialism, attuned to the prevailing optimism of the age" (p. 228); and when he claims that in the post-Civil War period the "ideology of the millennium merged without a break into what came to be called the social gospel" (p. 235). Furthermore, his picture of the millennial implications which many whites saw in the Civil War (p. 235) sug-

[31]  Persons, *op. cit.*, p. 176.

gests that the subject is worth investigating from a Negro angle, for there is some evidence to show that Negroes saw the Civil War as the coming Millennium. When one realizes that the church, orthodox and unorthodox, dependent and independent, open and secret, was, before the Civil War, the Negro's main form of expression, this is hardly surprising.

The Negro millenarians in America, before, during and after the Civil War, are amongst the most striking examples of the American churches of the disinherited. Yet, American, like British millenarianism, has never been a product only of the poor. Nor is it, as it may so easily appear, basically a product of frontier conditions. Whitney R. Cross has dispelled this legend in writing of the Millerites that they

cannot be dismissed as ignorant farmers, libertarian frontiersmen, impoverished victims of economic change, or hypnotized followers of a maniac, thrown into prominence merely by freak coincidences, when the whole of American Protestantism came so close to the same beliefs. Their doctrine was the logical absolute of fundamentalist orthodoxy . . .[32]

America, indeed, is the ideal place for the comparative study of religious movements of a millennial type. Rural and urban; rich, poor and middling; white, Indian and Negro, "advanced" and "primitive" peoples; orthodox and heretic: all the various elements which go to make up these movements, and whose exact proportion in them is in dispute, are here. Americans have little need to go outside their own boundaries to study them. But Americans cannot stay within their borders. As Charles Woodmason of the Anglican Church saw in 1765, when he investigated for London the heresies of the Carolina frontier:

Africk never more abounded with New Monsters than Pennsylvania does with New Sects, who are continually sending their Emissaries around.[33]

And it is these emissaries from Woodmason's time to the present day, whose influence, in such apparently different but inherently similar movements as the Pacific Cargo cults and the Kitawala of Central Africa, has added continually to the changing but constant pattern of the pursuit of the Millennium.

GEORGE SHEPPERSON
*Edinburgh University*

---

[32] See his important pioneering study, *The Burned-over District. The Social and Intellectual History of Enthusiastic Religion in Upper State New York 1800–1850* (Ithaca, N.Y., 1950), p. 320.
[33] Richard T. Hooker, ed., *The Carolina Backcountry on the Eve of the Revolution* (Chapel Hill, 1935), p. 78.

# III

# BRAZILIAN MESSIANIC MOVEMENTS

In order to understand Brazilian messianic movements one must distinguish those of pre-conquest and early colonial times from those that arose among the neo-Brazilian populations of the 19th and 20th centuries. The social setting of such movements, and the cultural traditions and socio-cultural characteristics of the groups taking part in them, were radically different in the two periods.

## I. INDIAN MOVEMENTS OF EARLY COLONIAL AND PRE-COLONIAL TIMES

Our earliest information is contained in the writings of Portuguese missionaries and early colonial travellers and explorers. These record periodical migrations of Tupi-Guarani tribes, at first from the backlands to coastal areas and later also along the coast, northwards. In both cases the migrations were often over very long distances. It was remarked that they occurred in a wave pattern: when one subsided another started. Moreover, a migrating band had usually come from territory far removed from contact with the band that had migrated last.

Some of the early Portuguese observers also recorded what they had been able to learn about the beliefs and customs of the migrating peoples, and about their social organization. Trained ethnologists are now of the opinion that the migrations were due to religious inspiration. According to Tupi-Guarani myth there have been two Creations. The first world was destroyed by flood. Its inhabitants were culture heroes who, having earned immortality through prayer, ritual dancing, and moral conduct, escaped destruction by joining the Creator in his abode. This was conceived as being either at the earth's centre or beyond "a great river". The present world was set by the Creator on two cross-bars; when they slip, as some day they must, it will be destroyed by fire. Human beings may however survive the destruction if they perfect themselves, that is, if they rid themselves of evil through religious ritual. They will then be able to join God in his abode, the land without Evil, which lies to the East. But the journey will be long and difficult. Kurt

Nimuendaju Unkel, Leon Cadogan and Darcy Ribeiro have found these same myths among contemporary Indians.

Kurt Nimuendaju was the first ethnologist to suspect that the historical migrations of the Tupi-Guarani had a mythical basis. The migrations, reported by early informants as having occurred also before their time, that is, before European contacts, were definitely not casual. They were mass movements heading for the Land without Evil. To find the way blocked by the Atlantic was disappointing, but the Indians would simply conclude that they had mistaken the direction. Nimuendaju based his argument on information from a band that was continuing its ancestral migrations in the 20th century. He also collected evidence among the Apapokuva-Guarani, both of pertinent mythical belief and of historical migrations of their own tribe, and of some neighboring tribes, in search of the Land without Evil.

Nimuendaju found that such migrations were always led by a native prophet, usually the medicine-man. On the basis of visions and dreams the prophet would reveal to the tribe that the destruction of the earth was imminent and he would promise to lead them to the Land without Evil, their Paradise. The occasion was never one of population pressure nor of disturbance by war, famine, or disease. It is evident that when the Portuguese arrived the Tupi-Guarani were but newly settled on the coast, for they were ill-adapted to the environment. They lived mainly from agriculture and hunting, were poor fishermen and sailors and had no adequate craft for long sea voyages. The fact that they were fierce warriors and had driven away the former inhabitants of the coast suggests that had they merely been in search of new and richer territory they could easily have lorded it over the vast valley and forest regions of the interior. Instead they had moved on to an environment that was strange to them, and were continuing to move up the coast to the north. Nimuendaju could find nothing to account for their behavior except religious motivation.[1]

Leon Cadogan has found further confirmatory evidence for this thesis in the myths and legends that he collected among the Nbyá-Guarani of the Guiará region, on the borders of Brazil and Paraguay. These Indians, too, tell of a former world which was destroyed by a deluge, they named a number of culture heroes who had been able to join God by crossing the sea, and they believe that the present world is doomed before long to destruction. In Cadogan's opinion the Indian migrations both of early colonial times and pre-colonial times arose from these beliefs.[2] Another modern Brazilian ethnologist, Darcy Ribeiro, has documented the same myths and world-view among a contemporary Tupian tribe, the Urubu of the Gurupi River in northeastern Brazil. He has even a case-study of an Indian chief who set out on a journey

---

[1] Kurt Nimuendaju Unkel, *Leyenda de la Creacion y Juicio Final del Mundo*. Mimeographed edition, S. Paulo, 1944.

[2] Leon Cadogan, *Ayvu Rapyta: Textos miticos de los Mbyá-Guarani del Guairá*. Fac. Filosofia, bulletin 227, S. Paulo, 1959.

to meet God, following all the steps prescribed by tribal legend and tradition. His journey ended in tragedy.[3]

The "Santidades", mass movements of Indians occurring in the late 16th century, were of a somewhat different character. They were described in detail by the Jesuit missionaries, who complained of the disturbing effect that they had on missionary work. These movements sprang up usually among Indians who had been brought to the Jesuit reductions by force. The leaders promised not only to take their followers to the Land without Evil, but to free them from bondage, to restore old Indian traditions and religious ritual and to bring back an era of splendor and abundance. It must be stressed that in contrast to earlier Indian migrants, the Indians who took part in the Santidades had been subjected to forced acculturation. Their social organization had been disrupted, their leaders subdued, their medicine-men driven away, and their myths and traditions derided. Both in being a form of protest and also in other aspects, their movements resembled those of North American Indians subjected to similar conditions of deprivation and submission.[4]

In other words the Santidades were reactions against the social and religious order imposed on the Indians by their new colonial masters. Like their North American brethren the Brazilian Indians resorted to ritual dances, song and prayers, and resumed tribal customs and practices that the Jesuits had long banned. In their desperation they also recalled their myths and old-established cultural traditions. Their leaders, recruited either from among their own ranks or from other tribal groups, were followed without question into remote parts of the interior. Here the necessary religious preparations for the search for the Land without Evil could be carried out without fear of the Jesuits or the colonial authorities interfering.

It is important to note that neither of these two types of Indian mass movement in Brazil required any radical change in the old tribal organization or customs. Occasionally some recently acquired elements of Catholicism were incorporated into the old rituals.[5] But for the most part there was simply stress on the need to attain individual perfection through practice of the old ritual songs and dances that properly preceded a journey to meet God. In both types of Brazilian movements myth gave a clear picture of what Paradise would be like and a general idea of how to get there. The leaders were the *pagés*, or medicine-men, who by tradition had authority in religious matters. The lay chiefs, the *morubixabas*, were not displaced (in the case of the Santi-

---

[3] Darcy Ribeiro, "Uirá vai ao encontro de Maira", *Anais II Reunião Bras. de Antropologia* (Salvador, 1957), pp. 17–28.

[4] *Cartas Jesuiticas* II Cartas Avulsas, 1550–1568. Publ. Acad. Bras. Letras (Rio 1931), p. 382; *Cartas Jesuiticas* III Cartas, Informacões, etc. do Pe. Joseph de Anchieta S.J., 1554–1594 (1933), p. 331.

[5] *Primeira Visitacão do Santo Officio ás Partes do Brasil* (confissões da Bahia 1591–1592). Soc. Capistrano de Abreu, Rio, 1935, pp. 65–66; Ralph Linton, "Nativistic movements", in *Reader in Comparative Religion*, William A. Lessa and Evon Z. Vogt ed. (Row, Peterson and Co., Evanston, 1958), pp. 466–74.

dades their office was revived), but readily accepted the prophecies and directions of the *pagés*. Finally it must be remembered that these Indians were semi-nomads and were well accustomed to long war expeditions. The whole tribe had participated in these, the women following the warriors to carry and prepare their food. An expedition in search of the Land without Evil was felt to require a little more careful planning, and intensive spiritual preparation, but it involved minimal disturbance of the traditional ways and cultural patterns of the tribe.

## II. MESSIANIC MOVEMENTS OF THE 19TH AND 20TH CENTURIES

Later movements drew their following mostly from the neo-Brazilian population of mixed Portuguese, Negro and Indian stocks. Indians might be involved, as for example in the Rio Negro (Amazon) area, where some tribes came under Protestant influence.[6] In the northeast, where the first of the later movements occurred in 1719–20, and also in the south, *mestizos* of Indian origin could be found among the followers of messianic leaders. But by this period the remnants of the Tupian tribes had been expelled from the coastal areas and had taken refuge in the tropical forests of northern and central Brazil. Many Indian groups escaped decimation through war and disease only to be disrupted and assimilated. Some of the surviving groups may still have pursued the quest for the Land without Evil, but their movements did not interest the neo-Brazilian population.

The new messianic movements that sprang up among the peasantry of northeastern and later of northern Brazil derived not from Indian mythology but from Jewish traditions carried to the New World by Christianity. With the colonists came related legends that had grown up in Portugal.[7] Outstanding among these was the belief that King Sebastian, who had probably been killed in Africa while fighting the Moors, would return.[8]

Apocalyptic preaching by itinerant Catholic priests exercised great influence. The Brazilian author Euclydes da Cunha, writing of a 19th century movement in the northeast, has drawn attention to this.[9] Late in that century Protestant missionaries kindled apocalyptic fantasies among the populations of the south and even among the Amazonian Indians.[10] Throughout most of the country Pentecostal ministers today in the same way rest their appeal to the humble people largely on the prophecies of the Apocalypse.

[6]   Eduardo Galvão, "Aculturacão indigena no Rio Negro" *Bol. Museu Parense Emilio Goeldi,* no. 7 (September 1959) p. 53.

[7]   Norman Cohn, see above, p. 40.

[8]   J. Lucio de Azevedo, *A Evolucão do Sebastianismo* (Liv. Classica, Lisboa, 1947).

[9]   Euclydes da Cunha, *Os Sertões,* 15th ed. (Livr. Fco. Alves, Rio, 1940), p. 169.

[10]   Maria Izaura Pereira de Queiroz, "L'influence du milieu social interne sur les mouvements messianiques brésiliens", *Archives de Sociologie des Religions* no. 5 (January–June 1958), pp. 3–30.

It is sufficient here to refer the reader to the extensive literature on the movements that have arisen.[11] Two that occurred in the northeastern province of Pernambuco early in the last century were the incidents of Rodeador[12], and of Pedra Bonita.[13] These were distinctive in being the last millenarian movements to have a predominantly Sebastianic character. In the second there were even blood sacrifices of children offered in the hope of bringing King Sebastian back. The Sebastianic legend was present, but subordinate, in the later Canudos incident.[14] Father Cicero's movement, which arose in a nearby area early in the 20th century, and the Contestado incident, which followed, in southern Brazil, were apparently free of Sebastianic influence.[15] Then, also in the south, among German immigrants influenced by a Protestant woman, a movement of Mucker origin appeared.[16] Since then there have been sporadic movements spreading especially in rural areas. Around 1900 there was a wave of fervor, people assembling in the hills or at popular shrines to await the end of the world. Most of these movements were brought under control by the Catholic Church, but "saints" still arise among the common people with prophetic messages.

The ideology that has characterized these later movements seems not very unlike that of the Tupi-Guarani Indians, yet it has quite different origins. Social isolation, extreme poverty, and lack of real religious help have constituted conditions under which apocalyptic preaching makes an enormous appeal. Every now and then charismatic leaders have arisen in different areas of the backlands to spread the message that the end of the world is at hand, and that King Sebastian or some other messiah figure, or Jesus Christ himself, has returned to lead the faithful to the Holy land. There, after the submission of the heathen, the punishment of the wicked, and the conversion of the indifferent, the Kingdom of God will be established on earth, and the blissful promises of the millennium will be fulfilled. Crowds of people will believe in the message and sell or abandon their property, to follow the prophet as he moves about the country telling the peasants his elaborate fantasies, leading them in prayer, and persuading them to build new churches. Rumors of their activities and of miracles often reach far distant communities and induce more people to leave their homes to join the prophets' following. The

[11] For a complete bibliography on the subject see Maria Izaura Pereira de Queiroz. La "Guerre Sainte" au Brésil: le mouvement messianique du "Contestado". Fac. Filosofia Univ. S. Paulo, Boletim 187, S. Paulo, 1957.
[12] "Devassa acerca dos acontecimentos da Serra do Rodeador". Manuscript. Secão de Documentos, Arquivo Nacional, Rio, Volume entitled Governadores de Pernambuco. Correspondencia com o Ministerio do Reino 1820–21. pp. 4–144, 180–87, 234–69.
[13] F. A. Pereira da Costa, "Folk-lore pernambucano" Rev. Inst. Historico e Geografico Brasileiro, vol. 70, part II (1907) pp. 35–44.
[14] See footnote 9.
[15] See footnote 11.
[16] Maria Izaura Pereira de Queiroz, "Classifications des messianismes brésiliens", Archives de Sociologie des Religions, no. 5 (January–June 1958) pp. 111–120.

religious authorities have sooner or later become concerned but their efforts to expose the new popular "saints" as heretical have failed. Clashes have also occurred between fanatical bands and the civil authorities, with a consequent resort to forcible suppression. Father Cicero adroitly managed to stay in peace with the Catholic Church, but most of these movements ended in bloody religious wars. The harassed prophets would withdraw to strategic places in the backlands and resist troops sent against them. Some bands gradually dispersed, some were forced into submission, and some, resisting to the end, have been annihilated.

In contrast with the earlier Indian migrations, these Sebastianic and millenarian movements had a disruptive influence upon the peasant communities and set up a form of life and social organization that was wholly strange to their adherents. Continuous prayer and penance left no time for cultivating the soil. The bands subsisted on food and cattle supplied by new converts or collected by force as they wandered through the country. Rudimentary military organizations often emerged, with roving adventurers or even bandits taking key positions close to the "messiah". At the start of such a development local political leaders would often temporize with a band, or attempt to make use of it, later drawing back and calling for military intervention. Local outbreaks of violence were not uncommon in reprisal for offences committed either by the faithful or against them.

As has been mentioned, the aberrant practices of one early 19th century movement included blood sacrifice. In this case internal dissension reduced numbers, and the remnant was wiped out by a military expedition.[17]

## III. THE CLASSIFICATION OF BRAZILIAN MESSIANIC MOVEMENTS

Several cases have been fully reported and analyzed in the ethnological and sociological literature on Brazil, and a classification has been attempted by Maria Izaura Pereira de Queiroz, as follows:

1) native (The Tupi-Guarani migrations before and after the arrival of the Portuguese);
2) syncretic Indian-Catholic (which we have called Indian anti-acculturative reactions after exposure to Catholicism under early colonial conditions);
3) Sebastianic;
4) derived directly from Christian belief (Catholic or Protestant, including movements led by thaumaturges and popular "saints" of Catholic origin);
5) contemporary Catholic-Spiritualistic.

There is so much overlap among these categories that such a classificaion has little heuristic value. There is no doubt that the Sebastian legend derived from

Christian belief,[18] and as is pointed out above, the movements of Rodeador (by Pereira de Queiroz called Santa de Pedra) and of Pedra Bonita were at the same time both Sebastianic and Catholic and also resorted to the cult of popular saints. The Rodeador movement went so far as to propose a belated military Crusade for the liberation of Jerusalem and other holy places in Palestine.[19] The Canudos movement also, according to Euclydes da Cunha,[20] had a strong Sebastianic character, yet Pereira da Queiroz places it in category 4. She further makes a distinction within this category between movements that "derive from the great stream of Christian belief" (Canudos, Jõazeiro, Contestado) and those evolving from belief in Brazilian saints or thaumaturges. She thus treats the remnants of such movements as those of Father Cicero or of the monk João Maria as though they were independent movements. In this connection it should be noted that Father Cicero's followers never disbanded. After his death pilgrimages to his home in Jõazeiro continued as before, the only difference being that pilgrims instead of seeking his advice now pray for his return, for he is their messiah. The classification is invalid not only because given cases overlap the categories, but also because the latter rest on a jumble of different criteria, on ethnic affiliation, cultural process, and history.

The same author attempted a second classification according to the roles assumed by the leaders:

A. movements in which the prophet or leader identified himself or was identified by his followers with a divinity.

B. movements in which the leaders took the role of messengers of divinity (*envoyés divins, emissaires célestes*).

She then subdivided these categories as follows:

A-1. the leader (the *pagés*) professes to be a reincarnated culture hero or ancestral spirit;

A-2. the leader professes to be, or is taken to be, Christ (the Indian syncretist movements, those of Canudos and Father Cicero, the Mucker movement and contemporary Catholic-Spiritualist movements);

A-3. the leader comes to be regarded as the reincarnation of a saint, either a recognized Catholic saint or a popular thaumaturge who has died, such as Father Cicero or João Maria;

B-1. the leader claims to have received inspiration and supernatural power from the deities;

B-2. the leader claims to be the emissary of another leader (King Sebastian) who will return, and as such to have extraordinary powers;

B-3. the leader is a thaumaturge or popular saint (João Maria, Beato Laurenco, etc.).[21]

---

[18]  See footnote 8.
[19]  See footnote 12.
[20]  See footnote 9.
[21]  See footnote 16.

There is however no evidence in the literature to support such clear-cut distinctions. In setting up her category A-1, Pereira de Queiroz, may well have been misled by the bias of early informants, many of whom were Catholic priests with little understanding of the role actually played by an Indian leader. For example, a Jesuit priest named Leonardo do Valle wrote in 1563 that "what is called *Santidade* is the arrival of an unknown medicine-man who, as a saint-man and a prophet descended from Heaven, brings news about future events, and all this ends in anthropophagy and devilish evils". The most reliable account, that of Kurt Nimuendaju, tells us that "when a pagé through visions, dreams, or wrong interpretation of natural phenomena had come to the conclusion that the end of the world was imminent he assembled the young men of his band and set them to feasting and dancing to discover the proper route to the East". In the same region that he studied (Outiveiro and Guiará), a religious movement started in the early 19th century with several *pagés*, inspired by visions and dreams, prophesying the destruction of the earth. They rounded up their people and through song and religious dancing prepared them to go in search of the Land without Evil. This movement has been revived at intervals. These Indian leaders in fact never claimed to be supernatural beings. On the special occasions of preparation for migration they were still playing their customary role of religious leaders who had the power of communication, as oracles, with ancestral and other spirits.

In the only Indian syncretic movement in which the leader is alleged to have claimed to be Christ (in the Rio Negro region) there was recent Protestant influence. Even so the evidence of his claim is open to question.[22] Nor can Father Cicero be classed with Antonio Conselheiro (of the Canudos incident) and João Maria (of the Contestado incident). He never claimed to be the reincarnation of a saint, and he denied enthusiastic followers' claims that he had performed miracles. Still less did he identify himself with Christ or consent to others so identifying him. Finally, categories A-2, A-3, and B-3 overlap, for a thaumaturge may claim to be the reincarnation of a Catholic saint or of Christ himself, or to be a new saint.

We now propose an operational classification that combines the organic characteristics of a movement with the leader's role:

1. *Native or Indian movements*

a) Those inspired by Indian mythology and world views that antedate the arrival of the Portuguese and have persisted, among isolated Indian groups, into very recent times.

b) The Santidades, in which Christian influence may be detected but whose principal characteristic was that of a reaction against forced acculturation and disruption of tribal life. (The Rio Negro movement, under Protestant influence, is included here.) The main motivation of these movements was the realization of traditional fantasies about a mythical land. Arrival in this land would mean

---

[22]  See footnote 6.

the attainment of immortality, release from the ordinary burdens of life and escape from the misfortunes brought by the impact of Western civilization. The leaders assumed their traditional roles of prophets and religious guides.

2. *The so-called messianic and millenarian movements reflecting Western influence*

a) Those of definite Sebastianic inspiration (Rodeador's and Pedra Bonita's) in which the myth of the marvellous return of King Sebastian (of popular currency in Portugal until the 15th century), can be traced as instrumental, as providing the *leit-motif* for large gatherings and the performance of religious rituals. Their leaders would announce that the millennium was at hand, and that King Sebastian was returning to subdue the heathen, punish the wicked, and lead the faithful to the terrestrial Paradise.

b) Those in which millenarian ideology was paramount, although Sebastianic and other legends may still have played some part. The followers would assemble to pray and to ensure that they would be among the saved on the day that this world would actually come to an end and the Kingdom of God be established on earth. Their leaders would assume the role either of messiah or prophet or that of a new saint, their role in each case being to lead the faithful to the Promised Land and to conduct the rituals that would bring about the return of Jesus Christ and would prepare Christendom for the Final Day of Judgement. These were the main features of the Contestado and the Canudos movements. In the latter the leader was called Bom Jesus but although he may have identified himself unconsciously with Christ he never claimed to be the Savior. In the Mucker movement the leader was a German woman immigrant who did actually claim to be Christ reincarnated. The Catholic Church was able to channel some of these movements; for example in a case in Gravatá (Pernambuco) in 1900, in which the people had been led to a hill-top to await the end of the world, they were dispersed without incident, and the movement died out.

3. *Messianic movements without strongly millenarian features and either of pure Christian or syncretic inspiration*

In this category we may group together a number of small outbursts of religiosity accompanied by the appearance of thaumaturges and new saints. Some are of Catholic inspiration, others are syncretic, the influences being Catholic-Spiritualistic or, as in the case of a contemporary movement noted lately in the great urban centers of the Northeast, of Protestant-Spiritualistic-Catholic derivation, or the syncretic influence may be theosophical. These movements are as a rule short-lived. They have been confined to urban centers and have never stirred people to abandon their homes and occupations to follow the saint-leader. The leaders have been inspired to give obscure revelations and to make miraculous cures, for example, of cripples. They are kept continuously busy in advising throngs of visitors who daily seek their help in personal matters. When their prestige begins to fade or if the authorities intervene, as in the case of the "Saint of the Palm-trees" in Pernambuco about 1951, most of these saint-leaders vanish as suddenly as they appeared.

## IV.  GENERAL COMMENTS

Various authors have sought to explain the Brazilian movements. Most of these explanations have been of a reductionist character, holding that each outburst of religiosity was due to political and social unrest, to chronic deprivation or to acute deprivation caused by some calamity, to the arousal of mass anxiety and tension or to mass psychopathological disturbance; or they have seen each outburst as essentially a collective form of protest. Roger Bastide recently discussed Brazilian messianisms from a socio-structural point of view. He related them to the extreme stratification of Brazilian society, which relegates the people of the backlands to the condition of pariahs, exposed as they are to periodic famine after droughts and subjected also to the political nepotism of the landowners. At the root of these movements, he stated, is frustration and backwardness through participation in a kind of "archaic culture" which persists because of geographical and cultural isolation. He was however unable to explain why the Negro in Brazil, although relegated to the lower social levels and exposed to the most severe frustrations, has never resorted to messianic movements.[23]

No one could in good faith deny the relevance of these socio-cultural factors. Yet in my understanding of the matter, due consideration should be given to the aesthetic appeal of the idea of a perfect age, to the need for renewed dramatic experience, and to the appeal of new types of leadership along with the new social relationships that develop among the members of a movement. The Indian messianic movements both of the pre-colonial period and of the period of forced acculturation rested on the firmly established myth of the Land without Evil, just as the Christian movements rested on the myth of the millennium. The two types of movement genuinely aimed to take the faithful to some form of terrestrial Paradise or to aid in the inauguration of an age of bliss. Both types brought people together in large numbers and induced them to carry out religious rituals that were believed essential for attainment of their goal. Both the Indians and the neo-Brazilians would retreat to remote places where they could carry on protracted rituals, almost without interruption, until the time should arrive for beginning the journey to Paradise to meet God, or to Jerusalem. It was for this that the tribes gathered and the peasants came together from their isolated farmsteads, under a religious leader who would assume absolute control and set the pace for all the activities of the group or of the new community. Miracles, visions, dancing and feasting or flagellation and fasting, songs of mythical or esoteric

---

[23]  Roger Bastide, *Les Religions Africaines au Brésil* (Presses Universitaires de France, Paris, 1960), pp. 495 ff.; Wilson D. Wallis, "Socio-cultural sources of messiahs" in *Religion, Society and the Individual*, J. Milton Yinger ed. (Macmillan, New York, 1957), pp. 578–86; Bernard Barber, "Acculturation and messianic movements" in *Reader in Comparative Religion*, William A. Lessa and Evon Vogt, ed., (Row Peterson Co., Evanston, 1958), pp. 474–78.

content, hymns, processions and other religious and ritualistic activities, all kindled by fervor and religious exaltation, would take precedence over the previous routine of life. When a people's dominant world view has been one of impending cataclysm, as in the case of the Tupi-Guarani, or of a certain apocalyptic end along with expectation of the long-announced arrival of a messiah who will usher the faithful into Paradise, is it surprising that many individuals should find their hopes rising on very small pretext, and that they should go to extremes in seeking their fulfilment? Even slight changes in political, social or cultural conditions will be sufficient to bring about the conviction that the supernatural is about to take over, and that fantasy will become reality.

Most writers on the messianic movements have tended implicitly to assume that the people whose behavior they are analyzing shared their own world-views and naturalistic bent of explanation. Viewed from the outside, without commitment to the local social setting, the dominant cultural values or the particular functioning of these societies, messianic behavior may well appear pathological, to be explained only by some actual cataclysm or crisis situation, by some extremity arousing deep anxiety and frustration. Taking such a view, the social scientist slides into over-generalizations determined by his theoretical orientation or simply by his cultural bias. He will contribute nothing to a solution of the problem of why these phenomena in some societies and cultures continue to recur through time even though social, political and cultural conditions are changing.

It is clear that wherever a long-established tradition of hope exists, one that gives a dramatic explanation of the cosmos and allows of active participation in the drama in such a way as to fulfil people's fantasies and to take them out of the daily toil or routine of their lives, there any change in social, economic or cultural conditions will favor the rise of a messianic movement. Someone among the many religious people who are always dissatisfied with the functioning of institutionalized religion will become a thaumaturge and leader. The movement may take its color from the most recent version of the relevant legends, or from current political and social issues. Nevertheless the movements will in essence always be similar. The idea of immediate salvation or of an ideal age of bliss soon to be inaugurated will capture people's imagination. Religious leadership and religious rituals will be given precedence over all lay issues. A new type of communal life will be organized along some special lines of structure and value orientation.

The Rodeador movement is a good case in point. Testimony given by some of its members who were arrested reveals the essential gentleness of their conception of the Crusade by which they intended to free the Holy Land and to establish at Jerusalem the Kingdom of God on earth. All of them had believed that this would be achieved by supernatural means, without any occasion for bloodshed, that sceptics and opponents would be confounded and dazzled by the splendor of King Sebastian's return in full glory with his armies. Few of the prisoners were able to express their conception of the new era at all clearly; their hopes and ideas were vague and dreamlike. They could say very little except to repeat over and over again that people should rid themselves of sin and lead a pious life. Everyone would then in time have his reward. Even the reigning King of Portugal would share in the munificent dispensations of wealth and sainthood that King Sebastian would pour out. A recent political outbreak, that of 1817, had hardly affected the people of the area where the Rodeador movement arose. It is true that there are some indications of popular unrest on account of the repressive regime of the governor in office at the time and of the military draft system that was being enforced. But the main reason for enrolment in the movement lay in the promised realization of the peasant's religious hopes. At the beginning no break was contemplated even with the Catholic Church, everyone who wished to join the new holy community being required first to confess to one of the priests of the nearby parishes. Religious fervor was fanned by revelations, prayer, rallies, miracles, and by the two leaders' daily communication with the Holy Virgin. A military organization was also set up, the two prophets being ex-soldiers who made good use of their experience by instituting graded ranks, nightly marches, and parades for inspection of arms. Notwithstanding this, no harm was done to non-members nor to neighboring farms and hamlets. Initiation rituals were modelled after military ceremonial. Yet prayer and waiting for King Sebastian took precedence over any military activity. Even when the members were attacked by government troops they made no immediate move to retaliate, believing until the last moment that the soldiers would miraculously join the movement. In the light of the testimony given after arrest, which shows members had really believed that once the faithful were on the march there would be no need to fight, it would seem that their military preparations had in the main a symbolic value. The prisoners taken had all been certain that everyone would be converted to their faith and would voluntarily enrol in their Crusade.[24]

The course of another movement, that of Father Cicero, is also illuminating. This man, a regular Catholic priest, devoted himself to the humble, led an ascetic life, and took great pains to arouse religious fervor among the isolated populations of the interior. He was highly successful, and after the ravages of a drought had driven great numbers of sick and starving people to the vicinity of the village where he had settled, his reputation spread far and wide. Father Cicero's sermons were always based on the apocalyptic prophecies, urging his hearers to repent and to lead an ascetic life. He aroused people to organize processions, to build new churches and to engage in public flagellation. These and other extreme manifestations of fervor enlivened the

[24] See footnote 12. Also René Ribeiro, "O episodio da Serra do Rodeador (1817–20); um movimento milenar e sebastianista" to be published in *Revista de Antropologia*.

holy community that arose under his leadership. Soon "miracles" occurred and were well publicized. He became renowned as a thaumaturge, and Jõazeiro, the village where he had settled, became the religious capital, as it were, of a wide area, the site on which people's apocalyptic hopes centered. As the place grew, problems of local administration and political control emerged. Father Cicero coped with these by investing one of his followers as mayor, letting the political structure be shaped after the ordinary model of Brazilian institutions. Clashes with the Catholic Church were met by partial submission to the sanctions of the upper hierarchy until a modus vivendi was obtained under which his prestige and influence remained unscathed. When the State government challenged his political as well as his religious control he armed his followers, raised a friendly political faction to power, and kept it in power.

Over the years Father Cicero accumulated considerable wealth, some of which he doled out, rather parsimoniously, among the poor and the disabled. He also developed the policy of moderating the extremes of religious enthusiasm by channeling it into well supervised daily rituals. In short, except for the fact that religious control remained firmly in the hands of a thaumaturge, his holy community came to be ordered in the same way as the ordinary political and social structure which customarily functions in the rural areas of Brazil. Late in his life he temporarily jailed a follower who had slipped into practices akin to zoolatry. Finally he permitted this man to set up a satellite community in which the excess fervor of more extreme devotees was put to good use in hard agricultural labor under a kind of rudimentary communism. Thus during Father Cicero's lifetime his messianic movement had become thoroughly institutionalized. "Miracles" and extreme forms of religiosity were discouraged, and social relationships and the political machinery at Jõazeiro were almost indistinguishable from those prevailing in general in Brazilian peasant society. Yet the emotional atmosphere of the whole town remained deeply religious and pervaded with messianic hope. After his death the town became one of the centers of Catholic worship and pilgrimage, and legends about the thaumaturge continued to offer hope and help to the destitute and the faithful.[25]

Father Cicero is the only messianic leader in Brazil whose career can be followed and whose personality can be appraised through the record of personal interviews and from the testimony of his aides and followers. When the bias of the informants is discounted, he appears simply as a mystic who took to heart the Biblical message and who soberly decided to work for the restoration of apostolic simplicity and ideal social relations, under the aegis of primitive Christianity. The evidence collected thus far from his own personal papers and from the reports of those who knew him gives no indication of

---

[25] Abelardo F. Montenegro, *Historia do Fanatismo Religioso no Ceará* (Batista Fontenele, ed. Fortaleza, 1959).

psychopathological traits nor of paranoic delusions. His record as a seminary student however shows clearly his mystic tendencies. The same may be said of Antonio Conselheiro, leader of the Canudos movement that ended in tragedy. According to Euclydes da Cunha his behavior can be understood only when the whole set of social and cultural conditions in the area where he enacted his drama are taken into consideration; it can never be understood through any appeal to psychopathology.[26] Information as to other messianic leaders of minor stature remains scant or unreliable, although it has to be admitted that a number of different personality types is to be found. The problem of evaluating the roles of these personalities brings the cultural relativistic point of view to the fore.[27]

Attention has also been given to the personalities of followers of some of these movements. Several individuals who took part in the Panelas incident were examined by a noted Brazilian psychiatrist and were given tests at a psychological clinic. The evidence from their life-histories and from the tests demolished the assumption that they had abnormal personalities or suffered from any active psychosis. It pointed up the naivete of their beliefs and world-views as well as the importance of the social milieu in conditioning them to accept the message of their leader. The latter, by inference from the reports of his followers, is assumed to have been feeble-minded. But among the followers themselves only one case of mental defectiveness could be detected.[28]

The problem of individual motivation remains central whatever hypothesis as to the cause of messianic movements be entertained. Three hypotheses may be considered compatible with the Brazilian evidence. In the first place a traditional belief in an unstable world order and in a Land without Evil that can be reached by courageous mortals who will first purify themselves through ritual will tend to give rise to such movements. Secondly, a situation of social constraint forcing the collapse of cultural values may incite people to recall their legendary fantasies. Finally, social and cultural isolation and sluggishness may create an ideal climate for the reception of apocalyptic teaching. The fundamental motivations for the individual to join a messianic movement seem to derive from two kinds of dissatisfaction. He may be dissatisfied with the current social, economic, or political order, or with the rewards of institutionalized religion. In either case a desire for change may be aroused, and hope for the realization of familiar apocalyptic fantasies may then flare up.

Just as I was leaving Brazil to attend the conference at which these matters were discussed, a Recife taxi-driver handed me a printed leaflet entitled "Operations of the Celestial Government founded in Brazil on January 1,

---

[26]  See footnote 9.
[27]  Melville J. Herskovits, *Man and His Works* (Alfred A. Knopf, New York, 1948), pp. 63 ff.
[28]  José Lucena, "Uma pequena epidemia mental em Pernambuco: os fanaticos do municipio de Panelas", *Neurobiologia*, Vol. 3 (1940), pp. 41–91.

1960." Its contents throw light on the millenarian fantasies that may be harbored by people who work with modern machinery in a large modern city and who seemingly participate in the whole contemporary Brazilian urban culture. Here are some samples:

As we move towards the end of the 20th century the sayings of the Scriptures about the new Earth and the new Heaven and the coming of the Son of Man in the Majesty of his Celestial Father will be fulfilled ... The year 1960 will be the milestone marking the second advent of Jesus ... Other civilizations have been born, therefore how could the civilization of the New Jerusalem, the wife of the Paschal Lamb, fail to dawn?

The obscure and symbolic exhortation continues by listing 24 rules of pure moral conduct which are enjoined on all who wish to join this movement and become the elect subjects of "the heavenly government." The document concludes with this prophecy:

the Son of Man shall be hailed as King of Brazil and of the government of the World for centuries of centuries, and the New Earthly Jerusalem shall take its sons to the Heavenly Jerusalem. Then Heaven shall be joined with Earth under one government and one Judge, who shall be God among men.

The leaflet states that this message was received through telepathy by a certain Cicero José Farias, the leader of the "Christian Jesuit Legion," which released it as "the third letter of the Second Advent." It claims that the movement was started at Jõazeiro (State of Ceará) and that it has branches at Arcoverde (Pernambuco) and in some of the principal northeastern state capitals. Here we have a fascinating new case for study.

RENÉ RIBEIRO
*University of Recife*

# MILLENARY ASPECTS OF THE TAIPING REBELLION (1851–64) [1]

In advancing whatever pertinent knowledge I have acquired of this major upheaval of the 19th century, the Taiping Rebellion, I am constrained to use the definitions and concepts that others have developed in this colloquium. Comparative studies on an interdisciplinary basis are a new field of endeavour for me, but I shall be very happy if data about the Rebellion contribute to the general body of knowledge that is being assembled.

As regards time and the direction of time, the Taipings said that they were seeking to recapture an earlier stage of perfection. This perfect age antedated the Age of the Philosophers (6th c.–3rd c. B.C.), including Confucius and Lao-tzu, the introduction and development of Buddhism, and, of course, the growth of the Confucian cult and the Taoist Church. According to their theology, God the Heavenly Father, the Supreme Ruler east and west, had once been worshipped by all Chinese. To restore this original situation after 2000 years of subsequent apostasy, God decided to send down into the world Hung Hsiu-ch'üan, the titular leader, as the Heavenly Younger Brother of Jesus. The regime which he and his followers proclaimed in 1851, called the *T'ai-p'ing t'ien-kuo* (Heavenly kingdom of great peace) was to last for an indeterminate period. Little is made of the Last Judgment; I cannot discover that anything was even said about it.

The Taiping founders used religious beliefs and forms unashamedly for political purposes; the liang-ssu-ma, the officials of the lowest grade in the hierarchy who maintained closer contact with the mass of the regime's followers, exercised both religious and political authority. The Rebellion should be measured against Norman Cohn's definition of a millenarian movement.[2]

Let us take up Cohn's points one by one.

The salvation promised was certainly collective. The portions of the Old Testament selected by the rebels in their tracts show their fondness for the idea of a host – men, women, and children led by a leader – in frequent communication with God. It is not going too far to say that the Taipings imagined themselves the latter-day counterparts of the Children of Israel.

The salvation promised was terrestrial. It would materialize fully when

---

[1] Except for the transliteration of Chinese titles, the simpler form *Taiping* is used throughout the article in place of T'ai-p'ing, the correctly romanized term.

[2] See above, p. 31.

the Manchu dynasty had been swept out of China. Indeed, the new regime of the saved was inaugurated at the formal commencement of the Rebellion in January, 1851. An otherworldly heaven was reserved for those who died in battle.

A sense of imminence seems to have been completely lacking and out of context. The so-called God Worshippers (Pai Shang-ti Hui), as the rebels were called by others before 1851, were not told by their preachers that their salvation might come at any moment by Divine interposition. Instead, they were readied for revolt, to be able by their own efforts to act when the opportunity presented itself, as it did in Kwangsi in the fall of 1850.

Finally the salvation was not total, if I understand Cohn correctly. The end sought was practical and possible, but was not envisaged with a hyperbolic yearning toward perfection. On the other hand, the title of the regime had an interesting millennial flavor. It styled itself officially the *T'ai-p'ing t'ien kuo* (Heavenly kingdom of great peace). T'ien-kuo, the second half of the title, entirely lacked any Chinese antecedents, originating in a term apparently coined by 19th century missionary translators of the Bible for the New Testament "Kingdom of Heaven." The first half of the title, on the other hand, reflected the Chinese usage of centuries. The polysyllable T'ai-p'ing (great peace) can be described as a millennial term of great antiquity, for it was the name of the last and most utopian of the famous three ages mentioned in the Kung Yang interpretation of the Ch'un Ch'iu, one of the Five Classics.[3] T'ai-p'ing has been used at least five times as an era title in the reigns of Chinese Emperors; it occurs currently in the titles of business houses and restaurants.

It is best at this point to make clear what the Taiping ideology was and why these ideas came at a time to excite the effective action that they did. Who the leaders were and how they drew their followers to them should next be discussed. Finally a brief comment as to the outcome of the movement is called for.

The Taiping appeal to the Chinese can be divided into two elements, the

[3]  Huo Hsiu's commentary, 1st year of Yin Kung, *Kung Yang Chuan*. The Han Shu, the second of the twenty-four histories, in describing times in China before 700 B.C., has the following utopian characterization of *t'ai-p'ing*. "When there was a surplus of food (enough) for a three year period (from nine years') presentations of products of labor, it was called *teng* maturity. Two consecutive *teng* (that is, a period of eighteen years) was called *p'ing* 'peace,' when there would be a surplus of food (enough) for six years. Three consecutive *teng* (twenty-seven years) was called *t'ai-p'ing* 'great peace,' when there would be a surplus of food (enough) for nine years which had been accumulated during twenty-seven years. Thereafter, kindly virtue spread (among the people), and permeated them. So it was said: 'If there is a (true) ruler, it must require a generation before humanity will prevail.'" Han Shu 24A, 5b–6a, translated in Nancy Lee Swann, transl., *Food and Money in Ancient China* (Princeton University Press, 1950), 134. Quoted in Eugene Powers Boardman, *Christian Influence Upon the Ideology of the Taiping Rebellion 1851–1864* (University of Wisconsin Press, Madison, 1952), pp. 126–127.

non-religious and the religious. The two were usually combined and seldom
occurred separately in their published pronouncements. For the present purpose, though, it is expedient to present them separately.

The non-religious part of the appeal sprang from the experience of humbler
Chinese and was directed toward all classes of the population. The Manchu
regime was attacked on the ground that it was un-Chinese. Taiping propaganda went into detail in an effort to enlist what can be called an ethnic
consciousness.[4] It made a strong case against the Manchu government,
charging that it was inefficient and corrupt. The Taipings attempted to
anchor in Chinese tradition as many of their revolutionary and new theological ideas as possible.[5]

The religious part of the ideology shows certain evidence of Buddhist and
Confucian influence and possibly that of Taoism. Buddhist influence is reflected in terminology. As can be expected, Confucian attitudes appear in
the ideological creations of the Taiping Chinese but they are without millenarian import due to the practical, non-revolutionary, conservative nature
of Confucianism. The mystical fantasies of the Taoist Church certainly lent
themselves to millenarian imagery. The tracts of the rebels, documents which
best reveal the ideas that interested them, show, however, little trace of the
Taoist line. For our purpose the Christian part of the Taiping religion over-
shadows all of the non-Christian Taiping part and is germane.

To judge from the use made of Christian ideas in their tracts, the Taipings
only employed a small part of the wealth of principle and illustration available
to them in the Bible. Why? Possibly because they couldn't understand the
more subtle parts of the Scriptures due to imperfect translation, insufficient
explanation, and the different cultural tradition from which the Bible came.
A more compelling determinant seems to have been deliberate choice. Let
us see what the Taipings took.

Most of what the Taipings borrowed came from the first five books of the
Old Testament. The Mosaic idea of God as the Creator and the only God to
whom sacrifices might properly be made is conspicuous. He is jealous of
homage shown to other deities but displays forgiveness and has to be regarded as the God of *all* men to fulfil the myth of his universality for the
Chinese as well as for the Hebrews. God communicated with Taiping leaders

---

[4]  See Arthur W. Hummel, ed., *Eminent Chinese of the Ch'ing Period* (U.S. Government Printing Office, Washington, 1943–44), Vol. II, p. 878, for an account of how
the Manchus had taken advantage of internal confusion to deprive the Chinese of their
empire. A good example of a typical Taiping pronouncement is the "Edict received
from heaven to punish the Tartars and publish the order everywhere," a translation of
which appears in Boardman, *Christian Influence*, pp. 151–154. The original is available
under the title Feng-t'ien t'ao-hu hsi pu ssu-fang yü in Lo Yung and Shen Tsu-chi,
*T'aip'ing t'ien-kuo shih wen ch'ao* (Anthology of the poetry and prose of the T'ai-p'ing
t'ien-kuo) (Commercial Press, Shanghai, 1935), 1st ts'e, 4a, l. 1 to 7b, 1.5 under this title.
(Pages are numbered from the beginning of each document.)

[5]  Boardman, *Christian Influence*, p. 35 has a footnoted summary of their argument.

in times of stress and was believed to intervene personally at crucial moments.

The Taipings made use of three stories of the Pentateuch: the Biblical account of creation, Noah and the Flood, and the exodus from Egypt. The last was cast into meter, three characters to the line, in the style of the familiar Three Character Classic used to teach Chinese children characters. By far the most important portion of the Old Testament utilized by the rebels was the Ten Commandments. These were modified in an interesting manner to suit Taiping needs and apparently became an instrument for the discipline of masses of Chinese.[6]

Again, to judge from their tracts, the Taipings borrowed from the New Testament aspects of the idea of God there presented, the basic facts of Christ's life, and a few elements of Christ's teachings. Ideas of Heaven and Hell, of evil spirits and of Satan, all but the last of which had their Chinese Buddhist or native Chinese counterparts, were congenial to Taiping use. The Taiping God was the father of all men and could be approached directly by any believer. The belief in modes or functions of God implicit in the theory of the Trinity was even taken over but was not understood. On the other hand, Christ was not regarded as divine; he was simply the Heavenly Elder Brother of Jesus. The story of Christ's crucifixion, resurrection, and ascension is worded so as to establish the fact of salvation for virtuous believers. As important an event to Christians as the resurrection was represented by the insurgents as an example more of a return to earth than a guarantee of life everlasting. This made possible their theory of Christ's descent to earth in 1837 and other appearances among men in the years that followed.

The Biblical idea of sin was conveyed to the Taipings through the Chinese character *tsui* which meant primarily a crime, fault, or offense. The deeper connotations of the term *sin* were not understood; sin was called simply "transgressing the laws of heaven."

Apparently the organizers of the Taiping movemen⁺ realized the importance of an adequate eschatology and therefore set about constructing a system of reward and retribution in the hereafter. When complete, the system was employed to enforce their own ordinances and especially to inspire the utmost effort of their soldiers during battle. The Chinese form of Mahayana Buddhism could have been used for such an eschatology but the Taipings were committed by the terms of their dogma to the exclusion of Buddhist ideas. The way was clear for full utilization of ideological resources afforded by the Bible. The Old Testament was not of much use, for retribution is there carried out by enemies, pestilence, and the forces of Nature, operating on this earth and in this life. The Old Testament is almost devoid of references to heaven; Sheol, the Old Testament term for the underworld, shows as a concept limited attention as compared with the Avernus of the Aeneid or the Inferno of the Divine Comedy. Sheol is no more than the abode of

[6]   Boardman, *Christian Influence,* pp. 61–65.

the dead and its inmates if wicked experience no punishment other than oblivion.

In contrast, the creators of the Taiping eschatology found the New Testament a fertile source of example and imagery. Here was the "Kingdom of Heaven." In Matthew's Gospel procedure for reaching heaven is fully outlined and hell is represented as more than Sheol, for it is clearly the scene of punishment for wrongdoing. The Acts of the Apostles and the Epistles of the apostle Paul promise eternal life for believers. Revelations, a particular favorite apparently of Hung Hsiu-ch'üan, the spiritual leader of the movement, has an extravagance of figure and a profusion of physical detail that, despite inevitable mistranslation, appealed to the Taipings.

What did the Taipings do with the eschatological terms and ideas available to them in the New Testament? To begin with, they appropriated the "Kingdom of Heaven." T'ien, the character for "heavenly," was then prefaced to names of institutions and personages of the new order, e.g. "Heavenly Dynasty," "Heavenly Army," "Heavenly Elder Brother," and so on. They go on to describe heaven as the scene of endless bliss. In equal measure hell is portrayed by them as a place of punishment and unending misery.[7] Together with the formulation of the idea of a hereafter, one also gathers that the regime strove to establish an ideal commonwealth on earth and thus had a very practical end in mind.

Who were the leaders of the Rebellion and how did they draw their followers to them? Hung Hsiu-ch'üan, the visionary and titular leader, was a Hakka from a small farming community near Canton who tried unsuccessfully on four occasions to win the designation "Hsiu-ts'ai" in the official civil service examination in his home province Kwangtung. As a result of "visions" or hallucinations that followed his third unsuccessful attempt to pass the examinations and his later experience in interpreting his visions in the light of what he read in Christian tracts and was taught by Issachar J. Roberts, an American missionary in Canton, in 1847, Hung became convinced that he had been chosen by God to restore all of China to the true worship. He was reported by his cousin Hung Jen-kan to have said, "I have received the immediate command from God in His presence: the will of Heaven rests with me. Although thereby I should meet with calamity, difficulty and suffering, yet I am resolved to act."[8] Hung was aided by a convert and relative Feng Yün-shan to whom must go major credit for preaching the new faith and

[7] Boardman, *Christian Influence*, pp. 86–87 has illustrative quotations from Taiping tracts.

[8] Theodore Hamberg, *The Visions of Hung Siu-Tsuen and the Origin of the Kwangsi Insurrection* (Yenching University Library: Peiping, 1935), p. 22. The reader should consult an interesting article by a Cantonese psychiatrist who throws light on the reported mental illness of the Taiping leader. P. M. Yap, "The mental illness of Hung Hsiu-ch'üan, leader of the Taiping Rebellion," *Far Eastern Quarterly*, XIII. 3 (May 1954), pp. 287–304.

organizing communities of God-Worshippers in a mountainous area of Kwangsi, the province where the rebellion against the Ch'ing dynasty began. Hung was aided by Yang Hsiu-ch'ing, a community leader among the charcoal burners of the Thistle Mount area of Kwangsi where the God-Worshippers were organized. Yang displayed later unusual ability as a military commander but, more important for our purposes, also developed a talent as a shaman who claimed to receive communications from God and from Jesus the Heavenly Elder Brother at critical points in the military progress of the Rebellion. Yang's authenticity as a source of these communications or, better, as an oracle, was recognized by the titular leader, a fact reflected in his appointment as the Taiping equivalent of the Holy Spirit. Other leaders in the first years of the Rebellion were Hsiao Ch'ao-kuei, a brother-in-law of Hung, and a wood-cutter; Wei Ch'ang-hui, an educated Hakka *tsui-li* or petty official and a native of Chin-t'ien, the village where the Rebellion started; and Shih Ta-k'ai, a rich, educated Hakka farmer who developed considerable military ability. All except Feng und Hung came from Kwangsi where the memory of the exploits of Taiping leaders has been kept green into the 1940s.[9] Several years after the rebels had succeeded in establishing themselves in Nanking, captured in 1853, two other officials played prominent parts as leaders. One was the gifted Li Hsiu-ch'eng who rose from the ranks of Taiping soldiery and had no part in the religious leadership of the Rebellion. The other was Hung Jen-kan, a second cousin of the titular leader, who received the same instruction in I. J. Roberts' mission as Hsiu-ch'üan and was separated from the main body of God-Worshippers in the first year of the Rebellion. Jen-kan was a refugee from Ch'ing retaliation in Kwangtung against the Hung family, was accepted as a Christian by the Christian community of Hongkong, and during the years 1855–58 was employed there as a catechist and preacher by members of the London Missionary Society. Hung studied theology as well as secular subjects and made many acquaintances among the foreigners. While studying foreign administrative methods he came to appreciate the merits of Western political institutions so that later he advocated the adoption of many of them by the Taipings. In 1859 Hung was able to rejoin his old associates in Nanking and very shortly afterward was elevated by his cousin Hsiu-ch'üan to the post of Prime Minister. Probably Jen-kan received this exalted rank not because of the religious knowledge which his study and associations in Hongkong had

---

[9] Some years ago I was told by Chien Yu-wen, a well-known Cantonese historian of the Rebellion, that the military government of Kwangsi province furnished him with transportation and other support for his historical investigations in the Thistle Mount area in 1944. The degree of provincial interest in the Rebellion may be measured by the fact that Mr. Chien's investigations took place not only in wartime but during a year which saw Japanese invasion of Kwangsi and American withdrawal from Liuchow, an air base situated not far from the Thistle Mount area near a city to which the Taipings once laid siege.

given him but because educated Taipings with family connections that promised loyalty to Hsiu-ch'üan were at a premium. Hung Jen-kan was the author of an official Taiping document, *A New Work for Aid in Administration,* in which he recommended Taiping adoption of a number of Western political institutions and made suggestions about the separation of the judicial and executive branches of government and the establishment of a patent office, railroads, steamship companies, shipyards, a post-office, a police force, a banking system, information collecting agencies, a limited bill of rights, and profit inducements for the furtherance of private enterprise.[10]

Jen-kan's proposals were not adopted, for by 1859 the rebels were so occupied with military matters that there was little opportunity for civilian reform. Even if there had been, Jen-kan's personality was such that he would not have used religious means of furthering Westernization. Indeed, in the last years of the Rebellion – it was overthrown in 1864 – Hung Hsiu-ch'üan monopolized the religious leadership of Taiping headquarters in Nanking. Any delegation of religious authority was by this time unthinkable. Jen-kan and Li Hsiu-ch'eng in these last years tried to force the titular leader into a more active role but he refused such a role, became increasingly withdrawn and abstracted, and took his own life several months before the fall of Nanking to Ch'ing generals. Li Hsiu-ch'eng and Hung Jen-kan after their capture left official statements which are of historical value.

I have not previously discussed the source of the germinal ideas of the Rebellion which insofar as the contribution of a unifying influence are concerned were religious. Secular and nationalistic discontent was expressing itself in the activities of anti-dynastic secret societies, but these were localized efforts that were never able to organize a military movement that could cross provincial boundaries.

Though there were plenty of Moslems in China by the time of the Rebellion and though Catholic Christianity, under official ban, was known to Chinese, the ideas that produced unified military action came from 19th century Protestant books and, to a lesser degree, from an American missionary, Issachar J. Roberts. The written evidence, whether from advocates, critics, or neutral foreign observers, supports this.

Why did such millenary thought and agitation occur? The categorical answer can be made that in China unlike Brazil such millenial thought and agitation are not normal. The period 1820–1851 was for a variety of reasons not a normal span of years in Chinese history. There were social and spiritual

---

[10]    Ssu-yü Teng and John K. Fairbank, *China's Response to the West, a Documentary Survey 1839–1923* (Harvard University Press: Cambridge, 1954), pp. 57–59 has translated excerpts from a *A New Work for Aid in Administration.* See also footnote 12, p. 8 of *Research Guide for China's Response to the West* (Harvard Univ. Press: Cambridge, 1954) by the same authors. Jen-kan's career is given in fuller detail in So Kwan-wai and Eugene P. Boardman, "Hung Jen-kan, Taiping Prime Minister, 1859–1864," *Harvard Journal of Asiatic Studies,* 20. 1 & 2 (June 1957), pp. 262–294.

anxieties that could not be "assuaged by other means than millenial dreaming." The occurrence among the early group of rebels of convulsive, ecstatic experiences, and the presence of an atmosphere of religious revivalism were normal for such a period of pre-revolutionary unrest. The fact that Hung Hsiu-ch'üan was able to be as effective as he was attests the normality of usually abnormal religious ideas in these times.[11]

Sylvia Thrupp refers to the fact that Christianity is designed in large degree to arouse spiritual anxiety. Did the Taipings use their brand of Christianity for this purpose? The answer is yes, in that the Taipings sought to convince their followers that they were sinful. Once conscious of his sin, the suppliant was told to kneel and pray to God for forgiveness, using either his own words or a written form that was supplied. Afterwards he was directed to wash himself clean with a basin of water or, if opportunity presented itself, to bathe himself in a river. When he had obtained freedom from sin in this manner, the suppliant was directed to pray morning and evening and before meals, to keep the Sabbath every seventh day, to obey the Ten Commandments, and to avoid worshipping "perverted gods" or doing evil things. The obtainment of divine favor and of life after death in heaven would result from following such a course of conduct. Belief in the Atonement was encouraged, though, as mentioned previously, Jesus was not considered divine. It should be emphasized that the Taipings were committed to bringing about a heaven on earth in the form of their type of theocratic state. To this end a rather remarkable program of reform including land reform was formulated – remarkable in view of the refusal of Chinese members of the Ch'ing bureaucracy, virtually the only educated Chinese, to join the movement. So Taiping religion existed for two purposes, to provide other-worldly solace and to inspire the realization of a Taiping heaven on earth.

---

[11] "The life and career of Hung Hsiu-ch'üan provides one of the clearest examples in history of the process by which vast social, economic, and political forces impinge on the mind of an unusually perceptive and possibly unstable person, and having worked in him a transformation of mind and character, are through him gathered together and given meaning, and then released as an indomitable psychic drive to bring about social change. It is only in this light that Hung's place in history can be understood. Chinese authors have as a rule overlooked his mental illness, while many foreign authors have regarded him as a madman, although others also speak of him as a genius. But the principle of cultural relativity applies to insanity as to other aspects of human behavior. In the case of Hung evaluation of his conduct and thinking is a rather delicate task, not only because of his own special cultural background, but also because he lived in a period when the whole of Chinese culture was in violent transformation. But such an evaluation is really not important. The manner in which he arrived at his renovating ideas might have been grossly abnormal by ordinary standards, but it should be remembered that, while his religion ended in rejection and his revolution in failure, yet, in the light of history, many of the aims he cherished were also those sought by later Chinese leaders in the gradual process of the adaptation of China to the modern world. That is the measure of his genius, and the meaning of his madness." P. M. Yap, "Mental Illness of Hung Hsiu-ch'üan," *op. cit.,* pp. 303–304.

Reference is made to the occurrence of millenary expectations (see above, p. 20) in a situation in which specific secular discontents had built up a revolutionary situation. Such a description fits the Taiping revolutionary or pre-revolutionary position. Further, the ideas at issue were brought into action consciously to serve the reform and anti-dynastic purposes of Hung Hsiu-ch'üan and his coterie. Except for a few phrases and reference to forgiveness from sin, he and companion authors of the Taiping tracts left out the body of the teachings of Christ. For example, the Parables, the Sermon on the Mount, and the Golden Rule do not appear, a situation that indicates the exercise of conscious choice.

Did the promised millennium serve as a loophole for the admission of alien, i.e. Western influence? I have indicated above in discussing the influence of Hung Jen-kan that it could have but did not.[12]

The question was raised in our discussions, as to whether there was a ritual means of identifying loyal followers of a movement. Baptism, in the Taiping movement was made the ritual means for such identification. In the early days of the movement the applicant for baptism, placed before a table upon which there were two lamps and three cups of tea, repeated a general form for the confession of sins and was asked to answer satisfactorily certain general questions. When these had been answered, the neophyte knelt, the man in charge of the ceremony poured over his head a cup of water from a larger basin and then, when he had been baptized, the person baptized said, "My previous sin is washed away. I have put aside the old and am made new." The convert then got up, drank a cup of clear tea, and washed his breast with water to show that he had cleansed his heart. Then, if there was a river nearby, he went to this river to practice immersion, to confess his sins, and to pray to God to pardon them. Converts who had been baptized were entitled to receive various standard prayers for use morning and evening and at meals.

The further question was raised, whether thought incited Taiping action or action incited thought. My answer is that of course both happened, but that in my opinion thought oftener incited action. I cannot neglect also reference to the tension between disappointed candidates in the examination system and successful literati. The disappointed candidates sought an outlet in Taiping millenary theory and, in the case of Hung, as previously mentioned, the tension produced a nervous breakdown and reintegration of his personality to the point where he was equipped to lead the revolutionary movement.

It remains to discuss in general fashion whether Chinese traditions of protest by local revolt or other means play a part in the picture. There is in Chinese history a tradition of protest by local revolt which goes back to the

---

[12] Boardman, *Christian Influence*, pp. 74–76.

years between the earlier and later Han dynasties (ca. 23 A.D.). The revolts of the Red Eyebrows and the Yellow Turbans, both secret societies, prominent in Han civil wars, is a case in point. In the later years of the Yüan dynasty this kind of revolt was reinforced by what can be termed a nationalistic sentiment directed toward driving out Mongol overlords. This sort of sentiment was revived in the latter part of the Ch'ing dynasty, that is after 1800, when the Manchus were in decline and when the vigor which had been shown by monarchs such as the K'ang-hsi and Ch'ien-lung emperors no longer manifested itself in their successors. The first of such anti-dynastic and social protest movements of the 19th century was the movement known as that of the White Lotus or White Lily Society which occurred at the turn of the century. To speak in general terms, in the latter years of a typical Chinese dynasty, revolt, according to Chinese historiographical theory, may occur and is sanctioned as a means of expressing Heaven's displeasure with the behavior of the current ruler. The Taipings, however, were not pretending to fulfil the mandate of Heaven and install a better Chinese emperor nor were they seeking to place a purely Chinese emperor on the throne in place of a Manchu barbarian. No, their aim was an unusual one entirely out of the Chinese tradition. Members of rebellious secret societies could only join their movement if they met its rigorous tests and subscribed to its goal of a new heavenly kingdom in China. It is for this reason that the Taiping Rebellion has been of such interest not only to students of millenarianism and of Chinese revolutionary history but of revolutionary history in general.

EUGENE P. BOARDMAN
*University of Wisconsin*

# MESSIANIC MOVEMENTS IN THE CELEBES, SUMATRA, AND BORNEO

In the following pages an attempt will be made to describe the development of Messianic upheavals in three separate areas in Indonesia during the early decades of the present century: (1) the *mejapi* incident among the Bare'e Toradja of East-Central Sulawesi (Celebes), (2) the *parhudamdam* movement among the Karo-Batak of North-East Sumatra, and (3) the *njuli* phenomenon of the Lawangan Dayas of South Kalimantan (Borneo). The pattern of millenarian expectations in each of these areas embodies elements that can be understood only in terms of the distinct cultural characteristics of the ethnic group in which they occurred, although it will also be suggested that the catalytic agents that produced the Messianic "response" in each instance, possessed sufficient similarity to allow them to be considered together. In this manner the present paper also seeks a connection with an earlier analysis of Messianic expectations in Java.[1]

## I

Our first concern is with the Bare'e linguistic division of the East Toradja ethnic group, the members of which have been the subject of one of the most exhaustive analyses in the voluminous Dutch ethnological literature on Indonesia.[2] The Bare'e live virtually in the center of Celebes, around Lake Poso and between the Laa, Poso, and Kalaena rivers and their tributaries. They were traditionally settled in widely scattered and strategically located villages of up to several hundred people in size. The village population constitutes in a sense an extended family, members of which acutely feel that they are, however distantly, related to each other by ties of blood. Connubial prohibitions appear to be comparatively few and flexible and extend primarily to forbidden intermarriages between comparatively closely related members of different generations (e.g. unions between uncle or aunt and nephew or niece, or grandfather and granddaughter). As a result of

[1] Justus M. van der Kroef, "Javanese Messianic Expectations: Their Origin and Cultural Context," *Comparative Studies in Society and History*, vol. I (1959), pp. 299–323.
[2] N. Adriani and A. C. Kruyt, *De Bare'e Sprekende Toradjas van Midden-Celebes* (De Oost-Toradjas), (2nd ed., Amsterdam, 1950), 3 vols. The description of Bare'e Toradja society in this essay is based on this work unless otherwise indicated.

population pressure on the land, or because of quarrels between factions in the village a group of inhabitants may leave and elsewhere form its own community. In due course there arises a complex of villages, emanating from a "mother" village, members of which form a unit with a distinct name. In the village the heads of households are the principal source of authority. One of them is the *kabosenja* or chief, a cooptative office, in the sense that an older chief selects and prepares his own successor with the concurrence of the other villagers. The *kabosenja*'s actual powers are quite limited. Though the Toradja also used to recognize the authority of certain kings, called *datu* or *djena*, their influence, mainly of a traditional nature, is of little relevance here. Cultivation of rice, the principal food crop, takes place in slash-and-burn fashion on plots of land traditionally regarded as communally owned by the village (through the mythical bequest of the first ancestral pair of humans that settled the community) and apportioned to families who work in close cooperation with each other. The yield of hunting and fishing supplements the diet, while in recent decades, with increasing individuation in land tenure and cultivation methods, trade in copra and forest products has added an important new dimension to the Toradja economy.

Fundamental to our understanding of the *mejapi* phenomenon is the manner in which the needs and inclinations of the Toradja individual, who is described as having "a strong egocentric tendency" by Kruyt and Adriani, are balanced by or made to harmonize with the dictates of the community. The Toradja village is more than a human aggregation, it is also a religious congregation, the members of which feel united with one another and with the mythologized ancestors by an all encompassing sacred order in which the critical moments in human life, from birth to death, the cultivation of food on communal land, and the approved code of conduct in peace and war all play pivotal roles. In agriculture, the building of dwellings, or in the hunt, mutual endeavor and assistance is the rule, strengthened by the sense of family unity that traditionally permeates the members of a village; the Toradja is not apt to undertake any venture of importance without drawing his immediate relations into the matter. As a Toradja *kajori* (folk verse) has it: [3]

> We are each others' brothers and sisters
> let us not leave each other
> If the sea becomes restless
> we will go together
>
> Together we form one lake
> on my side everything is calm
> Only when you separate yourself
> would things become unruly.

[3]  W. A. Braasem and R. Nieuwenhuys, *Volkspoëzie uit Indonesië* (Groningen, Djakarta, 1952), p. 200.

The environment in which the Toradja child is raised tends to strengthen a sense of interdependence with the group. There is very little privacy in a Toradja dwelling and the section of it that is withdrawn from immediate contact with the rest of the community yields its secrets readily to the listening passer-by. Parental quarrels, jealousies, economic difficulties, sexual relations, debts, problems of warfare – all of these the child is privy to at a very early age, and the events in and general condition of his household and community become, of necessity, the child's earliest and most important framework of thought and action.

But there is another side to the coin, for much in Toradja life predisposes toward a denial of this same communal unity. Educationally the later stress on subservience to *aluk* (religiously sanctioned custom and social demand) and the primacy of participation in group activities is counteracted by the extreme freedom in the first seven or eight years of life of the child. As soon as the Toradja child can more or less help itself it is virtually left to its own devices in household and village, and is required to render only periodic small services to parents and other members of the immediate family. For the rest "the child goes its own way and educates itself, learns what it wishes and lets go what it does not want to," remark Adriani and Kruyt. A kind of self willed individualism, inclining toward the extreme of egotism, may be regarded as potentially present in the result of this early educational freedom. Another analysis of Toradja child psychology stresses the child's acute sensitivity to the absence of a firm family foundation in Toradja life, so that the child's uncertainty about the consequences of family quarrels and disturbances is augmented by the general formlessness and excessive permissiveness in its early development.[4] In consequence the later imposition of communal demands fall with considerable abruptness on the growing child: circumcision, teeth filing, required work on the land and – in an earlier day – participation in war, marriage, common work effort in the erection of dwellings – all these events and mechanisms of identifying the child with the group cross the earlier egocentrism and repress it with their cumulative weight. This process should not be seen as encountering hostility and resistance only, however, for the very formlessness of existence may drive the developing ego "into the arms of the collectivity," in which it can safely submerge itself. As Fischer, commenting on this transition in the life of the Toradja child has put it: "It is the anxiety of being alone in the literal and figurative sense of the word which urges them on not to be different from the others, for the consequences that would bring, one does not dare face."[5]

Whether this educational development allows us to draw conclusions for

---

[4]   J. Kruyt, "Iets over de geestesstructuur der Inheemschen van Midden-Celebes," *Nederlandsch Tijdschrift voor Psychologie,* vol. 5 (1937), pp. 194-214.
[5]   H. T. Fischer, *Kinderaantal en Kinderleven in Indonesië* (The Hague, 1950), pp. 48-49.

the periodic instability of Toradja communal life is of course hard to say, but certain it is that the Toradja lives – and sometimes not too easily – between the realization of the all embracing importance of communal demands in his own survival pattern, and the inclinations toward self-willed solutions and highly egocentric forms of behavior. An awareness of the relative instability of social foundations and the tension that this may produce should probably be seen as an important motif in Toradja culture. Nothwithstanding the realization of the importance of communal cohesiveness in the life of the individual the continued bifurcation of the Toradja villages is an evident fact. Sometimes population pressure on the land leads to the departure of some villagers and the founding of a new community, then again it is the emergence of rival factions around prominent members of a village society that leads to a split. From time to time a single household, no longer feeling at ease, might decide to pack up and settle in a different community. Undoubtedly such moving away was facilitated by the sense of having family bonds with members of other villages belonging to the same kinship complex, so that communication with the all important world of familial and ancestral spirits (to be discussed presently) would not be disrupted too greatly.

Whatever the cause of the sundering of communal ties the process itself is well known and an examination of myths describing village and lineage origins confirms it. For, "everywhere there are tales of humans who live in the forests and hold themselves apart" from other villagers. This withdrawal mechanism, the awareness of which is sharpened by the clash of individual inclination and communal demand in the development of the Toradja personality, is perhaps most fully expressed in the *mejapi* phenomenon. The term *mejapi* means "to hide oneself," usually behind or beneath some kind of protective cover. From time to time the Toradja may withdraw from the rest of society, either individually or in groups, and go to live in an isolated spot in the forest. Ordinarily *mejapi* occurs after a dissatisfied villager has managed to obtain a small following. The source of the dissatisfaction may be as minor a grievance as the simple daily round of village life can provide, but whatever the reason *mejapi* is usually a blow to village authority, especially the authority of the *kabosenja*, who as preserver of tradition, is the embodiment of communal *aluk*. Sometimes the exodus may take place under a feigned leader, while the real instigator, who may have had a quarrel with the village chief or his relatives, remained behind the scenes. The protest gesture of *mejapi* therefore comes as a shameful experience for a village headman, and, given the comparatively small size of the Toradja village, as a threat to the continued viability of a community as well. Thus it became incumbent upon the *kabosenja* to persuade the dissidents not to leave, or else to overtake them in the woods to which they had gone and convince them to return. On occasion violence was the result of such efforts.

The *mejapi* phenomenon, apart from reflecting the delicate balance between communal pressure and individualistic assertiveness in Toradja society, must also be seen in terms of the comparative instability of the authority of the village headmen. As was indicated above the *kabosenja* is at best a *primus inter pares*, whose sphere of authority is continuously circumscribed by tradition and by the concensus of the heads of households who deliberate with him. But in all matters, whether it concerns the apportionment of communal lands at sowing time, the building of a village shrine, or the arrangements for a marriage, the headman has no real coercive authority for "in everything the villagers remain free." The *kabosenja* then, must with great tact and patience, guide and persuade everyone. Should a *kabosenja* become too forceful factions may emerge, a rival chief may become prominent, and a *mejapi* or a permanent split in the community may be the result.

So considered the *mejapi* phenomenon is an almost institutionalized gesture of rebellion against a form of communal authority which by its very nature must be weak and so adept in the arts of gentle persuasion that periodic failure with a resulting protest is almost inevitable. There is yet another element in Toradja culture that has bearing on *mejapi* however, namely the concept of the spirit world and the role played by the Toradja *tadu* or sjahman in mediating between this spirit realm and the world of the living. In order to understand this aspect a brief look at the Toradja religious system is necessary.[6]

According to the types of supernatural forces believed in Toradja religion has three divisions. The more popular branch is concerned with the worship of and control over ancestral spirits, especially spirits of closely related past forebears who were known to be strong and influential in their respective lifetimes. Every member of a household can address himself to such spirits, but family and in some cases village heads are wont to be chosen to communicate with the more important ancestral deities. A second division involves supreme deities, such as Lai, the "Father God of Heaven," and Ndara, the "Mother Goddess" of the Earth, who play but a minor role in Toradja religious life, notwithstanding their exalted position. Village headmen and the *tadu* act as mediators between these supreme gods and men. Related to this division is the third and perhaps most important branch, the system of religious therapy carried out by priestesses who influence the realm of spirits of the air (*wurake*). The *tadu* then are concerned both with more "universal" and supreme gods and with spirits that transcend families or even villages. Theirs is the realm of the Upperworld of souls, and of the Underworld with its "City of the Dead." Above all this third branch is "therapeutic" for the *tadu* may strongly influence the souls of the living; indeed, by taking a spiritual journey herself, she is said to be able to snatch or persuade departed souls to return to their bodies below and so restore health. The peculiarities

[6]  See in this connection also R. E. Downs, *The Religion of the Bare'e Speaking Toradja of Central Celebes* (The Hague, 1956).

of the Toradja sjahmans and the symbolic bisexuality which is connected with their practices have already been described elsewhere,[7] suffice it to point out that the Toradja is accustomed to have frequent contact with the world of the dead and with the forces that govern it, and that he looks especially toward the *tadu* (who are always women, or if men, must dress and act as women) to influence these forces for his benefit. For the realm of all the spirits, whether ancestral or more "universal" (collectively designated as *lamoa*), involves not only his physical well being but the established social order and its fortunes as well. Thus, though the *tadu* may be said to spend much of her mediating efforts in the realm of the *wurake* and in journeying toward Upper- and Underworld, her role in communicating with family ancestral spirits is not minimal. All of the supernatural is believed to inter-act with the world of men, and the Toradja's consciousness of this lends force to the sanctity of established custom. If the established traditions are upset, the expected anger from the side of ancestral and other traditional spirit forces heightens the need of the *tadu* to balance the accepted order once again.

A critical point of juncture of the supernatural with the natural order is the headhunt as it was at one time practised in the Central Sulawesi area. For the Toradja headhunting is a religious obligation. War and the taking of heads associated with it was believed to preserve the welfare of the com-munity, particularly the individual health of the villagers. One usually hunted the heads of neighboring villagers or of the inhabitants of regions with which a traditional revenge pattern had been established, originating in some distant quarrel. With the scalps and heads of the defeated enemy the ancestral spirits residing in the village shrine were nourished. Should such "food" not be forthcoming, then, so it was believed, the ancestral spirits would start "eating" the villagers and disease and death would be the inevitable result. This "nourishing" aspect of the headhunt is also reflected in the headhunt ritual, which has the character of a symbolic transition from a condition of undeveloped childhood to maturity, indeed to collective immortality, through a cosmic defeat of death. It is not accidental that the Toradja terms for harvesting and headhunting are similar.[8]

The immediate etiological factor in the particular *mejapi* eruption with which we are concerned was the interaction, and in some cases the violent collision, of all the above named aspects of Toradja culture with the sudden manifestations of active Dutch colonial control in the Central Celebes around the beginning of the present century. The "Westernization" process of the

---

[7]    Justus M. van der Kroef, *Indonesia in the Modern World* (Bandung, Indonesia, 1954–1956), vol. 2, pp. 182–197 (chapter VI, "Transvestitism and the Religious Herma-phrodite").
[8]    R. E. Downs, "Headhunting in Indonesia," *Bijdragen tot de Taal-, Land- en Volken-kunde,* vol. 111 (1955), pp. 46–51.

Bare'e speaking Toradja took place in three phases: (1) from about the middle of the 19th century to about 1900 Dutch authority over the Central Celebes existed, at best, in name only, (2) from about 1900 to approximately 1907 a far-reaching penetration of both civil and mission influences began to take place and it is in this period that the *mejapi* reaction takes on distinct accultural overtones, and (3) from about 1907 to the present, the disruption and modernization of Toradja society proceeds at an ever more accelerating pace, but the accultural frustration phenomena acquire a different mode of expression. Each of these stages, including the important *mejapi* movements of 1902 and 1907, may now be examined in greater detail.

While in the course of the second half of the 19th century the Dutch, in effect, laid claim to the entire area which came to be known as the "Netherlands East Indies," this claim of sovereignty, though usually jealously guarded in foreign diplomatic relations, was not supported by an active, *de facto* control by the Dutch authority over vast reaches of the many Indonesian islands, large and small, beyond Java, until the beginning of the present century.[9] In the Central Celebes the Netherlands East Indies' government had in the 1860s periodically sent its observers, but as late as the 1880s a sympathetic Dutch official posted near, but not in, the area is described by Adriani and Kruyt as a person who "realized that the Government had nothing to say here", and who therefore "did not assume the appearance of having any authority." As happened in other parts of the Indonesian archipelago, it was only when foreigners, in this case two Australians looking for gold, settled in the area and the government became afraid that Britain or Australia might make claims on the Central Celebes, that the Dutch moved in. In 1894 the first Dutch junior civil servant settled in the Poso area but neither he nor his successors were allowed by the government to interfere in internal Toradja affairs. Through ruses some Toradja heads were persuaded to sign a contract with the Netherlands East Indies' government, the contents of which – especially the clause proclaiming that the government owned all the Toradja land – failed wholly to be understood. This first phase of Toradja contacts with the Dutch may be said to have come to a close with the opening of a mission post in Poso in 1892 by the Dutch Mission Association (*Nederlandsch Zendelinggenootschap*) of Rotterdam, and with the first efforts to persuade the Toradja to abandon their ancestral cults – efforts which were, in these early years, virtually without success. Toradjas found it particularly difficult to understand why the Dutch would leave their country at all, if as they said, things were so much better there than in the Toradja world. Appeal to an unknown God, moreover, struck the Toradja as irrational: they worshipped their own ancestors, as the

⁹ G. J. Resink, "Veronachtzaamde Uitspraken," *Indonesië,* vol. 8 (1955), pp. 1–26 and Justus M. van der Kroef, "On the Writing of Indonesian History," *Pacific Affairs,* vol. 31 (1958), pp. 352–371.

Dutch did theirs; between them was no commerce. As late as 1905 not a single Christian convert had been made.[10]

After the turn of the century and the official abandonment of a non-interference policy by the Dutch colonial government in its relationship with the many scattered population groups under its nominal control, a new phase in the acculturation process of Toradja society set in. In 1903 the district of Central Celebes was established, civil control was regularized, a start was made on the suppression of head hunting, and more and more Toradja leaders were forced to acknowledge Dutch suzerainty. Violent conflicts between scattered village units and colonial military began to break out and although the Toradja ruler of Luwu acknowledged the sovereignty of the Dutch Queen, the "Toradjas did not understand the significance of this statement." Uncertainty and anxiety in the Toradja community made further "pacification" increasingly difficult and as skirmishes continued "the actions of the Netherlands Indies Government," as Adriani and Kruyt put it, "aroused fear everywhere." Even when by the end of 1905 violent resistance seemed to have come to an end, Toradja village chiefs resisted the demands of the Dutch: construction of roads under a newly imposed tax paid in labor (the so-called *herendiensten*), building new dwellings, planting the rice fields by a certain time, prohibition of headhunting – all these and others met with silent ill will. With great rapidity the Toradja was now uprooted from his traditional environment. To facilitate supervision the government forced the Toradja to abandon their inaccessibly located villages and to settle in the open on the plain in new dwellings. It undertook, with various degrees of pressure, to propagate the wet rice (*sawah*) cultivation, whereas the Toradja was accustomed to plant his rice by the "slash and burn" or *ladang* method. It forced taxes in labor on all able bodied men, for projects the significance of which was not understood. Still other taxes were imposed, with a socially even more disruptive effect. For example, an income tax, payable in money, was levied on all able bodied Toradja over eighteen. But even to determine accurately what individual income was and is in a society where communal control if not ownership extends to all lands and often to cattle, and where the village heads sometimes, as a matter of convenience, allowed all village possessions to be registered in his name only, proved to be a hazardous task, filled with injustice. Worse, in order to earn the money with which to pay his taxes, which varied from 5 guilders to half a guilder per person per year, the Toradja male, who up to this time had virtually lived outside a money economy, was now compelled to cultivate and sell crops, or to forage in the forest for products marketable along the coast. Men thus came to be forced to spend weeks, sometimes months, in the interior forest, gathering the

---

[10] For these early mission efforts see also N. Adriani, *Verzamelde Geschriften* (Haarlem, 1932), vol. 1, pp. 208–267.

necessary damar and copal, while wives and children were for that period virtually abandoned and lacked the barest provisions.

Particularly significant was the extent to which the accelerated impact of government and missions undermined the ancestor worship, one of the fundaments of traditional society. By prohibiting the headhunt the colonial government seriously impaired the sense of communal stability and spiritual continuity. There were many outbreaks of various illnesses, due to the enforced relocation of Toradjas and the changed style of living, which the Toradjas themselves attributed to the fact that communal ancestral spirits could no longer be nourished by the heads of slain enemies. Certain burial customs were declared forbidden for hygienic reasons, but the government appeared to be unaware that without these funeral procedures, such as the gathering and cleansing of the bones of the dead, the *Toradja* believed that the dead could not be united with their ancestral spirit. The introduction of money taxes and regular money transactions and the propagation of new methods of rice cultivation equally attacked the ancestrally hallowed system of economic production. A pall of uncertainty began to hang over much of Toradja society in these years. The consequence was a new interest in the missionaries, not because of the Christian religion, but because someone was needed who might provide direction in the largely still mysterious and chaotic new order of things. The need for leadership drove some to the new, but rendered others susceptible to the more traditional mechanics of coping with a frustrating or unsettling experience. It was this susceptibility which made the *mejapi* outbreak of 1902–1908 possible.

In 1902, in the Pakambia region of Central Sulawesi a man, named Salalempa and a woman named Liombee initiated a *mejapi* action of considerable proportions.[11] Liombee, apparently a *tadu*, was said to have particularly close communion with the ancestral spirits and in the evening she would go forth, dressed as a warrior, uttering strange sounds as if a spirit were speaking through her. On such occasions no light was allowed lest disaster overtake everyone. Liombee acquired quite a following with her tales of having met the spirit of the grandfather of one, or of the deceased mother of another villager, and once she prophesied that one of the principal chiefs in the Pakambia region upon posting himself in a specified locale would receive from his grandfather spirit a golden hat as soon as Liombee fired twice with a rifle in the air. Neither this, nor other prophesies ever came true, but this did not apparently lessen Liombee's popularity, for by this time her pronouncements had come to acquire a more distinct millenarian

[11] A. C. Kruyt and N. Adriani, "De Godsdienstig-Politieke Beweging 'Mejapi' op Celebes," *Bijdragen tot de Taal-, Land- en Volkenkunde van Nederlandsch-Indië uitgegeven door het Koninklijk Instituut voor de Taal-, Land- en Volkenkunde van Nederlandsch-Indië*, vol. 67 (1913), pp. 135–151. I have relied on this account in the next three paragraphs.

character and excitement increased. Aided by Salalempa she now declared that soon all humans would be allowed to enter the Upperworld without having to die. It would now be unnecessary to sow the fields or tend to livestock and all available food could be consumed with little thought of the future.

On the upper Jaentu river Liombee's followers at her instruction now built a large shed and here by the hundreds they waited for the coming metamorphosis which would make them into souls. A large number of small earthen vats and baskets had been made for the benefit of the ancestral spirits who, so it was believed visited regularly. An abundance of rice and meat had been brought along for the purpose and was quickly eaten, without the expected transformation having occurred. The participants, who had come from considerable distances in and about the Pakambia area, now became impatient, but still able to channel popular sentiment Liombee and Salalempa declared that the location was probably improper and that the prophesied event should be expected on Mount Tawi. There too a long wooden structure on stilts was erected. Along the walls long cars had been placed, and the faithful were instructed to "row" with all their might, since this would cause the building to be lifted into the air and all occupants would thus enter upon the hoped-for journey to the Upperworld. It may be noted that the idea of "rowing" to the spirit world is also encountered in the work of the *tadu* who travels to the spirit world by means of a boat manned by other spirits. As the followers redoubled their efforts excitement grew, and from time to time the leaders stepped outside the shed and called to the rowers inside that the poles on which the shed was constructed were beginning to separate themselves from the earth.

The disappointment, when it was realized that the building and occupants remained on the ground, was great and soon led to violence. The deceived rowers united against Liombee and her fellow villagers and fighting broke out in which one village was entirely destroyed and the inhabitants fled into the forest where additional numbers perished. Yet despite the obvious fiasco of this initial *mejapi* movement the expectations that had been aroused by it refused to die. As late as 1908 the inhabitants of the Buju Mapipi village, who had been among the first to support Liombee and Salalempa, were still attempting to establish direct contact with the ancestral world. Special structures in remote places in the forest continued to be built and groups of villagers absented themselves there, awaiting the hoped for transformation. Departure from the village was now prompted by an important additional reason: it was said that the spirits of the dead had forbidden the living to subject themselves to Dutch authority, and in order to escape the wrath of the Dutch government the living would be taken directly into the Upperworld. A new organized *mejapi* movement began to take form under the leadership of one Makusi. An entire *mejapi* village was constructed under his direction, and here it was said the ancestral spirits descended for brief contact with the living every day. Some 100 people appear to have lived in this settlement. The community had no cultivated fields. Its members must have lived on the gifts of visitors, although they themselves declared that the food was brought by a special "ship from heaven", and that no one should be allowed to use curse words since that would cause the ship to capsize. No attempt was made to construct defenses for the community, for a *lamoa* (spirit) had descended at one point during the proceedings, and speaking in a drumming voice, had guaranteed the protection of his followers. Makusi himself appears to have had special communication with the *lamoa*. On the spirit's instructions he had surrounded himself by seven women who were said to be his special disciples.

The Dutch government eventually became aware of this new *mejapi* movement under Makusi, for word about the nightly dancing and singing that took place in the forest had spread. A Dutch official went to the village and persuaded Makusi to show one of his instruments of communion with the *lamoa*. This turned out to be a "letter," a sheet of paper with some unintelligible scratches upon it, which Makusi said had been given him by his *lamoa*. The Dutch official, seizing the letter, declared that he would make a test to verify the letter's origin. If the spirit had indeed been the author, the paper should not burn when exposed to fire. As the paper went up in smoke Makusi's prestige was dealt a blow from which it did not recover. Soon his followers drifted back to their homes, the village was demolished and Makusi himself apprehended and exiled. The Pakambia Toradja who had been most actively involved in the *mejapi* incidents, and who as late as 1907 had killed off a Dutch patrol in their area, were systematically "pacified," by a military expedition. With this the *mejapi* phenomenon appears to have passed into history.

The third phase in Toradja acculturation, which began with the ending of *mejapi* and the increasing acceptance of Western schooling, perhaps allows us to see the *mejapi* reaction as the last determined attempt by the Toradja to counter the unsettling influences of a new age by the mechanics of the traditional supernatural order. To this end use was made of the technique of collective protest, with which the Toradja is best familiar, that is, "to hide oneself," thus registering one's discontent. Inevitably the *mejapi* under discussion here took on a pronounced religious-political character, for it was not only the living, but also the sacred ancestral spirits who as guardians of the social order were affected by the coming of the Dutch, so that religious belief came to be articulated in political terms also. The discrediting of the *mejapi* action led by Makusi did more than render meaningless this hallowed technique of protest, for in the context of the pattern of Toradja interpersonal relations the failure of *mejapi* means much more. It disrupted decisively the delicate balance between communal pressure and individual demand, nullifying on the one hand the authority of the ancestral spirit world, the mainstay of communal cohesiveness, while on the other it understood the futility of traditional protest action against the prevailing social reality. The Toradja *aluk*, in this third phase of modernization, becomes increasingly a hollow shell, which the individual may manipulate to his own advantage, but to which he feels no strong commitment. In the years after the First World War the hunger for schooling in the Toradja country becomes impressive, and in subsequent decades as the social and economic resources of the traditional Toradja world become more and more exhausted, there begins a migration of Toradja to the South, especially to the "metropolis" of Makassar, where problems of urbanization further complicate the development of the younger Toradja group.[12]

Yet notwithstanding the demand for education and the seeming zest for the more tangible aspects of Western influence an inner commitment to the new order remained lacking. There was little or no realignment of values: in 1950, after nearly five decades of intensive missionary activity, only an estimated 8% of the population had been baptized. Though the traditions of the *aluk* have broken down, especially among the younger generation, neither the accultural influences of the missions nor of the government necessarily created a new orientation: "there emerges a social group, which despises paganism, but does not accept Christianity. Without inner conviction they profit from the opportunities which the pagan cults offer. Under the influence of education, a complex of social factors and political movements, there emerges a type of modern, uprooted pagans."[13] Among these folk *aluk* is regarded instrumentally and opportunistically, as for that matter are other religious affiliations in the area such as Islam and Christianity; the religious systems today serve primarily as a kind of rationale for political action, which, as a result of the further incisive disturbance brought by the Japanese occupation during World War II (1942–1945), the Indonesian Revolution (1945–1949) against the Dutch, and various insurrections since Indonesia formally attained her independence in 1949 (e.g. the movement of Muslim extremists under Kahar Muzakkar, or the federalistic "Permesta" upheaval, which have thousands of followers today and continue to disrupt all of Celebes), has greatly intensified and at least in part fills the present ideological vacuum.

---

[12] H. J. Heeren, "De Trek der Toradja's naar Makassar," pp. 52–63 in G. H. van der Kolff, ed., *Sticusa Jaarboek 1952* (Amsterdam, 1952).

[13] J. M. van Lijf, "Tana-Toradja 1905–1950," *Indonesië*, vol. 5 (1952), pp. 367–369. It may perhaps be mooted that this failure to accomplish a realignment of religious values was at least in part due to a deliberate policy of religious eclecticism of the Christian missions. "Important ceremonies to which the people of Poso were greatly attached and which could be vested with a Christian mantle were allowed to remain," and from the start people were left "to the old ways and customs as much as possible so that they felt at ease." A. C. Kruyt, "The Influence of Western Civilization on the Inhabitants of Poso (Central Celebes)," pp. 7–8 in B. Schrieke, ed., *The Effect of Western Influence on Native Civilizations in the Malay Archipelago* (Batavia, 1929).

## II

Virtually concurrently with the upheavals caused by *mejapi* in Central Celebes disturbances broke out in the Batak society, which is centered around Lake Toba in Northern Sumatra. These disturbances, known as the *parhudamdam* movement, were precipitated – as in the case of the Toradja – by the accelerating and unsettling influence of missions and civil government among the Batak, although – unlike the case of the Toradja – there appears to be a longer religious-historical perspective in the Batak accultural protest action.

The term "Batak" designates a number of ethnically related population groups (Toba-, Karo-, Simelungun-, Pakpak-, Angkolao-, and Mandailing Batak).[14] Additionally there are Batak groups which later left the Toba region, while the migration of all of these Batak subdivisions to the coastal regions of Sumatra, and indeed over much of Western Indonesia, has long been an important cultural dynamic in Batak culture. It is with the Toba and Karo Batak that we will primarily be concerned in this section. In many respects the Batak show great similarities: language (allowing for minor dialectic variation) and myth, many aspects of law and social structure, and the relation of man to the supernatural are much the same. All Batak regard the Toba-Batak area as their origin, they accept common mythologized ancestors, and most have been stirred by the same accultural influences. There are also differences: the Toba-Batak are primarily flooded field agriculturists, the Karo also practice dry cultivation, while the Simelungun or East Batak depend almost entirely on the dry cultivation. Throughout the Batak country the *marga* or patrilineal clan is the basis of the social order, an assymmetric connubium involving an exchange of "male" and "female" gifts is common, while both *marga* structure and connubium underscore a symbolic religious dualism of a type frequently encountered in Indonesia. Customarily the Batak live in *huta*, small villages comprising up to 50 nuclear families, surrounded by the fields. Population pressure or quarrels and jealousies (the Batak's aggressive "individualism" is commented upon by virtually all foreign observers) cause frequent and permanent departures from the *huta*, the establishment of new *huta* and subsequently the formation of a new *marga*. New and old *margas* retain complex religious and connubial relationships. With some qualifications marriage is patrilocal while *marga* membership permanently affects the males and affects women until marriage, when they take the name of their husbands. The frequent bifurcation of *huta* and the formation of new *marga* gives a certain instability to Batak society. Relationships between *margas* are characterized by "jealousy and exclusivism . . . especially when it involved disposal rights over the land,"

---

[14]  On the Batak generally see M. Joustra, *Batakspiegel* (Leyden, 1926), and J. C. Vergouwen, *Het Rechtsleven der Toba-Bataks* (The Hague, 1933).

remarks one authority,[15] and certainly among the Toba Batak (in contrast to the Mandailing) social structure is not very rigid and communal leadership allows for considerable flexibility.[16] The individualism of the Batak, little curbed by strictures on mobility, has been correctly seen as an important dynamic in his recent economic development.[17]

Founding a *huta* is perhaps the most generally accepted way in which to acquire social prestige. Almost any malcontent may persuade a few followers to move away with him and found a new village. In the *huta* the descendants of the *huta* founder constitute something of an elite, above the commoners group of later settlers, and the prisoners of war or those in debtor bondage, who have servile status. But except for the last group class distinctions are not strict and only minimally influence the connubium. In the *huta* the nuclear family is the pivot of the socio-economic order, although the traditional Batak dwelling may comprise several related nuclear families, each occupying a section of the house. Land is held, worked and transmitted through the nuclear family and the male line, though it could not traditionally be alienated permanently from the *marga*. The *radja* (chief) *huta* transmits his position to his immediate relatives and such a chief's family may acquire added prestige by becoming, in time, also the founding family of a new *marga*. In the *margas* themselves there is no single overcapping authority, although the *radja marga*, the founder (or his descendant) of the *marga*, may have special authority in a number of matters such as land tenure. The prevailing pattern of fluidity and mobility in interpersonal relations gives Toba Batak society a kind of "federated," centrifugal character, in which the more centralizing controls, as in the case of the Bare'e Toradja, are comparatively ineffective. Of old the inner conflicts that this centrifugal tendency has produced in Batak society have been commented upon by foreign observers. William Marsden in his *History of Sumatra,* written in 1783, notes that the Batak "are . . . extremely jealous of any increase of their relative power and on the slightest pretext a war breaks out between them . . . some rajas possess a much more extensive sway than others; and it must needs be so, where every man who can get a dozen followers and two or three muskets sets up for independence." [18]

[15]  W. K. H. Ypes, *Bijdrage tot de Kennis van de Stamverwantschap, de Inheemsche Rechtsgemeenschappen en het Grondenrecht der Toba- en Dairibataks* (The Hague, 1932), p. 8.

[16]  J. Keuning, "Toba-Bataks en Mandailing-Bataks. Hun Culturele Samenhang en Daadwerkelijk Antagonisme," *Indonesië,* vol. 7 (1953), p. 165.

[17]  See e.g. A. J. van Zanen, *Voorwaarden voor Maatschappelijke Ontwikkeling in het Centrale Batak-land* (Dissertation, Leyden, 1934), esp. chapter 3.

[18]  William Marsden, *The History of Sumatra* (3rd. ed., London, 1811), p. 375. G. L. Tichelman, "Notes on the Central Batak Country," *Bulletin of the Colonial Institute,* Amsterdam, vol. 3 (June–August, 1940), no. 3–4, p. 194, notes that "The Bataks have never formed a homogeneous whole. In days of yore . . . wars and rumors of war were seldom absent. Women gathering in the crops in the fields were guarded while they worked by their husbands and brothers armed to the teeth."

The self-assertive, centrifugal aspect of Batak life is perhaps also illustrated by such practices as *musuh berngi*, "to make a stand." Traditionally, if a Batak felt slighted by his fellows or had not, in his opinion, received just consideration from his *huta* or *marga* he declared himself to be an enemy of everybody, "making a stand" against the world by affixing to his door a strip of cloth or paper called *pulas* upon which, in symbolic fashion, he had depicted acts of murder, arson and other calamities. Nor did he remain satisfied with this – he might in fact carry out or feign to carry out some of his threats described on the *pulas*. The result of the *musuh berngi* was usually that society took note of his grievance and attempted to placate him.

Another example of the same tendency, and one which, if anything, is even more prominent today, is the institution of *mardjadjo*. The Batak adolescent leaves home for an unspecified period of time, to live and work among strangers; today this may involve a lengthy sojourn at some nearby city with varied, though irregular, periods of employment. These are the Batak's *Wanderjahre*, a period that presumably enhances his self-reliance and during which he is expected to reflect about his life. Personal choice of one's future presumably figures not insignificantly in such reflections. There is a Batak proverb that says: "Rough and hard are the branches; yet the ape lives among them; cold is the water, yet the fish lives in it," meaning that each feels best in his own element.

Yet despite the criss-cross of mutual antagonisms in the social sphere a concept of a higher magico-religious unity and centripetality is also evident. Like many Indonesians the Toba Batak is aware that the microcosmic order of men, guided by custom and ritual, completely meshes with and is influenced by the macrocosmos of various supernatural forces, and that both find their meeting ground in the figure and symbolism of the "High God," called Ompu Tuan (or Debata) Mula Djadi na Bolon, which means "Grandfather Lord Origin of Being."[19] By his very eminence Debata seems virtually removed from the common world of men, and the other deities of the Upper-, Middle-, and Underworld in which the Batak has divided the universe speak much more vividly to the imagination. Among the Upperworld Gods of special significance are the Debata Na Tolu or the "Three Gods" (Batara Guru Doli, Soripada, and Mangalabulan), who correspond to the Hindu trimurti of Brahma, Vishnu, and Çiva, and who testify to early Hindu-Indian influences in the Batak country. Mention needs also to be made of the many spirits, some good but mostly malevolent, who occupy the Middle World. They, along with a simple cult of worship of ancestral spirits, constitute the animistic heart of popular Batak religion, which traditionally was dominated by the male priests called *datu*, who fulfilled primarily a mediating function

[19] Ph. O. Lumban Tobing, *The Structure of the Toba-Batak Belief in the High God* (Diss., Amsterdam, 1956), esp. pp. 175–177.

and the feminine sjahmans (mediums) called *sibaso*.[20] Today the terms *datu* and *guru* have become interchangeable, with the latter being more favored, and the male *guru* has even risen in prominence at the cost of the female *sibaso*, acquiring the functions of the latter, such as knowledge of sacred custom. The religious round consists of the propitiation of these spirits at sowing and harvesting and on other critical occasions in life, while the journey of the human spirit to the Underworld, the Batak Hades, traditionally involved the close supervision of the *sibaso*.

Despite this profusion of supernatural beings the Batak cosmology is essentially pantheistic; neither man, nor the spirits, nor indeed the High God stands apart from nature, but, as in the case of other Indonesian cosmologies, the idea of a transcendent and all pervading unity in reality lies in back of all concepts of the supernatural.[21] The High God is of course the spiritual or supernatural expression of this unity, but the idea also has its counterpart on earth and in Batak society itself with its frequently mutually antagonistic *margas,* its chronic splitting of *hutas*, and its aggressiveness and individualism always close to the surface of social life. In the Batak world it is the figure of Si Singa Mangaradja, the legendary "priest king" who is the embodiment of ethnic unity in diversity. Because of Si Singa Mangaradja's role in the development of the *parhudamdam* movement his historic character must briefly be considered here.

There has been a good deal of controversy over the Singa Mangaradja's origin. The term itself is not Batak but Sanskrit and means "Lion King". It denotes a hereditary office of all-Batak leadership in religious and at one time probably also in political matters. It is not inconceivable that the office, if not the title, originated during the period of strong Hindu-Indian influences in the Batak country. These influences, especially noteworthy between the seventh and fourteenth centuries, proceeded from the East Coast inland and left behind not only impressive statuary and ornamentation, but also skills to fashion certain agricultural implements, new crafts and technology, and above all important concepts and nomenclature of the supernatural, such as Batara Guru, next to the High God the most important and certainly the most widely understood deity, and the first manifestation of the Batak trinity. The identity between Batara Guru and certain pre-Hindu religious concepts in Indonesia is well known, so that the popularity of Batara Guru among the Batak is not in itself surprising. It is necessary to suggest, however, that the Hindu-Indian penetration into the Batak area may

---

[20] On Batak religion generally see Joh. Warneck, *Die Religion der Batak, ein Paradigma für die animistische Religionen der Indischen Archipels* (Leipzig, 1909) and W. A. Braasem, *Proza en Poëzie om het Heilige Meer der Bataks* (Amsterdam, Djakarta, Surabaya, 1951), pp. 19–21.

[21] *Cf.* Justus M. van der Kroef, "Animal Folklore of Indonesia," *United Asia*, vol. 11 (1959), pp. 250–254.

have had important political consequences: it brought a measure of unity among the divers Batak *marga*, which even at this date, had in all probability begun to acquire some of the characteristics of the larger regional division (e.g. between Toba and Karo Batak) evident today. This unity was acquired or imposed at the cost of subservience to the Hindu or Hinduized states of South and Southeast Asia, which at one time had their outposts or tribute-paying subordinate principalities all along the Sumatran coast. Thus the Batak paid tribute via Baros, a half legendary kingdom, to the suzerains of "Greater Hindu India." Baros's history is far from clear; for long periods it was probably a semi-independent Hinduized merchant principality in Central Sumatra, drawing resources from the interior and trafficking with the many similar coastal monarchies in the precolonial Southeast Asian world. Later, with the spread of Islamic influence, it became dependent on Acheh, in North Sumatra, but it retained considerable autonomy under its own rulers. Whether the rulers of Baros themselves bore the title Si Singa Mangaradja, or whether they appointed as their liege subject someone with this title in the surrounding Batak area is not certain. But the identification with and legitimization of the ruler by the Godhead, which was standard practice in the Hindu and Hinduized world, clearly also occurred in the case of the Singa Mangaradja: it is probably correct to see him, with Joustra, as "the son of Batara Guru and nothing less than the earthly manifestation of Çiva himself" [22] – as the personification of cosmic unity and stability, the deified pivot of the social order among the Hinduized Batak.[23]

But Hindu influence was to wane with the shifting fortunes of Southeast Asian states, while the comparative isolation of the Toba Batak region barred a steady Hindu acculturation process too. Si Singa Mangaradja, though Hindu in origin, became a Batak institution, the idea of political unity of all the Batak groups probably running counter to the other decentralizing tendencies of Batak life. Reaction to Hindu-Javanese influence in the neighboring Minangkabau region of West Sumatra [24] may have temporarily placed the Singa Mangaradja in the 14th century in a position of new prominence and on a plane of equality with the Hinduized Minangkabau rulers, while still later, after Islam had increasingly begun to supplant the Hindu influence in the Indonesian archipelago, a new dependency of the Singa Mangaradja on strongly Muslim Acheh to the North probably came into existence. But these politico-cultural changes only minimally affected the ethnic identity of

[22]  M. Joustra, "De Singa Mangaradja-figuur," *Gedenkschrift van het Koninklijk Instituut voor de Taal-, Land- en Volkenkunde van Nederlandsch-Indië,* (The Hague, 1926), p. 220.
[23]  Warneck, *op. cit.,* p. 115 Braasem, *op cit.,* pp. 31–33; on the Hinduization process generally see J. C. van Leur, *Indonesian Trade and Society, Essays in Asian Social and Economic History* (The Hague, Bandung, 1955).
[24]  *Cf.* L. C. Westenenk, *De Hindoe-Javanen in Midden- en Zuid-Sumatra* (Weltevreden, 1920).

the Batak. In time Si Singa Mangaradja's position became something like that of the living representative and descendant of an all Batak culture hero, the embodiment – in the supernatural sense – of autochthonous Batak identity and unity, and in this fashion Batak folk tales came to interpret his past. Some related him to Alexander the Great (who has played such a major role in Malayan court mythologies generally), others described him as of Achehnese royal birth, yet others held him to be the result of a union between a wood spirit and a Batak woman, while still later, in the 19th century and in consequence of the first mission influences in the Batak area, Si Singa Mangaradja's origin came to be described in semi-Christian terms (e.g. he is the son of a "shining apparition" and a woman, whose husband at first did not want to accept him as his son; later the Singa Mangaradja wanders about the country performing miracles, bringing peace, and so on). It should be pointed out that some of these mythological explanations of the Singa Mangaradja's origin place his birth not in antiquity, but only about two centuries or so ago. Whether we must therefore see some kind of historic break in his position, or a meeting of different accultural concepts in an ancient, but latterly more prominent form of Batak leadership, is difficult to tell.[25]

In any event, from about the 17th century onward there is a line of historic Si Singa Mangaradjas, the last of whom was killed by a Dutch military patrol in 1907. Between the first of this line, whose origin and exploits lie wholly embedded in legend, and the last, little is known. This is how he is ordinarily regarded: he is known to reside at Batakara at the sacred Toba Lake, his ancestors and he himself speak through datus and mediums; prescribed offers of goats and a black horse must from time to time be brought to him. His intercession is solicited in prayer to effect an abundant harvest. He has instituted many customs and invested the major Batak radjas with their authority. One of his line, called Ompu Tuan na Bolon ("Grandfather of the Great Lord"), who lived early in the 19th century, was killed by his nephew, a wondrous and miracle working boy who had been exiled to the Minangkabau, and after having risen to power there returned to revenge himself on his uncle. Not all Singa Mangaradjas were revered; some in popular opinion, were weak or tyrannical men, whose words "were injustice." But beginning in the second half of the 19th century the Singa Mangaradja becomes the uncontested focal point of resistance to Christian mission activity among the Batak, and later to increasing Dutch civil control. It is in this context that

[25] C. M. Pleyte, "Singa Mangaradja, de Heilige Koning der Bataks," *Bijdragen tot de Taal-, Land- en Volkenkunde van Nederlandsch-Indië uitgegeven door het Koninklijk Instituut voor de Taal-, Land- en Volkenkunde van Nederlandsch-Indië*, volgreeks 7, vol. 1 (1903), esp. pp. 1–8; Joustra, "De Singa Mangaradja figuur," *op. cit.* pp. 211–220; M. A. Renes-Boldingh and C. Loemban Tobing, *Bataksche Sagen en Legenden* (Nijkerk, 1933), pp. 75–91; and Karl Helbig, "Der Singamangaradja und die Sekte der Pormalim bei den Batak," *Zeitschrift für Ethnologie*, vol. 67 (1935), pp. 88–104.

he must be seen as the primary ideological source of the *parhudamdam* agitation.[26]

In many respects the process of Western influence in the Batak region was similar to that among the Bare'e Toradja: there is the same decades-long period during which contact with the Dutch authority is minimal, and there is the same abrupt acceleration of accultural forces at the close of the 19th century. When, for example, the celebrated naturalist Franz Junghuhn crossed into the Batak region in 1840 – one of the first Westerners to traverse large sections of the land of the Batak – he found Dutch authority for the whole area represented by one district officer and twelve Indonesian soldiers at the coast.[27] But unlike the Central Celebes, Christian missionary activity among the Batak began years before the establishment of effective civil administration. In 1851 the Dutch Bible Association sent out H. Neubronner van der Tuuk to prepare a translation of the Bible in the Batak language. Van der Tuuk, a great linguist, was the first European to reach the sacred Lake Toba, where he met the then reigning Singa Mangaradja, and despite their mutual antagonism in time he even came to be regarded by some Batak as a long-lost older brother of the latter. In 1862 Ludwig Nommensen and the *Rheinische Mission* began their decisive Christianization efforts and in the following years Batak society was rent apart between gradually increasing numbers of Christian converts and those who under Ompu Pulo Batu ("Grandfather Stone Island"), the tenth and last Si Singa Mangaradja, rallied against the mission, their Christianized fellows and all alien influence.[28] When in 1876 the mission increased its concern with the Toba Highland country violence broke out. A Dutch patrol of company strength now moved against the insurgents with great severity; Nommensen himself records how in many districts not a single *huta* was spared.[29] Seemingly accepting the inevitable, some Toba chiefs now allowed both a missionary and a civil officer to establish themselves in their midst, but covertly resistance continued. In 1883, unquestionably with the aid of the Achehnese, Si Singa Mangaradja undertook a new massive action against the Dutch. Thousands of Bataks led by him attacked the mission post, burned it, and then surrounded the small Dutch military detachment. The latter's intrepid stand, and the subsequent wounding of the Singa Mangaradja turned the tide, however, and soon the insurgents were in full flight. New punitive measures were now imposed by the government, but still the unrest continued and in 1889 a new expedi-

---

[26]   Helbig, *op. cit.*, pp. 90–94; Pleyte, *op. cit.*, passim.
[27]   Paul van 't Veer, *Geen Blad voor de Mond. Vijf Radicalen uit de Negentiende Eeuw* (Amsterdam, 1958), p. 83.
[28]   On the opening of the Batak country see C. M. Pleyte, "De Verkenning der Batak-landen, een bijdrage tot de geschiedenis der ontdekking van het Toba-Meer," *Tijdschrift van het Koninklijk Nederlandsch Aardrijkskundig Genootschap*, vol. 12, 2nd series, (1895), pp. 71–96, 727–739.
[29]   J. Keuning, "De Toba-Bataks, Vroeger en Nu," *Indonesië*, vol. 6 (1952), p. 173.

tion proved necessary, although effective resistance was by now pretty well broken. In 1907 Ompu Pulo Batu was killed in a skirmish and his immediate family was interned by the Dutch. No new Singa Mangaradja was proclaimed; Ompu Pulo Batu's two eldest sons were educated at government expense and later entered Dutch service.[30]

But while the legendary priest-king was gone, in the popular imagination he still lived and hundreds, if not thousands of Batak rallied around his cause in a few sects and movements. Of these the still existing sect of the *pormalim* may be mentioned in passing. The last Si Singa Mangaradja is generally regarded as the founder of this sect, the members of which are scattered all over the Toba highlands, singly or in whole *huta*. The sect first appeared in the late 1870s. A *guru* (teacher) called Somailang is said to have acquired leadership of the sect after the Singa Mangaradja's demise, although other *pormalim* imply that the priest-king merely spoke through Somailang (who was later exiled by the Dutch) and his successors. To the *pormalim* Si Singa Mangaradja is not merely a messenger of God, he is the living High God himself. The word "pormalim" has nothing to do with the Malay term *malim* (priest) but comes from the Batak *malim* which means "to be independent" or "to be different from other men." In their beliefs and myths the *pormalim* show many Christian, but no Islamic, influences. Garbled concepts and names of the Old Testament are in use among them, while the tale of a virgin Nae Pulo Maria ("The woman of the happy island"), who bore a miracle-working son, came to be regarded by them as a parallel to the Christ story. As the *pormalim* put it: "We too have our Jesus and our Virgin Mary." Around 1880 an Italian traveller, Elio Modigliani, made a deep impression on some Batak leaders and Roman Catholic influences crept into the sect.[31] There was talk of a *Tuan Rum* (Lord of Rome, i.e. the Pope), and a Maryology now appeared, with statues, new prayers and processions. The confusion which this Mary cult brought, however, in the concept of Nae Pulo Maria (the last word is the Batak term for "to be happy" and does not necessarily denote Christian influence), as well as the subsequent atrophy of the Mary veneration itself, due to the absence of regular Roman Catholic influences, gradually led to a resurgence of Nae Pulo Maria in popular worship. The Mary cult virtually disappeared. Today the Singa Mangaradja, Nae Pulo Maria and some lesser Batak deities are worshipped exclusively; although outstanding early missionary figures and even an occasional Dutch officer could also acquire a sacred aura for a while.[32]

---

[30] *Ibid.*, pp. 172–174. On the death of Ompu Pulo Batu, who appears to have been accidentally killed while in the act of surrendering himself to a Dutch patrol see Radja H. A. M. Tampoebolon, "Het Sneuvelen van Si Singa Mangaradja", *Tijdschrift van het Nederlandsch Aardrijkskundig Genootschap,* vol. 61 (1944), 2de reeks, no. 5, pp. 459–482.

[31] For Modigliani's experiences see his *Fra I Batacchi Indipendenti* (Rome, 1892).

[32] Helbig, *op. cit.,* pp. 98–99.

*Pormalim* ritual and belief center around a special temple (*djamu pamudjion*), usually located in a *huta*, where once a week a service is held under a *guru* (women may be *gurus*). The temple area, which is forbidden to strangers, contains, according to Helbig, primarily some musical instruments and containers with the fermented lemon juice which is drunk during the service. A prayer is followed by a brief "sermon", which consists of admonitions to love and come to one another's aid, not to lie, and to be obedient (but not to "strangers"). After the ceremony follows the distribution of the *unte pangir* or lemon juice. The liquid is not only drunk, but one may touch another's forehead with it, or spray each other with it. Benzoin is burned on a small furnace and the aroma eagerly sniffed. A dreamy trance-like condition ensues in which the big drums gradually are heard. The *guru* now speaks and prophesies to the believers; Si Sanga Mangaradja is said to have seized hold of him. He prescribes work, or the sacrifices which Singa Mangaradja expects, and foretells illness and good fortune. The drumming and prophesying continue until everyone is exhausted and inebriated. Subsequently a horse or goat is sacrificed to Si Singa Mangaradja at a special altar constructed in the road between the houses of the village; there is dancing around the altar and the skins of the sacrificed animals are preserved for their sacred quality in the temple. Regular participation in these ceremonies makes the believer into an *orang pangulima*, "an invincible one." [33]

The *parhudamdam* movement shows some similarity with this *pormalim* sect, and like it must be regarded as part of the general accultural frustration phenomena centering around the Singa Mangaradja figure. It would appear that the immediate cause of the *parhudamdam* uprising was the increased civil administrative concern with the Batak country after the death of the last Si Singa Mangaradja and that it is a kind of intensification of the reaction pattern already in evidence prior to 1907. Between 1907 and 1917, when the *parhudamdam* phenomenon reached its zenith, Dutch colonial interference in the internal affairs of the Batak rapidly reached an extent far greater than anything experienced prior to this period. Up to about 1900 such scattered Dutch colonial service posts as were to be found in Central Sumatra could still be considered as a nuisance by the Batak, but so long as the missionaries were not molested no civil or military action need be feared and Dutch authority seems primarily to have been of a "show the flag" variety. Thus Dutch action against the Singa Mangaradja and his followers prior to the turn of the century should therefore be seen as having been provoked by the group of Batak irreconcilables themselves.

Around 1900 the Dutch themselves take the administrative offensive, however. The imposition of labor and money taxes on the Batak, the accelerated spread of schooling, the establishment of new security agencies

[33]  *Ibid.*, pp. 99–101.

which looked askance on the internecine quarrels and often bloody conflicts between *huta* and *marga*, the registry of land and the restructuring of land tenure patterns – all these turned Batak society upside down in a remarkable few years. The hostility of an important segment of the Batak to these changes, and the specifically anti-Dutch focus of this hostility, is quite evident. The *pormalim* for example, became noted as die-hard opponents of the new scheme of things, preferring prison to the payment of the hated *herendiensten* (labor tax levied on adult males).[34] Van Vollenhoven, the famed formulator and defender of Indonesian *adat* (custom law), notes the unrest in the Batak lands brought by the colonial government's land tenure reforms during these years: "the glow of burning sheds," the "excitement and unrest" following the government's decision to arrogate controls over un-cultivated village lands, the "Batak delegation to the Governor-General," and "the armed police and military who are required in connection with our agrarian regulations."[35] Other students of the *parhudamdam* eruption have pointed to the sharp increase in per capita taxes in 1914, as a result of which a population which had only just established contact with a money economy suddenly found its tax per head per year increased from 24 guilder cents to 75 guilder cents, a comparatively high expense for the average Batak in those years.[36] In the political sphere the tendency of the advancing colonial service to "confirm" communal chiefs in their authority, thus making them in effect adjuncts of that service, robbed the average Batak of his traditional, *adat*-sanctioned freedom of relations with the chiefs.[37] This process, espe-cially apparent in the Karo Batak region, tended to drive some of the Batak toward a protest action directed not only against an alien influence, but also against autochthonous institutions of Batak authority, thereby underscoring the further divisiveness of Batak society as a whole.

The *parhudamdam* movement began in 1915 in the boundary area between the Toba Highlands and the Baros districts (Tapanuli Residency), and from there spread in subsequent years through virtually the entire Batak country. By 1920 the main movement had come to an end, though sporadic indica-tions of *parhudamdam* continued until about 1930. The word *parhudamdam* is derived from a *lallwort* "Sigudamdam," which the followers of the move-

---

[34]  *Ibid.*, p. 102.

[35]  C. van Vollenhoven, *De Indonesiër En Zijn Grond* (Leyden, 1919), pp. 89–90. See also Alinoeddin Enda Boemi, *Het Grondenrecht in de Bataklanden (Tapiannaoeli, Simeloengoen en het Karoland)*, (Diss. Leyden, 1925), pp. 153–154.

[36]  N. Surman Loemban Tobing and E. Gobée, "Dari Hal Parsihoedamdam," *Koloniaal Tijdschrift*, vol. 8 (1919), p. 395. Another version has it that Parhudamdam followers would only have to pay 6 cents taxes, others 6 guilders. This promise made many converts. J. H. Neumann, "De Perhoedamdam in Deli", *Mededelingen Tijdschrift voor Zendingswetenschap*, vol. 62 (1918), p. 188.

[37]  H. J. A. Promes, "De Economische Ontwikkeling in de Batak-landen in de Eerste Helft van deze Eeuw," *Tijdschrift voor Economische en Sociale Geografie*, vol. 46, no. 8 (August, 1955), p. 162.

ment frequently utter during their feverish rituals and collective excitement. It might be translated as "indicating people who are noted for their frequent use of the term sigudamdam." [38] *Parhudamdam* followers declare however, that these and other manifestations of glossolalia ("speaking in tongues") among them have a higher, sacred significance not known to unbelievers. In some parts of the Karo Batak country the movement was designated as *agama baru*, i.e. "the new religion." As in the case of the *pormalim* sect the *guru* and initiates of *parhudamdam* used mythologized explanations to account for the origin of their movement. One common explanation was that God (whether the "High God" Debata, or the comparatively more popular Batara Guru is not certain) came into conflict with Queen Wilhelmina because of the heavy taxes the Dutch levied on the Batak and that *parhudamdam* is God's answer to these injustices. Another version has it that after the Dutch captured Si Singa Mangaradja he was thrown into the sea, and at the bottom met God, who took pity on him, taught him the new religion, and then despatched him topside to teach the Batak the new creed which would free them from the Dutch. Apocalyptic themes are present in other explanations: a great flood and "rain of stones" is imminent and God chose the Singa Mangaradja to teach the Batak a new religion which would save them from the coming holocaust.[39]

In the course of its development the *parhudamdam* beliefs probably became more varied. Reference is made to the fact that the *agama baru* will be revealed in several (some say three, others seven) layers, the first of which, called *agama pengerentes* (from *ngerentes*, i.e. "to cut a path through the forest"), will have male *guru* as its teachers. Later phases may be revealed by female *guru* and by a male teacher with webbed hand and feet who wears a necklace of small bells and who will grant a believer any wish he makes. Unbelievers are designated by the term *piske* (i.e. "the Christians") or as *hapir* (from *kafir* or "unbeliever"). *Parhudamdam* was spread by travelling *guru*, who stopped in various *huta*, and after having received permission from the *radja huta* began to proselytize. In the study of van den Berg, referring to *parhudamdam* among some Karo Batak, this proselytizing commences with the *guru* being brought bananas, rice, tobacco, three roosters, and other articles as the curious and would-be-converts gathered

[38] "Parhoedamdam-Beweging," *Encyclopaedie van Nederlandsch-Indië* (2nd ed., The Hague, Leyden, 1919), vol. 3, p. 343. According to G. L. Tichelman, "De Parhoedamdam Beweging", *Mededeelingen van de Vereeniging van Gezaghebbers B.B.*, December 1937, no. 45, p. 2 (*overdruk*) there are other interpretations of the origin of the term *parhudamdam*. One has it that the term is derived from the Malay *berdendam* ("to have a grievance"), another that the term comes from the Batak *hoedamdam* ("I destroy") but the term does not appear in dictionaries. According to others the term is derived from Si Damdam, the name of a leading disciple of the last Singa Mangaradja.

[39] E. J. van den Berg, "De Parhoedamdam Beweging," *Mededelingen Tijdschrift voor Zendingswetenschap*, vol. 64 (1920), pp. 22–38. In the description of *parhudamdam* rituals and beliefs in the next paragraphs I have relied on this article.

around him. With the edibles brought him the *guru* prepared a meal, over which he uttered a magic formula. Then by eating the food one became a member of the sect, hence the saying "*ipan agama mbaru enda*", or "one eats the new religion." The method of eating this sacred food is different from the method of eating prescribed by *adat*. The latter stipulates that one eats facing downward, the *parhudamdam* meal must be eaten face upward, and upon finishing one must with both hands demonstratively close the mouth. After the meal a sacred liquid, consisting of diluted lemon juice, was distributed, and the *guru*, dipping his hands in the liquid briefly seven times, touched head and shoulders of his converts. Then it was time to bathe. In a body the converts descended to the bathing place and there washed themselves, taking care, however, to cover the lower part of the body with clothing (unlike the usual, completely nude method of bathing). The *guru* again uttered a formula, a mixture of Arabic, Malay and the local dialect, calling upon God as "owner of the fatherland (*umpung tanchajar*) to send his protection to his followers.

After the ritual bathing the *guru* assembled the converts around him and began to instruct them in *ngeratip* (acquiring invincibility), using special gestures with the hands and calling on Si Singa Mangaradja. While the *guru* chants a monotonous *taba* (magic prayer formula) his seated followers first begin to move their bodies rhythmically up and down without leaving their places. Gradually as their excitement increases they sway back and forth more and more rapidly, jumping up and down until they fall down exhausted. In this condition they are asked individually by the *guru*: "Who are you?" and the reply may be "Marimbuli Bosi" (the name of the son of the virgin Nae Pulo Maria venerated by the *pormalim*) or the name of some other legendary heroic figure. Responses such as "arimo" (tiger) or "djaksa" (magistrate) are also common. (One convert who replied "Tuhan Debata," i.e. the Lord God, drew an enormous following in subsequent weeks). This is also the occasion for the glossolalia from which the *parhudamdam* takes its name. After each convert had spoken "in tongues" the *guru* suddenly exclaimed "ampun" (forgiveness) and the excitement died down. Seizing a handful of rice, and throwing it up in the air the *guru* now laid down the commandments to be followed. There were strictures against murder, theft, adultery and lying. For the next seven days men and women must avoid each other and when bathing always keep the lower body covered. No one might walk under an overhanging branch of a tree or under a flower bud, unless leaves or some other cover were held over one's head. Certain food was prohibited, including pork, small frogs and certain cucumbers. No one should talk about the new religion with the *piske*, and the *guru* cautioned that thieves and poisoners and other criminals could not be admitted to the sect (this as advice to some converts who would begin to act as *gurus* themselves and spread the new dispensation). Soon the end of the world would come. Si Singa Mangaradja would protect his followers, but in order to make sure that after the apocalypse one's existence would continue pleasantly, every one should carry some rice and salt, and some scrapings or splinters of one's house and utensils (hair or feathers of one's cattle or fowl) because from these one's property would be abundantly restored. Finally the *guru* provided each convert with a small bamboo knife of about four inches in length and having seven notches upon it. This knife had magical properties: one's enemy would see before him a knife of enormous length or the knife could change one's appearance in his eyes.

As the new religion spread through many *huta,* propagated by self styled *guru,* the unrest in the Batak country mounted. In some places the labor tax was resisted, elsewhere agriculture and trade came virtually to a standstill while Christianized Batak who remained aloof from the movement were attacked. Rumors of an impending return of the Singa Mangaradja combined with secret conclaves of *parhudamdam guru* and speculation that a huge Batak uprising was in the making increased the excitement. A Dutch district officer was murdered by *parhudamdam* followers and with speed and severity the government acted to forestall further outbreaks. Scores were arrested and military patrols again and again penetrated deep into the Karo and Toba country. Gradually order was restored but apocalyptic expectations remained high. Some *gurus* promised that membership freed one from all sorts of inconveniences, others claimed to have been cured by gurus, and the sacred food given to converts came to acquire such an aura of sanctity that one enterprising Batak even began to sell small packages of it. But after this the movement soon lost most of its popularity, although the name *parhudamdam* continued to be heard through the 1920s.

The reasons for the gradual demise of the movement can be summarized as follows. Firstly, a significant portion of the Batak remained aloof from *parhudamdam,* and particularly the Christianized Batak openly expressed their hostility to it. The movement thus lacked a broad, all encompassing nationalistic character, which could have overcome the traditional huta-marga jealousies as well as the existing Christian-non-Christian divisiveness. Secondly, the increasingly more frequent "pacification" forays by the Dutch colonial military proved the futility of any resistance to the Batak – one *guru* after the other, one *huta* or *marga* radja after the other became the dutiful accomplice of the new colonial administrative order, or else simply acquiesced. But thirdly, and perhaps most important, the *parhudamdam* movement erupted at a time when important new developmental dynamics had already been deeply stirring Batak life, giving the Batak community a new value orientation which rendered *parhudamdam* ineffective and made it appear outmoded to many Batak even at the height of its short lived popularity. This is not the place to discuss the remarkable economic development of the Batak country which began especially in the first two decades of the present

century after the individualizing effects of Christianization, Western schooling
and increasing contact with the world outside the long isolated Batak country
had brought about a social and economic revolution.[40] Suffice it to note that
with extraordinary eagerness and aggressiveness the Batak seized the opportunities presented him by the increasing number of Western contacts: in
droves he migrated [41] to the East Coast and beyond Sumatra to try his hand
at commercial agriculture, wage labor, trade, petty industry, military life and
civil government service. He became even more "school minded" than the
Toradja, and with his near neighbors, the Minangkabau of the West Coast
of Sumatra, he began to exert an influence on the developing political and
national economic consciousness of the emergent Indonesian nation far out
of proportion to his numbers. The new materialistic acquisitiveness of the
Batak dismayed the missionaries and in fact led to a breach in the organization of the Batak evangelical church. Batak individualism, the cultural
dynamics of which have been repeatedly noted in previous pages, thus
seemed to become a force that found more satisfactory objects of self-
realization in an ardent embrace of the new, than in an organized expectation
of apocalyptic revenge that would restore the old.

But as in the case of the Toradja the acceptance of the West has taken
place in essentially positivistic terms, i.e. the technological achievement and
organizational skills of the West have been readily accepted, but despite more
than seven decades of intense mission activity Christianity has made no
significant advance in the area. Nor has Islam been particularly successful.
The phenomenon of the "modern pagan" noted in the case of the younger
generations of Toradja is perhaps even more prominent in the Batak area.
What has persisted, and what possibly fills the religious void, can best be
described as Batak ethnicism, an ideology or rationale of the unique Batak
historic and cultural identity among the various population groups of Indonesia, a kind of ethnic nationalism that is no longer significantly supported
by traditional autochthonous concepts of the supernatural,[42] but by quite

[40]  Cf. A. J. van Zanen, op. cit., passim; J. A. Promes op. cit., vol. 46 (1955), pp. 159–
165; vol. 47 (1956), pp. 97–102, 126–134, and J. de Ridder, De Invloed van de Wes-
tersche Cultures op de Autochtone Bevolking ter Oostkust van Sumatra (Diss., Wageningen, 1935).

[41]  Clark E. Cunningham, The Postwar Migration of the Toba-Bataks to East Sumatra
(Yale University Cultural Report Series, New Haven, 1958), esp. pp. 82 ff. The Batak
migration unquestionably aggravated profound socially disorganizing forces already
present on Sumatra's East Coast, the result of the influx of contract laborers from Java.
See J. Tideman, "Landlooperij ter Oostkust van Sumatra en de middelen ter bestrijding
daarvan", Koloniale Studiën, April 1921, pp. 1–18 (overdruk).

[42]  On the nature of this Batak ethnic nationalism see also G. L. Tichelman, "Lokaal
Patriotisme in het Timoer-Bataksch Gebied ter Sum. Oostkust", De Indische Gids, June,
1937, pp. 506–511. Noteworthy in this connection is the changing appreciation of Si
Singa Mangaradja over the years. In a newspaper for Christian Batak in 1922 the editor
could still refer to "the Majesty of our Grandfather, King Singamangaradja, the un-
surpassed ruler . . . the king who never dies" (cited by M. Joustra, "De Singa Mangaradja-

secular, avowedly materialistic ambitions for the betterment of the individual and of the Batak group as a whole. As in the case of the Toradja this ethnic or regional nationalism has come to be suffused by the cross currents of modern politics in Indonesia, and it is not surprising that both the Batak and the Toradja have prominently figured in the warlike civil disturbances against the central Indonesian government in the last few years.[43]

## III

In analyzing the *njuli* movement in Southern Borneo we are impeded by the paucity of materials and by the comparative speed of the processes of cultural change, which has made the Messianic expectation of the Lawangan Daya a shortlived historic oddity. Even so the *njuli* phenomenon is, or was, an integral element of the total traditional Lawangan culture pattern, while the reasons for its occurrence and even some of the details in its manifestation allow us to draw significant comparisons with millenarian movements elsewhere in Indonesia.

The Lawangan are one of a number of tribal subdivisions of the larger Daya population group, long domiciled and spread throughout Borneo.[44] The word "tribal" here merely denotes affiliation with a human group said to have a common ancestor, the members of which feel bound, to greater or lesser degree, by an original blood relationship, which is still supported by common linguistic, ritualistic, religious, and legal precepts of a fundamental nature. Located in the South-Central section of Indonesian Borneo, along the banks and between the great rivers and their tributaries that move toward the Java Sea, and not far from the Southern Coast, the Lawangan may be classified with other groups into the larger Ot Danum division, one of the six principal divisions of the Daya ethnic group.

---

figuur," p. 218). In subsequent years only older Batak appear to have kept their veneration for the Lion King. A request made by some *pormalim* leaders to the Dutch Governor General to have the eldest son of the last Singa Mangaradja formally invested as his father's successor was denied. Shortly before World War II a young Christian Batak declared that most of what the Dutch officials heard about the Singa Mangaradja was just talk and that the younger generation "had not the slightest interest in the Singamangaradja idea." H. C. Zentgraaff and W. A. van Goudoever, *Sumatraantjes* (5th edition, The Hague, 1947), pp. 142–143. The national Indonesian government, however, in line with its emphasis on the exploits of presumably authentic Indonesian heroes has given new prominence to Si Singa Mangaradja, and he is now classified along with Diponegoro, Imam Bondjol, Pattimura and others as worthy of special veneration on certain public occasions and in history texts.

[43] On the role of this regional nationalism in the recent disturbances in Indonesia see Justus M. van der Kroef, "Indonesia: Centrifugal Economies," pp. 197–220 in James W. Wiggins and Helmut Schoeck, ed., *Foreign Aid Reexamined. A Critical Appraisal* (Washington D.C., 1958), and the literature cited there.

[44] This description of the Lawangan is derived from Jacob Mallinckrodt, *Het Adatrecht van Borneo* (Leyden, 1928), 2 vols., unless otherwise indicated.

Daya society presents a picture of a kind of continuum, moving from a genealogical to a territorial form of social organization. The Lawangan, at the time that *njuli* arose among them (1920–1922), could be placed somewhere near the middle of that continuum. The Lawangan tribal identity with its common and sacred ancestral origin was still understood, but increasingly a territorial separation and individualism was making itself felt. Whereas in an earlier day all Lawangan had probably lived together in one large settlement, a continuous splitting of families and extended families, as a result of land shortages or internal dissension, had created the pattern of a large number of closely contiguous hamlets, of up to about 200 people in size, consisting of the well known elongated Daya dwellings, each housing several generations of an extended family. Settlements, purely territorial in structure and comprising primarily nuclear families did not as yet exist, although development in that direction, as evidenced by other neighboring Daya tribal divisions near the coast, was indicated. For some time, then, genealogical loyalty had been waning: tribal and lineage ancestral foundations were crumbling under the pressure of a more transient territorial affiliation. Along with it had come a changing appreciation of leadership. Traditionally the Lawangan communal heads were the descendants of the tribal or lineage founders, whose primary responsibility was the spiritual welfare of the community in its relationship with the supernatural. With the decline of genealogical ties a kind of leadership void came into being in which more novel forms of group direction might be expected to manifest themselves.

Three class levels might traditionally be distinguished among the Lawangan: (1) an aristocracy of tribal, lineage and family leaders, the direct descendants of the founders of their respective social units, (2) the free men, including strangers who had settled among the group, and (3) slaves, usually prisoners of war, who were the collective property of the community, and worked under the direction of the chiefs for common benefit. Collectively the freemen constituted the chief body of communal authority, of which the chiefs were but an executive expression. Connubial restrictions were few: marriage with slaves or between close relatives of a different generation was forbidden, cross cousin marriage was frequent and the connubium generally involved an exchange of gifts. Agriculture was a collective enterprise performed on land that could not be alienated from the community. Land was worked in family or even individual plots, and a special land "administrator-priest" (called *pengulu*), regulated the sowing and harvesting rituals, adjudicated disputes, and determined whether strangers might work the land and the size of compensation they would have to pay. In the period under discussion territorialization and individual tenure were making steady headway.[45]

The Lawangan view of the ultimate reality is, in common with that of

45 See also G. J. Vink, *De Grondslagen van het Indonesische Landbouwbedrijf* (Diss., Wageningen 1941), pp. 30–31.

other Dayas, essentially monistic: all of nature is an expression of a single invisible life-giving and directing force called *doo-oos* which manifests itself qualitatively in the same way in all things, whether man, animal, vegetable or rock. Expressions of the *doo-oos* can be manifold, however, and include a host of supernatural beings from major deities, who are the manifestation, also in their mutual interrelationship, of certain mysterious and immutable dynamics of the *doo-oos* (such as the interplay of symbolic opposites in reality, a belief found among other Daya, and indeed throughout Indonesia),[46] to lesser spirits of a more restricted functional nature. The *doo-oos* substance of certain objects, such as the head obtained in headhunting, is of special significance. Equally important are the enduring *doo-oos* substances of souls of the dead, and among the Lawangan the skull of the tribal ancestors served as the means of keeping in touch with the departed forefathers. Above all the Lawangan are concerned with the preservation of balances in the various manifestations of *doo-oos*: sowing and harvesting, birth, death and marriage, all are acts that may upset the magic equilibrium and thus require restorative rituals. In such matters the tribal and lineage chiefs act as priestly mediators, they lead in the ceremonies that determine the relationship between the community as a whole with the supernatural.[47] In addition the Lawangan are familiar with both male and female sjahmans, who can establish contact with the spirit world, can exorcize the evil spirit and thus restore health when individual illness strikes, and guide the souls of the dead to a hazily defined "country of the dead" located at a mountain named Bukit Lumut. It is especially the sjahman's ability to keep in touch with and guide the spirits of the individual dead, to determine their readiness for the journey to Bukit Lumut, and thus to unite the community of the living with the departed, that is of significance in the *njuli* phenomenon. For the Lawangan feels as much in touch with the dead as with the living. The ancestral realm and what is happening there permeates his entire thinking, and folksayings and legends are to an important degree concerned with the relationship between the dead and the living.

The pattern of Western penetration into the Lawangan area was broadly similar to that described for the Toradja and the Batak. Although as early as the 1820s some officals of the Dutch government created the impression that all or most of Borneo was under Dutch control, it was not until the closing decades of the 19th century that this control became something more than nominal, and that, also because of English interests in the island, closer supervision over upstream Daya territory became regular administrative

---

[46] See for example H. Schärer, *Die Gottesidee der Ngadju Dajak in Süd-Borneo* (Leyden, 1946) and Justus M. van der Kroef, "Dualism and Symbolic Antithesis in Indonesian Society," *American Anthropologist,* vol. 56 (1954), pp. 847–862.

[47] J. Hoek, *Dajakpriesters. Een Bijdrage tot de Analyse van de Religie der Dajaks* (Diss., s. l., 1949), pp. 100–110.

policy.[48] Even so actual interference in Daya affairs did not start until the beginning of the present century, so that for years many Daya vaguely realized that their original freedom had come to an end, while being kept in the dark as to the exact nature and the demands of the novel forces that were circumscribing their lives. On the coast settlements of Indonesians, Malayans and Chinese increased in size and numbers and along with the Dutch began to exert their influence on the Daya of the interior. A lively trade in wood products and copra, the monetization of a sector of the traditionally self-contained Daya economy, the spread of Islam by Indonesians on the coast, the prohibition against headhunting and tribal war, the Christian missions and the schools – all these gradually overturned Daya institutions, weakening tribal and genealogical bonds, promoting individualism in social and economic life, forcing an accommodation with the new cultural elements. Typical of the latter was the fact that some Lawangan after becoming Islamized did not leave their original community, but remained as a separate, compact element in their traditional society with their own head (*wakil*), thus daily demonstrating that the framework of interpersonal relations might be kept without accepting the traditional supernatural sanctions of those relations. The new exclusive territorial structure of Daya communal life thus became more prominent.

In this maelstrom of ideas and institutions old and new, the government's redoubled intervention in Daya life after World War I added to the confusion. In 1920 surveying began preparatory to the imposition of a new, so-called "land rent" tax, and immediately rumors spread that the Dutch government intended to expropriate all Daya land. New roads that had to be built by means of *herendiensten* caused additional resentment, amplified still further by a new tax on slaughtered cattle in 1924. The eruption of the *njuli* movement among the Lawangan falls exactly within this period of new taxation, but it is also clear that a number of vaguely formulated Messianic and apocalyptic notions had begun to circulate throughout the Lawangan area before this time and helped prepare the ideological groundwork of the movement. One of these earlier ideas had its inception among some Lawangan situated near the Mahakan river around 1900, and revolved around the belief that a piece of resin had suddenly become longer under the influence of the tones of a flute someone had played nearby, and that this lengthening of the resin forecast a lengthening of human life, indeed, to immortality. Other Lawangan near the Barito, Ulu Sungei and Pasar rivers appear to have joined in this "resin movement" in subsequent years. The exact nature of the resin movement and the reasons for its demise are by now impossible to determine, but as an indication of the heightened expec-

---

[48]    Graham Irwin, *Nineteenth-Century Borneo. A Study in Diplomatic Rivalry* (The Hague, 1955) and C. Nagtegaal, *De Voormalige Zelfbesturende en Gouvernementsland-schappen in Zuid-Oost Borneo* (Utrecht, 1939).

tations among the Lawangan in this restless era the incident is not without significance.[49]

The term *njuli* is derived from *suli*, which means resurrection from death, and the core of *njuli* belief was the impending return of the souls of the dead from Bukit Lumut to their respective villages on earth and the establishment of a new era of bliss.[50] A former paradise condition appears in some Daya legends, where it is described as having been lost because of quarrels or disobedience to the law, with the result that henceforth man cannot be "cured from death." *Njuli* activity was centered among the Lawangan, though other groups such as the Ma-anjan Daya, and even Christian Dayas participated.

The movement appears to have originated in a popular resistance action against one of the indigenous ruling families during the late 1880s, and it is possible that some of the instigators were dissatisfied members of the Bandjermasin court. There is little certainty on this point, however, and the principal manifestations of *njuli* occurred between 1920–1922 when its leader was a Lawangan communal chief named Tumenggung Badar, who assumed the title "Kakah Gajah" or "The Great Grandfather." It was apparently Badar who organized the *njuli* movement around the Samarikung legend. This legend deals with the exploits of a hero named Mbung Munur, who owned a gong with which he kept death out of life. Mbung Munur, not satisfied with his immense powers, also wanted to experience death. With the aid of an apparition on Bukit Lumut he was able to die, taking the gong, now rendered ineffective, with him. On Bukit Lumut, Mbung Munur gathered and still gathers all the souls of the dead around him and he is now known as Mansan Samarikung, the Lord of the Dead. Many have attempted to steal the gong from Samarikung and thus bring back the power to keep death out among men. None has been more diligent in such efforts as the heroic Ajus, a giant who is "much attached to earthy pleasures." But every time that Ajus comes close to the gong Samarikung bewitches him and he slides down the mountain again. But one day Ajus will succeed. Ajus will cut off Samarikung's head, descend to the world, and then the ancient heroes and ancestors will come back, bringing with them the "*ongkek sokek*" or magic basket which will give forth anything that one wishes. No longer will taxes have to be paid to the Dutch.

Tumanggung Badar made it known that he was not only Ajus but that he had killed Samarikung and would shortly journey to Bukit Lumut to get the gong and liberate the ancestral dead so that they could return to earth.

[49]    J. Mallinckrodt, "De Njoeli-beweging onder de Lawangan-Dajaks van de Zuider-en Ooster afdeling van Borneo," *Koloniale Studien*, vol. 9 (1925), pp. 396–424.

[50]    The description of Njuli belief and practice is based on J. Mallinckrodt, "De Njoe-lie-beweging onder de Lawangan-Dajaks van de Zuider- en Oosterafdeling van Borneo, *op. cit.*, pp. 396–424 and W. K. H. Feuilleteau de Bruyn, "De Njoeli-beweging in de Zuider- en Oosterafdeling van Borneo," *Koloniaal Tijdschrift*, vol. 23 (1934), pp. 41–65.

In the movement Badar appears to have been primarily concerned with the ritualized means of bringing the ancestral spirits down; more "temporal" matters such as the organization of the believers and collection of payments were left to five other leaders of the movement who bore resounding titles. These five met with Badar at frequent intervals. The actual proselytizing was left to still another group, the so-called *penguru*, trusted teachers, who arranged for the nightly seances that characterized the movement. Those indicating their wish to participate had to purchase a kind of oil, called *ollau panjuli*, which would bestow supernatural powers on the user. The *njuli* seances were held in a shed at a lonely spot in the forest. The five "temporal" *njuli* leaders seated themselves in the four corners of the building and in the center, where a gong stood ready. At the four corners strips of rotan pierced the wall and were attached outside. After the center leader had blown on a flute, the four assistants at the corners pulled the rotan cables and made the shed shake. In total darkness Badar entered, exchanging a prescribed Muslim greeting with the assembled, "Salam alakium, salam Allah." Badar then seated himself on top of the gong, and after eating some of the prepared food began the main purpose of the meeting, the *ngasi njuli* or instruction.

During *ngasi njuli* Badar explained that there had been seven major earthquakes in history, each having been preceded by efforts of the spirits to give a new foundation to the world. An eighth and last quake is now being prepared; after it has taken place the ancestors will return to earth. The period of the eighth quake is a terrifying one, with alternating droughts, storms, and floods, but at the end of it "death will have ended." It really was unnecessary to continue the ancestor rituals, declared Badar, in view of their imminent return. Moreover, he declared, he had acquired the skull of Samarikung, the Lord of Death, when he killed the latter, and skulls would no longer be necessary to keep in touch with the ancestral spirits. But only those who belong to the *njuli* movement would see the ancestors and would escape being harmed by them as they return. To that end the *njuli* followers must wear a strip of white cloth around the wrist. (A white band is usually worn when in mourning, in order to ward off attack by the souls of the dead. For the soul is said to see everything in reverse, i.e. it sees black, not white, and since black is the color of and denotes the soul, another soul that is met will believe that it is meeting one of its own kind and will not harm one). After these and similar explanations Badar abruptly left. The remainder of the seance was given over to an orgy of eating, drinking and sexual activity by the participants, at the conclusion of which a bath was taken while the "temporal" leaders of the cult uttered garbled Arabic formulas.

As the movement, spread by the *penguru,* acquired new followers, new themes also appeared in it. Threats were made against those who remained aloof: it was said that all unbelievers would soon die and turn to dust and would be forever excluded from the union with the returning ancestors. During the meetings some members acted as if they were spirits who had briefly returned from Bukit Lumut and explained that they were the ancient heroes temporarily resurrected from death. The preparation of the meetings became more elaborate. A carabao was slaughtered and all participants bathed in water that had been mixed with the animal's blood. Vigils were now being kept near the rivers to signal the coming of the ancestors, who would use a boat. The leaders of the movement seemed to grow in number and even a female sjahman with her assistants, whose husband was covertly active in *njuli*, became prominent in it. Economic dissatisfaction was no longer an immediate cause for a *njuli* meeting. Also after a harvest, when there was usually an abundance of food, *njuli* activity might be observed, and de Bruyn is probably right in saying that the harvest ritual, with its emphasis on the role of the ancestors and on traditional usage, was probably an appropriate setting for the introduction of *njuli* ideas. Still the movement never came to any organizational focus. For one thing Badar's prophesies never came true, of course. Moreover, the scattered and isolated nature of the Daya communities involved in *njuli* prevented effective communication and control by the leadership. Then there were too many leaders, and the motives of some (for example, of ex-communal leaders with a grudge) being eventually devaluated by the populace. Still another reason was probably the very eclecticism of *njuli*, in which the central ancestor cult came to be suffused by so many foreign cultural elements that its role as a specifically nativistic reaction was lost. Salutation, prayer formulas, and some rituals as well as the *penguru* system denote Islamic influence; recent Christian converts, much impressed by the Book of Revelation in the Bible, also joined, bringing their particular point of view to the movement. A kind of simple communism in property and a promiscuity of women followers, both of which find some reference in a number of traditional Daya practices, were carried to considerable extremes, however, in some instances of later *njuli* activity, rendering the movement less and less understandable in its traditional terms. Both the *njuli* meetings and the *njuli* leadership progressively vanished later in the twenties, without any incidents of violence.

Indonesian Borneo is still a sparsely settled "frontier" region where only the last three or four decades have begun to bring decisive changes in the internal relationships of indigenous society. Still, even "in Indonesia itself", to cite a recent medical researcher, "only little is known about the Dayas." [51] It is especially the economic side of Daya life that has contributed to their advance. The Lawangan and their neighbors have been increasingly drawn

---

[51]   P. A. Hoogenkamp, *Ontwikkeling, Voeding en Voedingstoestand van Zuigelingen en Kleuters bij de Ngadju-Dajak op Kalimantan-Selatan (Zuid-Borneo), Indonesië* (2nd ed., Amsterdam, 1956), p. 30.

into the network of copra, forest products, and even rubber cultivation and marketing that has so rapidly developed in the area around the South China Sea in the last decade, and that has provided such a markedly different cultural matrix. An aggressive, acquisitive materialism, and a new, politically significant, individualism are conspicuously progressing and of ancient tribal traditions and ancestor lore there remains sometimes not even a memory. One recent investigator concerned with the Lebang Daya has noted that among them he "could not find anyone who could give me information about their 'adat' (myths, origins, etc.)".[52] His comment may be fairly taken as an indication of the course of future development of the Daya generally.

IV

Space forbids a comprehensive comparison of these three movements, but some important similarities may perhaps be noted by briefly analyzing five interrelated factors: (1) the nature of Western influence, (2) the formation of personality in relation to institutionalized forms of protest and advancing individualism, (3) the magico-religious role of ancestor veneration, (4) the character of millenarian leadership, and (5) the concept of the objective, apocalyptic or otherwise, of the respective movements, held by the followers of these movements.

1. *The Pattern of Western Influence.*

There is no doubt that in all three cases the intensification of Dutch control, preceded by or in conjunction with the work of Christian missions, was the catalytic agent in the eruption of Messianic sentiments in more or less organized fashion. There is a notable similarity in the manner in which these Western influences made themselves felt. For decades in the last half of the nineteenth century, Dutch supervision was nominal; varying with the area it had primarily a nuisance value. Western influences in this period were certainly present, but were essentially experienced as rather distant echoes by the Indonesian groups concerned. These influences were strong enough to prevent them from being eradicated by the action of the indigenous peoples themselves, yet they were never strong enough or explicit enough to be properly appreciated or to call forth a significant counter-reaction. Then, with considerable abruptness, and as a result of a deliberate abandonment of the policy of "non-interference" in the island areas beyond Java – a policy which had been faithfully adhered to for most of the 19th century – Dutch controls over and intervention in the internal affairs of the peoples of

[52] F. H. van Naerssen, "Een Streekonderzoek in West-Borneo", *Indonesië*, vol. 5 (1951), p. 144.

Sumatra, Borneo and the Celebes increased sharply. "In 1870", declared a Dutch colonial government publication issued in 1914 and dealing with the rapid expansion of colonial authority, "the situation in and the knowledge of the greater part of our outer possessions was still such, that in general something was known only about the population located closer to the coast, while as regards that which remained hidden in the deep interior, only vague and unreliable information came to us." But now (1914), the report went on, "even in the great islands of the outer possessions our authority has expanded in such a way that officials are established in the very heart of the interior . . ." [53]

The indigenous reaction to this comparatively sudden change was the millenarian movement, a reaction amplified by ignorance and fear of the abrupt acceleration of forces which had hithertofore been present, but relatively dormant. For years no clear confrontation with, or understanding of these forces had been possible, only garbled notions and uncrystallized expectations had existed, and Kruyt is probably correct in insisting that millenarian movements may occur precisely under such conditions of prolonged unfocussed and unsublimated culture contact.[54] I do not wish, at this point, to reiterate my argument on behalf of a "holistic" approach in directed culture change,[55] but it would appear that the three movements here described confirm the dangers of a policy of "indirect rule" (for so long the proud principle of Dutch colonial statecraft) and suggest the possible advantages of a total, "flood-like" process of change and more radical realignment of values.

The influence of the Christian missions offers some contrasts, but the net effect of the Christianization effort was a disintegrating one. By its policy of eclecticism the mission among the Bare'e Toradja aggravated the accultural unbalances of "indirect" civil rule, so that when this rule became more decisive, the mission was unable to provide any ideological rationale of the new political order. Among the Batak the accultural reaction was partly reflected in the absorption of garbled Christian concepts (as in the *pormalim* sect) by xenophobic ideologies, and more importantly in the further liberation, under Christian aegis, of a traditional, aggressive individualism. In the

---

[53] *De Buitenbezittingen 1904 tot 1914. Mededeelingen van het Bureau voor de Bestuurszaken der Buitengewesten Bewerkt door het Encyclopaedisch Bureau,* (Semarang and Surabaya, 1914) Afdeling X, Deel I, pp. 1–2. Indonesian reaction to increased Dutch administrative interference was unequivocal. Well into the second decade of the present century various insurrections occurred throughout the length and breadth of the archipelago. *Cf.* C. Lulofs, *De Onlusten in de Buitenbezittingen* (Batavia, Weltevreden, 1914).

[54] A. C. Kruyt and N. Adriani, "De Godsdienstig-Politieke Beweging 'Mejapi' op Celebes," *op. cit.,* pp. 144–145.

[55] See my "Patterns of Cultural Change in Three Primitive Societies," *Social Research,* vol. 24 (1957), pp. 427–456 and "Culture Contact and Culture Conflict in Western New Guinea," *Anthropological Quarterly,* vol. 32 (1959), pp. 134–160.

context of heightened economic activity, this soon outran the mission's approval, and also by its avowed materialism even led to a conflict between modern, "acquisitive," Christianized Batak elements and their earlier mentors of the *Rheinische Mission Gesellschaft*. In both instances the increasing emergence of "modern pagans" testifies to the extremely modest success of the missionaries. In the case of the Lawangan both Islamization and Christianization accelerated the disruption of the traditional genealogical bonds of Daya society; both these creeds, in the words of Mallinckrodt, "push the individual in the foreground as regards the community." [56] Of a significant restructuring by the missions of the accultural hostility and frustration as evidenced in the millenarian movements there is not the slightest evidence.

## 2. *Personality Structure and Institutionalized Protest.*

Among the Bare'e Toradja, no less than among the Batak, the balance between communal pressures and individual resistance to such pressures is often a precarious one. The comparatively great freedom of early childhood among the Toradja, colliding with the sudden imposition at a later age of social responsibilities, cannot be separated from *mejapi* as an accepted means of registering one's dissatisfaction with the group. A certain parallel suggests itself here between the relatively abrupt imposition of these traditional social responsibilities on the Toradja child, and the suddenness of strict and novel Dutch controls over the internal affairs of Toradja society as a whole. The institutionalized form of protest in the case of the former reappears in the case of the latter, and thus the Toradja found the manner of his millenarian protest to the Dutch already at hand, so to speak. In the case of the Batak we encounter a whole complex of factors (the motives underlying the founding of a new *huta*, the institution of *musuh berngi* or "to make a stand," the jealousies between *marga*, the practice of *mardjadjo* or leaving home) that mold the individualism, the aggressive questioning of authority, indeed the "contrariness", that is said to mark the Batak personality: "The assistant-resident (civil service official) of Siantar once told me," writes Kraemer, "that he annually received more than 5000 petitions from Bataks, who

---

[56] J. Mallinckrodt, *Het Adatrecht van Borneo, op. cit.*, vol. 1, p. 99. For a related development with distinct messianic overtones on the small island of Nias off the West coast of Sumatra see T. Muller, *Die 'Grosse Reue' Auf Nias. Geschichte und Gestalt einer Erweckung auf dem Missionsfelde* (Gutersloh, 1931). In this connection a question may be raised about the relatively integrating role of the foreign religion in the millenarian movements here discussed. Christianity, in the case of *parhudamdam* and Islam, in the case of *njuli*, both contributed ideas and in ambivalent fashion aided the messianic reaction formation. But at a certain point, it may be mooted, this contribution becomes destructive. Thus, as was indicated earlier, the very profusion of Islamic ideas and practices in *njuli* robbed it of its essentially nativistic character and so speeded njuli's decline. In the case of *parhudamdam*, however, the avowed antipathy for the *piske* as well as the ideological strength of the Singa Mangaradja idea provided a more stable core.

appealed against the verdicts pronounced by the *rapats* (district courts)." [57]
In both the Bare'e and Batak societies the chiefs have but limited authority
and the idea of secular leadership as a kind of *primus inter pares* appears
to be the rule.

It would be hazardous indeed to generalize about the psychological factors
that are relevant to *mejapi* and *parhudamdam*, but it is perhaps permissible
to suggest that the "proclivity to protest", as it appears in many of the culture
traits of the Bare'e and Batak, predisposes the personality toward a course
of Messianic action. This predisposition reflects and is reenforced by the
inadequacy of personal relationships with authority: *mejapi*, for example,
testifies to nothing so much as to the lack of a meaningful and satisfying
integration of the personality with the pattern of social obligations that
is imposed with such traumatic swiftness on the growing child. But such
protest action, it may be mooted, is not free from feelings of anxiety. The
Messianic movement (like the *hula*-founding process or the traditional *mejapi*
action) provides the means simultaneously to "protest" the existence of such
feelings of anxiety, and to assuage these feelings by participation in a new
substitute collectivity. The condition of omnipotence which is reflected in
the glossolalia of the *parhudamdam* follower works toward the same relief
of an oppressive condition of insecurity.

For the Lawangan the picture is not so clear, but it would seem that the
weakening of the traditional magico-religious ties places the individual in an
increasingly less stable position, in which wholly unrelated and sometimes
incomprehensible demands are made of him, and a confusion of values
becomes more and more conspicuous. The new organizational haven provided
by *njuli* and its sublimating mechanisms, must have exercised a powerful
appeal to those living in a psycho-cultural no man's land.

### 3. *The Role of Ancestor Veneration.*

The communal ancestors are of importance in all three Messianic movements described, but their role in each individual case is different. In *mejapi*
the object of the movement is to get the living into the spirit world where
the ancestors dwell, while in *njuli* the purpose is to get the ancestors down to
earth from their mythical mountain, and ancestor veneration is no longer
necessary. In the former movement again the ancestral spirits are said to
have forbidden their living descendants to have any commerce with the
Dutch, in the latter a condition of invincibility is attained along with the
paradisiacal bliss resulting from the appearance of the ancestors. In the
*parhudamdam* movement the accent lies elsewhere: the family ancestors as
such play no specific role of importance, it is rather their collective manifes-

---

[57]  Hendrik Kraemer, *From Missionfield to Independent Church* (The Hague, 1958),
p. 51.

tation in the single tribal progenitor figure of Si Singa Mangaradja, the *"Ur"* Batak, the symbol of ethnic unity so to speak, that needs to be emphasized here.

In all three societies, though to a greater extent in the cases of the Lawangan Daya and of the Bare'e Toradja, individual and collective well-being is appreciated in terms of a balance with the realm of ancestral spirits and influences. Whether this realm is inhabited by many diverse elements or whether it can be interpreted at a higher, centripetal level such as that provided by the Batak idea of the "High God" or by the Singa Mangaradja figure, is a matter of minor significance. For this ancestral world is essentially the source of ethnic identity and uniqueness, which must inevitably come into play in accultural confrontation and which, if it is attacked in any fashion, produces unbearable feelings of anxiety in the individual. If one may speak in psychoanalytic terms for a moment, the ancestral realm, as it is manifested in sanctified *adat* or symbolized in a culture hero, is the principal source of Super-Ego formation. The reaction to the progressive obliteration of this source is not only a principal psycho-cultural dynamic of the millenarian movements here described, but as has been indicated elsewhere,[58] is a major factor in the current process of disorganization and political instability in Indonesia as a whole.

### 4. *The Messianic Leadership.*

Broadly speaking religious leadership among Lawangan, Bare'e and Batak is of two types: first, the communal variety (exemplified by the *kabosenja* among the Bare'e, the *datu* among the Batak or the *penguru* among the Lawangan), concerned with a mediation between the supernatural and the human group as a whole, especially at critical times such as harvesting or during an epidemic; secondly, the sjahmanistic kind (such as the Bare'e *tadu*), capable of acting as mediums, of taking a spiritual journey to the world beyond, and usually but not exclusively occupied with individual therapeutic measures. Competencies overlap in all three societies: the Lawangan sjahman may deal primarily with affairs on Bukit Lumut, but a Lawangan communal chief is hardly indifferent to Samarikung, the Lord of the Dead. In the movements here described both types functioned. Thus Liombee, with whom the first *mejapi* action against the Dutch is associated was apparently a *tadu*, while Tumanggung Badar, the leader of the *njuli* movement in 1920–1922, was a Lawangan *pembakel* or communal chief from Tweh. Some female sjahmans indeed acted as "fronts" for communal chiefs in the spread of *njuli*. It is more important to note, however, that much of the millenarian action was either started or else greatly amplified

58    Justus M. van der Kroef, *Indonesian Social Evolution. Some Psychological Considerations* (Amsterdam, 1958).

by self-styled teachers (broadly designated as *guru*), seers and other would-be charismatic figures. Thus, after Liombee's demise it was Makusi who brought the *mejapi* movement forward, while much of the propagandizing of *njuli* was carried on by Badar's *penguru*. Especially in the case of the *pormalim* and *parhudamdam* activity, it is the self-proclaimed *guru* who, in conjunction with *marga* and *huta* chiefs, and undoubtedly supported by an occasional *datu* or *sibaso*, had the greatest "Messianic" impact.

This phenomenon of the independent, self-declared charismatic leader is of the utmost importance in an understanding of the Indonesian millenarian movements, for Indonesia's cultural climate is unusually receptive to such figures. Even in the so-called Hindu period in Java and Sumatra (roughly between the 7th and 14th centuries A.D.) we find next to the Çivaitic and Buddhist clergy many *mpu* or *rsi*, secluded contemplatives, teachers and "holy men", whose reputed mystical and charismatic abilities were also in harmony with the older animistic-pantheistic views and practices of indigenous society. "Unbelievable was the veneration of the populace for them," and Stutterheim is undoubtedly correct in seeing the later respect for the Muslim *kiajih* or scholar of the writ as a continuation of this earlier devotion for the *rsi*.[59] In the 15th and following centuries the Islamization of Indonesia gets underway, and the *kiajih* and *ulama* (particularly if they are associated with simple Islamic schools giving instruction in the sacred texts) begin to attain that high level of veneration that is still so evident in Indonesia today. This veneration, though structured by Muslim religious organization, is still seen by the populace in the mystical aura of old. The great Islam scholar Snouck Hurgronje typified the traditional charismatic regard for the Indonesian *kiajih* well when he wrote that as far as the Indonesian is concerned the *kiajihs* "more or less control the treasure chamber of Allah's mercy . . . Their prayers bring blessings or curses, healing or sickness. Even the breath of him who is familiar with the sacred writ and fulfils his ritual obligations brings benefit to the ignorant." [60]

A typical illustration of how self-proclaimed *gurus*, making use of latent millenarian expectations, may keep a society in ferment is the Batara Gowa movement in the Southern Celebes. Batara Gowa is the name as well as the title of the kings of Gowa, a formerly independent principality in Southern Celebes. In 1767 the then ruling Batara Gowa was exiled to Ceylon by the Dutch East India Company, and almost immediately a long line of impostors, some of whom claimed to have returned from exile (the actual Batara Gowa had died on Ceylon in 1795), demanded the throne. One of these, Sangkilang by name, actually became ruler for a while, and his son, known as the Karaeng Data, claimed to be Batara Gowa's son. All through the 19th century

[59] W. F. Stutterheim, *Het Hinduïsme in de Archipel* (2nd. ed., Groningen, Djakarta, 1951), p. 133.
[60] Cited R. A. Kern, *De Islam in Indonesië* (The Hague, 1947), p. 92.

prophets and *gurus* appeared, claiming to be the exiled ruler, his son, or Karaeng Data's son; as late as 1904 a Buginese, named Labadu, created a stir by claiming to be Karaeng Data's grandson. Most of the claimants attracted a following and sold amulets; one of them predicted an apocalypse in which all whites would perish, another styled himself "king of the cholera," declaring that an outbreak of this dreadful disease was imminent. Armed conflict with the Dutch usually ensued, invariably ending in disaster for the impostor and his followers. But with almost clocklike regularity new claimants would appear and attract a small army of devotees.[61]

Whether we turn to Gowa, or to the Singamangaradja expectation of the Batak, or to the Ratu Adil ("Just King") tradition on Java, analyzed elsewhere,[62] we encounter the same pattern of charismatic readiness, the same indefatigable confidence in spiritual things hoped for, in millenarian evidence not seen. The pattern seems sometimes to be as vivid today as in decades past: here we read of a villager named Uman and his wife Nji Uum, who appear in Djakarta to spread their new religion, dressed in white and carrying "a sharp weapon meticulously wrapped in white cloth" as a talisman with them; there we are informed of the spread of the new mystical Pangestu movement, which offers "a correct and genuine interpretation" of Islam and Christianity as based on divine revelation received by its chief priest, R. Sunarto, since 1932 in Solo, Central Java; again one reads that the old, communalistic, Messianic movement on Java known as Saminism continues to find new adherents and is now in fact allied with the Indonesian Communist Party; from Samarinda, Borneo, there comes the report that 76 girls have become obsessed by spirits while at school; and elsewhere one is told that the Indonesian spiritualist Pak Subuh, (R.M. Mohammad Subuh Somohadiwijojo), founder of Subud (a curious mixture of Couéism, Javanese mysticism and Moral Rearmament ideology) has founded a center in New York City and is about to open the Second International Congress of Subud in Coombe Springs, England.[63] When several American experts who worked on the

---

[61] J. Tideman, "De Batara Gowa op Zuid-Celebes," *Bijdragen tot de Taal-, Land- en Volkenkunde van Nederlandsch-Indië uitgegeven door het Koninklijk Instituut voor de Taal-, Land- en Volkenkunde van Nederlandsch-Indië*, vol. 61 (7de volgreeks, 7de deel), (1908), pp. 350–390. An analysis of the reasons for the persistent charismatic agitation in connection with Batara Gowa falls outside the scope of this paper. Apart from the element of fraud, attention should be paid to the centric position of the king in Gowa society. The king, strengthened by his magical ornaments, was believed to be the pivot of the universe; without him the normal order and the means of acquiring sustenance from the soil and from the sea were held to be impossible. The desperate need to fill this vacuum created by the removal of the legitimate Batara Gowa was probably a basic reason for the agitation.

[62] Justus M. van der Kroef, "Javanese Messianic Expectations," *loc. cit.*, pp. 299–323.

[63] *Indonesian Observer* (Djakarta), January 19, 1959, p. 3; June 22, 1959, p. 1; August 4, 1959, p. 2; November 9, 1959, p. 2; December 10, 1959, p. 2. On Saminism today see Suhernowo et. al., *Golongan Masjarakat Samin* (Jogjakarta, Balai Persiapan Pekerdjaan Sosial, 1955). On Subud see J. G. Barnett, *Concerning Subud* (New York, 1959).

construction of an ICA-sponsored cement plant in East Java became ill, and the "mental condition" of the Indonesian workers at the plant became "unruly," one finds a distinguished Indonesian physician and parliamentary deputy urging "a para-psychological study of the matter," since there are indications of "the possibility of the existence of magic powers like those existing in the Egyptian pyramids, at the plant site." [64] "Indonesia", as one Djakarta bi-weekly put is, is indeed, "perhaps the only state in the world which aims at consciously bringing a spiritualist element into the affairs of state." [65]

Thus the "routinization of charisma," as described by Weber, is in the case of the millenarian movements of Indonesia poorly developed, with the result that as movements they are apt to be but "a transitory phenomenon." [66] But the popular sense of Messianic expectations that envelops and suffuses the principal dynamics of Indonesian cultural change remains highly developed. In the long run neither the charisma, nor its *guru*, but the readiness is all.

## 5. *The Image of the Movement.*

There is no apparent uniformity in the three movements as to the ultimate objective of the millenarian action. In *parhudamdam* and in *njuli* there is a clear preparation for an apocalypse, in *mejapi* there is no trace of it: one simply escapes to the ancestors and is relieved from further pressures by the Dutch. A clear xenophobia, expressed as a desire to get even with the whites is actually only present in *parhudamdam*, where the evident antipathy for the *piske* (Christian) summarizes the entire range of antagonistic attitudes. It is more latent in *njuli*. Just what the millennium is like is left as vague in the *njuli* as in the *mejapi* idea, except that the Dutch and their handiwork will presumably be no more. In the vagueness of the idea of the realized millennium Javanese Messianic expectations do not differ from those of the three movements here described.

And as in the case of the Javanese Ratu Adil-Eruçakra-Mahdi complex of Messianic beliefs the stasis factor should also be stressed here. For the Lawangan man's task in life is first and foremost the maintenance of the delicate balance between himself, as one aspect of the monistic ultimate reality, and the remainder of that reality expressed in various supernatural forces. Wellbeing is here defined, as in the traditional Javanese world view, as stasis, as that condition of metaphysical equilibrium which, if it is upset, brings misfortune to all. For the Bare'e Toradja, as for the Toba Batak,

[64]   *Indonesian Observer*, December 17, 1958, p. 1.
[65]   *The Indonesian Spectator* (Djakarta), August 1, 1958, p. 10.
[66]   Max Weber, *The Theory of Social and Economic Organization* (ed. by Talcott Parsons, Oxford and New York, 1947), pp. 364–373.

preservation of this balance is often a difficult business: the Toradja's *mejapi* and the Batak's *musuh berngi* express the protest of an individual who seeks a new harmony with the collectivity – who wishes attention to grievance, compromise, a new balance. The realization or even the interplay of antagonistic forces is, however, not the important thing, for virtually all Indonesian cultures center their cosmologies on the fusion and higher harmony of cosmic opposites, in which all distinct self-consciousness, all separate, defined and yet so arbitrary boundaries of the one monistic reality, whether experienced by an individual or by a group, are erased.[67] The millenarian movements in Indonesia are, in the last analysis, but another form of the same equilibrium-seeking dialectic which, in turn, is the essence of the ultimate reality as Indonesian thought conceives of it.

JUSTUS M. VAN DER KROEF
*University of Bridgeport*

[67]  J. P. B. de Josselin de Jong, *De Maleische Archipel als Ethnologisch Studieveld* (Leyden, 1935), pp. 12–13; R. van Dijk, *Samenleving en Adatrechtsvorming* (Diss., The Hague, 1948), pp. 34–49; and J. M. van der Kroef, "Dualism and Symbolic Antithesis in Indonesian Society," *op. cit.*, pp. 847–862.

# THE MILLENARIAN ASPECT OF CONVERSION TO CHRISTIANITY IN THE SOUTH PACIFIC

Much has been written about "Cargo Cults", the best known form that millenarism has taken in Oceania. Yet none of the synthetic studies that have been attempted to date has been entirely satisfactory. If one maps the emergence of the cults, it will be seen that they have occurred in a curiously irregular pattern. The question thus arises: why is there a Cargo Cult here and not there? This has been one of the problems on which I have pondered during my nine years of field work in Melanesia.

Studies have often been based on so restricted a concept of Cargo Cults as to make it difficult to discern the common features of the different movements. The many different aspects and variations of religious structures as they appear in contact conditions have too seldom been viewed as a whole. Up to now, few anthropologists have troubled to analyze Christianity in the area, as it has evolved over nearly two centuries. We talk of Missionization, as an external factor which plays havoc with traditional society. We look for the remnants of heathenism inside the existing Christian society. We rarely think of Christianity as a living factor inside the social structure, as being in many ways an entirely new phenomenon: the reinterpretation of occidental traditional religious ideas and structures by people who have chosen to make use of them as their own.

I am presenting here not any final analysis, but simply a working hypothesis for future research. Existing data are very self-justifying in nature; only field work of both an extensive and intensive kind can allow us to understand the precise value of such and such detail. I am persuaded that further research could ultimately in many ways deepen our understanding of culture change in the area. The cooperation of members of the new generation of islanders in the area could be of immense help.

I start with the question: how did the indigenous people react to their initial contacts with Christian missions? For an answer to this question we must turn first to the mission literature. Unfortunately this is rather poor for our purpose. Early mission reports were written for home congregations, in the hope of stirring enthusiasm and obtaining badly needed financial help. Only occasionally were missionaries given to social analysis. Nevertheless they always give some clues to the reaction of the people. Their evidence leads me to the hypothesis that from the beginning the people tended to view everything new that was offered them by the missionaries as a whole, as a "package deal".

With us, it took a whole generation of work in social anthropology to gain acceptance for the functional approach (that is, for the notion that each element of a culture has a function to perform within an integrated whole), then to supersede the first general ideas of the "patterning" of culture by the more precise concept of structure. I suggest that Melanesians and Polynesians discovered functionalism and structuralism for themselves through being confronted with the white man's culture and society. Among other fine points, they grasped that religion had a definite function inside our world. They realized that if they were ever to come to our level they would have to accept our religion. At first they ascribed to white men a kind of god-like status; but this view passed. The native people were soon trying to think out how they might become the equals of these pale-skinned, rich, powerful, at times naive or ruthless mortals. The simplest way appeared to be the adoption of their religion.

The best evidence we have on this point is in some quite recent Lutheran Mission reports stating that converts had expressed disappointment with the mission's attitude toward them. The reports attempt to analyze "from the inside" the converts' reaction to their disappointment. E. F. Hanneman and R. Inselmann have drawn on this material in studies that confirm each other with rare intellectual honesty.

The "inside analysis" was made through an interesting use of symbols at the 1937 annual conference of the New Guinea Lutheran Mission. In the brand new hut built for the Conference, a bush vine was placed so as to represent the moral division between the Mission and the people, created when the latter separated themselves from their pastors in following the local variant of a Cargo Cult, the Letub. The Church Assembly expressed its regret that such a division had occurred, and explained that it had arisen because the missionaries had kept for themselves the material wealth which should accrue to the Church membership as a whole from its acceptance of Christian faith. The missionaries agreed to patch up the apparent quarrel, but suspended sacraments as long as they were not sure of the community's will to follow a wholly Christian way of life. The following year the natives took the initiative of drawing a vine through the hall, as symbolic of continuing division between them and the missionaries; they were openly accusing the latter of hiding from the native members of the Church the secrets of European wealth.

This feeling was not new. It had already been expressed in 1933 in a pidgin address to Rev. R. Hanselmann, beginning, "*Bilong wonem mifela no sawe kisim as billing cargo? . . .*", which may be translated as follows:

"How is it we cannot obtain the origin of wealth? You hide this secret from us. What is ours is only rubbish, you keep the truth for yourselves. We know that all that is the white man's work is forbidden to us. We would like to progress, but the white man wants to keep us in our state of Kanakas. The Mission, it is true, has given us the word of God, but it does not help us black men. The white men hide from us the secret of the Cargo . . ."

Speaking of a still earlier time just after 1914, Hanneman tells how, after a period of active and passive resistance to European control and after a series of prolonged discussions among themselves, the Madang area people finally decided to obey administrative regulations and accept the Mission's teaching. For a time there were many happy collective conversions to Christianity. In Hanneman's view, more than half the population of the Madang district thought that through acceptance of European civilization and religion they would gain automatic access to the white man's food, tools, money, clothes, domestic comfort, mental faculties and strength of character. The Christian God was to give them the white man's riches and abilities, in the same way as their former gods gave them success in their ceremonial exchange expeditions or protected their warlike incursions into enemy territory.

Hanneman goes on to show how this hope of access to the Cargo could influence outwardly Christian developments. The Kukuaik (beware) movement was born in 1940 on the island of Karkar, north of Madang, after the local missionary had preached about the return of Christ. Phenomena of quaking, glossolalia, and hysterics appeared, all in hope of hastening the coming of Christ and of the Cargo. In the same way, after the last war, it was said around Finschhafen that Christ had died again here and that his bones were being assembled to be sent to the U.S.A. Ten years earlier, at the village of Biliang, near Madang, the people celebrated an outwardly Christian ritual, in Sunday clothes, to request from God the coming of the Cargo.

Today, in this area, Cargo Cult leaders denounced over and over again what is in their eyes the falsity of missionary preaching, as the Cargo has never come. The respective attitudes of natives and Europeans on the matter are shown in a poetic exchange of symbolic discourse between natives of the area and a patrol officer: "A father has two sons; one inherits from his father a cargo ship, the other only gets a canoe", said the natives. The European officer replied, "The dove flies upwards, finding its food on various trees, but the duck's habit, when seeking food, is to stick its head in the mud." This was an unhappy answer, although not untruthful in the context of segregational attitudes which persist among the European population in New Guinea. Another remark made to missionaries in this area was: "What the Mission has given us is good. We like the word of God. But they have given us only one part, merely the shell. The kernel they keep for themselves." Such declarations are to my mind the most important evidence of the trend of native thought in the South Pacific.

How widely diffused are these attitudes? I do not propose to examine here the whole of the missionary literature, but will present only some of the evidence that it contains for areas that I know best, beginning with Tanna, in the New Hebrides. Mission reports are almost our only source for early European contacts in this area. We lack any first-hand record of the attitudes of the earliest converts.

Missionary work in Tanna was not always easy. Frank Paton quotes a serious catechism listener who asked to be paid for his attendance. This is by no means an isolated case; the first London Missionary Society people had the same experience in the Loyalty Islands. In some villages of North Tanna the missionary was told, "*Me fella want copra man, me fella no want missionary*".

This materialistic attitude was noted and partly satisfied through the organization of commercial stations by lay Presbyterians of good standing, by Forlong at Loanbakël, Bates on Aniwa, Carruthers at Lenakel. These men did good business at the same time as they tried to impress a Christian way of life upon their customers. This did not last, the traders on Tanna soon dropping evangelization and sticking simply to business. But the early missionaries had certainly realized that the natives had urges which were not merely spiritual. Outside Tanna missionaries were not always averse to trading direct. Well-known cases are those of Samuel Marsden in New Zealand, Pitman in Rarotonga, Pritchard in Tahiti, and some of the members of the Boston Mission in Hawaii.

The needs of the natives at their first contacts with our culture, though very small if measured in terms of money, were in some ways desperate, so deeply did their envy of the wealth of their new masters bite. The missionaries of the last century were overdressed and by the standards of the time lived in conditions of near luxury, their stipends being £ 200 a year. Judging by material remains of L. M. S. Mission Stations, for exampie, they displayed in Oceania the way of life of the English or Scottish Victorian middle classes. To the natives they appeared immensely rich.

The early missionaries were moreover responsible for creating the hope among the natives that they in turn could become rich through Christianization, for they doled out material goods as rewards for conversion and religious zeal. Buzacott has left us a record of presents given to the people in Rarotonga as a reward for their building a missionary college in 1844:

Piece goods and cloth from mission stocks, value £ 11.8.9
24 dozen knives (the gift of a friend)
4 bundles of children's dresses (gift of English friends)
Piece goods and cloth supplied by Buzacott, value £ 25.2.3.
3 large bullocks, value 30 dollars each, value £ 18.0.0.

5 boxes of American glass, value £ 10.0.0
50 hogs
Presents of bolts, hasps, white lead.

These presents represented good wages for the time. The published letters of Mrs. Watt, wife of the Kwamera missionary, on the south coast of Tanna, tell of rewarding promising pupils with clothing that was sent out around 1870 by the Glasgow Foundry Boy's Religious Society. Frank Paton also used gifts of clothing as a way of paying for work done for his mission. Most photographs published in the missionary literature of the time show converts of long standing as well dressed.

Material rewards could however be distributed only so long as converts remained a small minority of the population. As the body of converts grew, the material given them inevitably diminished, and when collective conversions occurred, the flow dried up altogether. This circumstance goes far to explain the later sense of disillusionment. Some missionaries I know have latterly tried to get converts to work for them without pay. This situation is accepted with less and less good grace, and is apt to be met with flat refusal.

Another material way of rewarding early converts may be discerned in the mission literature. The best help F. Paton got in Lenakel was from a man called Loohmae, who, with his friend Yawus, used the Mission to cover up his landgrabbing at the expense of a vanquished tribe; there were enough Old Testament texts to justify his attitude. Loohmae could thus count the rewards of his conversion in terms of coconuts and copra. He also however counted on going to heaven. When friends tried to persuade him to leave the mission to go to work for a nearby trader at a better salary he told them, *"Very good you work along money, by and by you go along big fire: Me work along Misi, me want go to heaven."*

The doctrine of hell fire was indeed a very significant element of mission teaching in this area, the Presbyterians insisting that everything heathen was from the devil. Satan came thus inadvertently to play as large a role as Jehovah. A man called Nabuk, just before he died, saw in a dream the people of the Lomwanyan group burn in hell and cry aloud for oranges. His friend Yawus then went to Lomwanyan and explained to the members of this group what would be their fate if they remained pagan. F. Paton gives the following story:

"While we were (on furlough) in Victoria a report got about among the Heathen that Jesus was coming on a certain day to take the worshippers to heaven, and burn up Tanna and all the Heathen. Some of the Heathen gathered their pigs together, and sat up all night watching; others began to kill and eat them lest they should be destroyed by the fire. Others again turned fiercely upon the Worshippers as the cause of all the trouble. In the midst of all this excitement, a labour vessel came. The Heathen told the recruiter of the report that Tanna was to be burned, and asked him if it was true. The recruiter, being a long headed man, replied: 'I don't know about Tanna, but I know that Queensland is not going to be burned', and hinted that it would be as well to make sure by recruiting for Queensland."

The doctrine of a vengeful God proved to be a dangerous one. Gordon, who preached in this vein on Eromanga in 1861, at the time that an epidemic of measles was running through the island, was murdered there a week later. It is a well attested fact that native people frequently blamed epidemics on the Christian God and on the inroads of Christianity in their traditional way of life. Turner and Nisbet in 1843, and in 1860 the famed John G. Paton, had to abandon Tanna because of this attitude.

With their narrow-minded theology, such nonconformist Protestant missionaries unwittingly transformed Christianity into a form of Monism. They themselves, did not realize how they had oversimplified their faith. They were convinced that the natives of the Pacific area were in the main mere children who had to be given a simple choice between good and evil. Almost every aspect of the customary life was condemned as the work of the Devil.

Their simple presentation laid great stress on the Apocalypse. Over and over again I have seen Presbyterian and Seventh Day Adventist teachers walking about the hills in Espiritu Santo and Malekula to show the heathen sets of brightly coloured pictures of the life of Jesus. The last picture of the set, by contrast in tones of black and red, always depicted the Day of Judgement according to the Book of Revelation of St. John.

We have thus isolated two aspects of how early native converts understood Christian doctrine as brought to them by 19th century missionaries: a) the Kingdom to come, glowing with happiness, material wealth, and, not to be forgotten, the promise of the resurrection of the dead; b) the fiery doom held out to non-believers. Both these elements appear in most of the Cargo Cults or other so-called nativistic movements that are described in the literature. Both occur in those I had the opportunity of studying personally in the field. The only change might be the replacement of Jesus's name by some other.

Let us now turn to the New Caledonia area, where there were both Catholic and Protestant missionaries. The initial reaction to the missionaries here was clearly to believe that they had godlike powers, even power over death. Catholic sources in New Caledonia tell us how in Balade, a district Captain Cook had already described as poor and desolate, the natives pleaded with the very first Marist fathers reproachfully, "Why are you miserly with us? You do not give us rain. Your brothers the white men keep it away from us in their country. Come and see our crops. They are dying so very much, the ground is dry." People would also come and ask the priests for the "water which called away death".

Later there was a hostile reaction, aroused in part by envy of the abundance of food in the mission stations. Brother Blaise Marmoiton was martyred in Balade after it became known that his dog had been trained to attack natives who trespassed on Mission premises.

The hostility soon turned to fear, when a wave of epidemics swept the islands. In Rarotonga, an epidemic of dysentery in 1830 killed a seventh of the population. In two districts "which had manifested much opposition to the advancement of Godliness", nearly everyone died. Ernest Beaglehole observes that "the sickness swept away all the leaders of the opposition and completely crushed the numerous parties which had set themselves against the establishment of Christianity and of law." The missionaries encouraged the belief that this was a punishment. Buzacott inquires:

"Are we wrong in coming to the conclusion which all the natives have come to: 'This visitation is from God?' ... For many years afterwards this judgement was used as a text, from which class leaders exhorted their inattentive scholars; parents were wont to warn their refractory sons and daughters by reference to it; and occasionally the voice of the missionary pleaded tenderly with ungodly youth, and entreated them to believe lest they too should fall into the hands of the living God."

Thus prophetism of a wrathful kind, in the Old Testament tradition, became part of missionary teaching in the area. It was strongest among the Protestants but competition between Catholics and Protestants probably made it fairly general. It is easy to understand how anathema were transferred from the heathen creed to the other new creed. With the arms trade flourishing, and new political ambitions governing at times the choice of Church, wars of religion became cruel, particularly in Fiji and the Loyalty Islands (Ouvéa, Maré).

The phenomenon that we must try to understand, however, is that of the many instances of mass conversion to Christianity. What were the underlying forces at work?

A modern myth collected on the Isle of Pines, south of New Caledonia, may give us a clue. It deals with the land of the dead, thought to be in the Bay of Oro, in the district of Tuete, northeast of the Island:

"It was the time of 'Queen Hortense' and her consort chief Samuel. The whole island was Catholic since a generation. A group of people from Tuauru on the island of New Caledonia proper had come to visit the paramount chief's court at Gadji. Some young men of this group went to fetch wood in the forest. One of them disappeared and was only found in the morning, as he tumbled half dead inside one of the village huts. Once he regained consciousness, he explained how he had followed an old woman and her granddaughter and got lost. In fact, the two women were not living beings but goddesses and they took him all the way to the bay of Oro. He found there a stockade, at the entrance of which was a French soldier on one side, and a black warrior on another side. In the fenced area were the dead, white and black being mixed, without any discrimination..."

The old myth of the land of the dead and the Catholic teaching that every one is equal before God had come together in this pathetic fashion. It must be noted that the period this myth recalls is one which saw the native population losing half of its land in favour of a political deportees' settlement and a strong army garrison. A few years later the greater part of this land was restored to the people. This favourable turn of events may have prevented a recurrence of such myth-making. The myth has nevertheless been handed on until today.

Somewhat similar feelings explain curious happenings around 1940 in the mountainous area of Northern New Caledonia. A traditional diviner named Pwagatch had been working for some years in the region, being called in from village to village to discover and eradicate newly introduced forms of witchcraft referred to by the name *doki*. His activity was frowned upon by both the administration and the missions. But the people seemed so glad to see their villages purified of sorcery, the men accused being purified through drinking a vegetable brew, that there were no disturbances. Pwagatch was therefore left at liberty. He ended his ten years' purification campaign by transferring his former very lax allegiance to the Catholic faith to the native Protestant Church, under the influence of Maurice Leenhardt. Then, during the war, when the island administration and the missions were distracted with other troubles, the old man became the unhappy tool of a visionary woman, self-appointed prophetess of a new variant of Christianity. She decided that Pwagatch was Jesus Christ reincarnated, and that there should be a great feast and dance. People assembled to eat all the food they had been able to collect. Henceforth, "Jesus was to feed them, the law of the mission and of the white man was ended". At this point, however, the principals of the affair were arrested.

The meaning of this story, which I have told elsewhere with fuller detail, appears to be complex. What is of particular interest here is that, in a matter of a few months, the regular procedure of conversion in small groups, with public baptism, spontaneously transferred itself to a new Messianism. This Messianism was more in line with the feelings of the people at the moment about the colonial administration and about the mission's apparent complicity with it. The procedure of conversion was adapted to a deviant form of Christianity. It is typical of the New Caledonians that the movement collapsed quite peaceably. They are too realistic a people to persist in a course that has lost efficacy.

Both the myth of the black and white dead and the hailing of Pwagatch as Jesus represent attempts to evade a situation which was felt to be oppressive. The personality of Maurice Leenhardt, a great upholder of the native cause in his time, was equal in native eyes to that of the Old Testament prophets, at least with those of kindlier and more humane vein. Leenhardt gone, none of the local missionaries, who were afraid of him, could fill this place. In their anxiety, the people had to resort to a living Messiah. This does not say much for their understanding of Catholicism, which they had accepted for over half a century. Yet actually they did nothing extreme; every action was on a symbolic plane, as though they were seeking a way of obliging Fate to comply with their wishes. Most manifestations of Cargo cults show a similar tendency to organize spectacular symbolic and collective series of actions, which it is hoped will be automatically efficacious.

Were mass conversions to Christianity then undertaken in the same kind of spirit? And if so, in what way did people hope the action would be efficacious? Two texts written by native informants from the district of Canala in New Caledonia will help us answer this question. The older text was collected by Maurice Leenhardt and is contained in his unpublished notes:

"A clod of earth thinks and opens up in the figure of a man. This figure talks, a body appears. He pulls out a flower in the form of a bell, presses on the petals which separate themselves slightly, adds a leaf, and this is then a second body born from the word of the first, the woman after the man. They give birth to sons who are the heads of clans. The parents having died and the children being jealous of one another, they dream, one of a sea snake, the other of a lizard. The children die, their totems remain. The children are bodies, their totems spirits who reveal the useful stones: yam cultivation stones, fishing stones. The dead parents help with all their heart the totem who receives the prayers of the children, because of the parents. Parents and totems work together to answer the son's prayers. Spells, wicked charms, yam or fishing stones, war magic, everything comes from them.

"The origin, the clod of earth, is now hidden; the children have eaten men and committed crooked deeds. So the heart, the love which stayed inside the clod, has remained closed in. The fluid does not go to them, the children, and they remain alone with their totems and their dead parents; but Jesus has taken away the fence, the fence which fell after the ill was done, to separate the names and hide the origin where love stayed away."

This text came out of half a century of resistance to Christianization in the region of Canala. Late conversion meant that in this case people kept a certain pride in their past. How in fact traditional beliefs coexisted with participation in the life of a Christian Church, is shown by the following story:

"During the year 1951, Sasine Boiso fell sick. He was a member of the clan named Thupira. On a morning of that year, he called pastor Tomedy and told him: 'Pastor, I want to talk to you about Kodu, our ancestral God. I know he is responsible for my illness. See, I dreamed this night and in my dream, Kodu appeared to me in human form, saying that if we do not hunt or fish for him, he will eat us all. I call you today to show you my thoughts before I tell them to my fathers: I want Kodu's life to end with the past. I shall ask my fathers to present you Kodu so that you shall pray on him and that his power ceases.' The Pastor answered: 'Sasine, if your fathers accept, I shall pray on Kodu.'

"Boiso spoke again and said: 'Pastor, I shall do this for my children. My sickness becomes worse every day. I have only a few days left to live amongst you. But I shall die after having seen you take Kodu and pray over him, so that my children shall worship one God only, Yahve. You must bring to an end the time of Kodu and his power.'

"Sasine Boiso called his fathers. They were four brothers. Three of them were Christians of the Protestant faith. The last one had remained heathen. He was the servant of Kodu, their God. It was in the eve of a day that Sasine decided to talk to his fathers. Their discussion lasted one night, a day and another night. The Christians accepted their son's proposal. The pagan resisted, saying: 'Who is the man who will come and destroy Thupiras?'

"Sasine Boiso's suffering was increasing. He said to his father, the heathen one: 'Father, have pity upon me. My pain is too great in waiting for the Pastor to do his work.' The morning of the second night of discussion, Korobani told his son: 'I accept your proposal.' He fasted, then called his brothers: 'Go and call the Pastor so that we can go and fetch grandfather.'

"They called the Pastor who went off with Korobani and one of the latter's brothers called Albert. They followed a mountain trail for about three kilometers. They crossed the summit of a mountain and reached a waterfall. Behind this waterfall were high cliffs overhanging caves. Old man Korobani showed the Pastor and Albert one of the cliffs where dwelt Kodu and told them: 'Let us not walk, but run, lest he escapes.' They ran and when they came to the spot, Kodu was not there. The old Korobani did not talk, but grew pale and shivered. Then he told his two companions: 'Let us run towards the second cliff; it seems Grandfather is escaping upwards.' When they got close to the cliff, Korobani climbed towards the top, while Albert and Tomedy were searching all round the cliff.

"Korobani discovered the ancestor. He jumped towards his companions and said: 'I have seen Grandfather up there.' The Pastor spoke and said to the two brothers: 'Do not speak, I am going up.' He climbed the rock and discovered on the top the mysterious stone. He asked then his two friends to keep their peace and prayed. Korobani climbed the cliff meanwhile to be present at the end of Kodu, the wild and fierce ancestor of the clan Thupira, who so many times during the ages gave proof of his superior power.

"The Pastor took hold of the stone Kodu and they returned to the village where they showed it to Sasine. After having thanked the Pastor, Sasine called all his children and family and said: 'Behold our God Kodu. He was in the past a warring God. He hunted men for his food. Today we dwell in the peace of Christ and our heathen wars have ceased. If we keep Kodu, he will eat us all. I am his last victim, do not count me any more. My sickness is worsening and I shall soon die. I was to be his last victim amongst us. Today everything comes to an end with the life of Kodu. From now on, he will no more be our God. You shall worship one God only, Yahve; listen to his word and follow his bidding which the Pastor shall teach you.'

"Having said these last words, Sasine Boiso passed away. The pastor took the stone to the sea and threw it away there."

This story, dating from only a few years ago, shows how the Pastor himself is integrated in a mythical world, where the stone God Kodu is a worthy rival of Yahve; how the priest of the clan remained heathen because of his function, while his brothers became Christians. It is nevertheless valuable to note that in the long run the continuance of both rituals was thought not to be conceivable and that the choice would be a Christian one. After fifty years of hesitation, acceptance of Christianity came to be considered as a total choice, adherence to the more important aspects of paganism inevitably spelling death.

This brings us to an essential aspect of the symbolism of conversion in Oceanian thought: life versus death. Maurice Leenhardt has on this point published some interesting descriptions of native dreams centering around the dangers of conversion in a specific context. We cannot analyze them further here. But the origin of the conversion of one dreamer, Kapea, who became a deacon, is of particular interest to us. In his dream, as he related it, "One day fishermen at Houailou saw a canoe coming from the south. They hailed the man in the canoe, who told them: 'I bring you the word of life.' Kapea, who was one of the fishermen, answered: 'The word of life! That is what we have been waiting for.'" This laconic conversation was the real beginning of Protestant evangelization on New Caledonia proper. Mathaia, the evangelist, came from Ouvéa, the northernmost island of the Loyalties, at the time Christian since nearly half a century. This contact with Houailou followed the pattern of traditional relationships between this district and Ouvéa. The details of the methods then evolved spontaneously by native pastors hailing from Mare, Lifou and Ouvéa make a fascinating story, unhappily too long to tell here.

"The word of life" has remained the key word in all religious discourse in the Protestant Churches of New Caledonia. Thus Maurice Leenhardt writes: "I only noted two sayings marking the stages of natives coming to Christianity. The first: 'I do not drink any more.' The second, and never has this order been reversed: 'I want to be alive.'"

According to the Journal of Taunga, London Missionary Society evangelist in Tuauru around 1844, the zest of his teaching lay in the message that the true God only was capable of giving salvation. The notion of salvation must have been very vague at this time. There had been little direct contact with whites except through some distribution of firearms to warring parties.

The term "alive" had later a very precise connotation. The tribes which accepted Protestantism around 1900 were those at the time the most in danger of losing their land to European settlers. The new form of Christian faith, brought by native evangelists, offered both a rallying point and a new hope for people who were being thrown out from their ancestral lands and regrouped in Reserves. Only a few had land rights there and kept relations with the old gods and totems. The new religion was the more appealing in that it was less authoritative than Catholicism. To desperate people it was a haven, a frame within which social cohesion could be reestablished. This "word of life" had for them exactly the meaning we would have put in it. It meant the refusal of social death, the hope of a better deal, and the will to be considered something other than ignorant savages. Such deeply rooted ideals gave native pastors and deacons courage to oppose, with dignity, any measures that they considered to be unjust. Some were deported; Pastor Setefano of Maré was murdered. In this case, early Christianization was definitely a subtle, in many ways efficient, and at times overt, form of resistance to the worst aspects of colonial rule.

Moreover, the insistence of the very first native pastors on learning to read, write and count, gave the people the means to a better understanding of European procedures, and particularly of checking on the more or less straight deals offered to them by the local European traders. Consequently many European settlers hated the native leaders of the church and charged them with being dangerous political agitators. From 1867, when a Catholic Father was brought to judgment for "incitement to rebellion", to 1917, when Pastor Maurice Leenhardt was accused of having fostered a native uprising, it was a byword that colonization could thrive only when missions had been destroyed.

It cannot always be demonstrated that conversion was due to such circumstances. Partly this is for lack of documentation, and partly it is because the situation has not always been so clear-cut.

On Espiritu Santo, in the northern New Hebrides, the coastal groups converted to Presbyterianism were extremely aggressive towards the unconverted natives of the interior. As I have shown elsewhere, their attitude was determined by the aim of becoming powerful enough to resist the inroads of the white man on their land rights and on their society generally. On the other hand, the unconverted feared that the Presbyterians would simply oppress them in ways that the coastal natives had often practised before. The local missionaries never realized that they were mere pawns in a complex game of power between Melanesian groups differing in their judgment about the imminence of European pressure. In short, conversion on Espiritu Santo was a means of establishing a generalized cohesion of a native society confronted by a dominant alien group.

Conversion in these circumstances had to be total. The whole of the native society was to be reorganized according to the pattern of the church; it was to be governed by its hierarchy of pastors, teachers and deacons, secular chiefs being there only as a "front" in case of administrative interference. Reorganization, to the native leaders, would mean strength; in many cases this was as far as their thinking went. Missionaries were not always responsible for the militant aspect of the work and planning of their converts. But there was something of the old temptation which gave rise to the Jesuit "reductions" in Paraguay. The Marist Fathers tried various forms of this type of Christian social organization in New Caledonia. It had a certain appeal to Catholic natives in assuring them of the protection that the mere presence of a white missionary gave. At the Melanesian mission on Mota Lava, in the Banks group, "Jarawia ... came to the Bishop with a plan of his own, of which he had already spoken to his countrymen (while) at Norfolk Island, and which amounted to a request to buy some land near the station on which he and others might settle and form a Christian village, to which all the group could come and live their own native lives, but giving up all that was distinctly heathen". Such collective conversions have occurred over the whole of the Banks group, and not only around Catholic or Melanesian Mission Stations.

It is notorious, however, that these large Christian villages are today the seat of numerous quarrels, particularly about land. The early missionaries had thought that it would be easier to establish the Kingdom of God in the Pacific than in suburban Scotland. How curious a Rousseauism, how curious a neglect of the Calvinist doctrine of Grace! The naive and triumphant Presbyterian or L.M.S. missionary of the years around 1900 was sitting on the very tensions he thought he had eradicated.

But for the time being there was some reason to be pleased. Everything was outwardly quiet and orderly in a Christian way. Teachers and deacons in the church were the real power inside the villages, traditional authority having disappeared or become subservient to them. Some of the methods used were the subject of numerous confidential dispatches between the British Government and the High Commission in Suva (Fiji).

On Tanna, the early years of the century were marked by the rapid conversion, to the Presbyterian Church, of the greater part of the population. Native informants refer to this time as the period of the "Tanna law". Administrative archives tell us how local courts had been organized, and how flogging or fines were inflicted upon Christian and heathen alike for immoral conduct, or simply for the carrying of kava roots on a path close to a Christian village. Informants who had experienced the "Tanna law" explained in recent years that if the "School", i.e., the Mission, had worked "straight", and had used progressive methods, "gone small small", everybody would have become Christian in course of time. They say that a general wish for peace, at a time of a severe death toll taken by internecine wars fought with firearms supplied by European traders, was responsible for earlier conversions. Then floggings expedited the process.

Missionaries of the time accepted the responsibility for having encouraged the setting up of courts. The abuses of these courts seem to have been in many ways the work of the local zealots; this attitude recalls the aggressiveness of Christian groups already noted on Espiritu Santo. It seems to be a fact that these courts were at the time popular, in so much as they furnished a means of cohesion, under the patronage and protection of the mission, a means of organization of the native coastal society against other abuses against which feeling ran strongly, those of European traders and recruiters. That is the reason why the period which official reports refer to as the one of the "native courts", is for native informants the time of the "Tanna law", when no European presided over their courts.

It should be noted here that in May of 1941 the majority of the Tanna Christians returned to paganism. They became and have remained staunch members of the sect of John Frum. This sect has revived the worship of Karapenmun, the god with whom John G. Paton had to contend in Tanna.

Mass conversions were stimulated also by more materialistic motives. They were followed by far-reaching changes in everyday life: changes in clothing, the learning of new building methods (using lime), by the appearance of European furniture and household implements in the converts' homes, and the acquisition of cattle and horses. Money economy was introduced through encouragement of coconut planting and copra production. There is abundant evidence of these changes in the mission reports, this aspect of mission work being easy to describe to home congregations.

The missionaries aimed at far more than improving the material conditions of life. A whole reorientation of the native society was envisaged. Consider, for example, the part of the New Hebrides where social recognition, prestige and control were functions of acquired rank inside a graded hierarchy generally known under the name of *Namangi*, grades of rank being paid for with pigs. The complex pattern of symbols and behaviour which this graded hierarchy justified, disappeared overnight with conversion. Leaders now had to be experienced not in pig rearing, but in the Work of God. Teachers and deacons were, naturally enough, the new men of authority in the new world of Christianity that had been accepted, with its promise of a glowing future. Later missionaries tried to install Christian chiefs so as to separate lay and religious functions. It is then that they found themselves in trouble with governments.

It has to be realized that a native group can of itself, with relative ease, decide to shed what would once have seemed to us anthropologists the most important and functional elements of its culture: on Espiritu Santo even such things as exogamy or bride price. There were dozens of such instances in New Guinea. The process of Christianization often involved sudden and radical changes, for which the missionary does not bear the sole responsibility. Usually kinship and matrimonial structures persisted unchanged; there would otherwise have been anarchy in social life, even among Christians. But so far as outward and spectacular aspects of their traditional culture were concerned, native converts have always been fairly ready to relinquish anything that in their eyes was inconsistent with adherence to Christianity.

Recalling Williams' information, E. Beaglehole describes in this way the last stages of Aitutaki's formal conversion, under the sole influence of a Polynesian evangelist, Papeiha:

"On the Sabbath on which he had the delightful satisfaction of seeing the whole of the inhabitants convene to worship the one living and true God, he (Papeiha) announced an important meeting to be held on the next day. At this meeting, he made two propositions: 'That all the *maraes* in the island should be burned, and that all the remaining idols should be brought to him' ... the second proposition was: 'That they should commence immediately building a house in which to worship Jehovah.' To both of these proposals, the assembled multitude yielded their cordial assent. As soon as the meeting broke up, crowds set off to burn up the *maraes*. District after district came in procession, chief and priest leading, to place their rejected idols at the teacher's feet, receiving in return a few copies of the gospels and elementary books."

In the same way, in each of the Loyalties, mass conversions preceded the coming of European missionaries and were due to the untiring and selfless efforts of Polynesian teachers. After a difficult beginning, it took less than two years to convert four-fifths of the island of Lifou. Once a civil war in the district of Lösi had come to an end, the teachers were recalled from the nearby island of Maré where they had taken refuge, and the island opened itself up to the work of Fao and his companions. The material results were shown by the building of monumental churches in every village.

There is still a better case in the records of the Methodist Mission, that of the spontaneous conversion of Ono i Lau, related by the Rev. Calvert. After a disastrous epidemic, it was decided that the priest should offer prayers not to the old gods but to the god known to be worshipped on another island as the only god, Jehovah. The providential arrival of a Tongan canoe, the crew of which were Christians, enabled these people to learn the authentic ritual. They then became zealous Christians. A few years later, they refused to allow Tui Nayau, the polygamous King of Lakemba, to take one of the local Christian girls as a wife. After this crisis, they developed revivalist symptoms. Loud weeping broke out and continued for some months despite the presence of a missionary who was sent in to try to control the excitement. The Rev. Calvert, who had at first doubted the reports he had heard, wrote that "The effect upon my poor frame was thrilling, but very enlivening".

Similar cases of spontaneous conversion are known from Tubuai and Manua. They gave rise to the plan of the London Missionary Society, and of other Protestant bodies, of sending native evangelists to open up new mission fields, before any European missionary was stationed. The native teachers interpreted Christian teaching in terms of symbolic phrases and spectacular acts, promising to save and to give a new life, and demanding sweeping changes in the habits of the people. Because of its integrated aspect, this total approach was exceedingly successful.

We must remember that the people of Oceania were confronted with a terrifying experience, that of their first contact with Europeans. The Europeans cheated, abused and kidnapped them and brought death through new diseases and new weapons. In the absence of any administrative structure to protect them, is it astonishing that the natives sought help and protection through conversion?

Is it astonishing, in the face of the prophecies made by the evangelists and confirmed by the missionaries, that wild hopes should be entertained about the golden and happy future reserved to Christian converts? Christianity was originally millennial. My contention is that, in its Pacific expansion, there has been in most cases an authentic revival of early Christian expectations, and that this relatively recent historical experience explains many aspects of the later falling away from the faith. Thus Cargo Cults and other nativistic movements should not be studied outside the frame of reference given by the early Christian history of the people. The manner of their contact with Christianity, whether direct or indirect, has been one of the principal sources of all their religious reinterpretations of the past and of the Christian faith itself.[1]

JEAN GUIART
*Ecole Pratique des Hautes
Etudes, Sorbonne, Paris*

## BIBLIOGRAPHY

Armstrong, E. S., *The History of the Melanesian Mission*, (London, 1900).

Beaglehole, E., *Social Change in the South Pacific: Rarotonga and Aitutaki*, (New York, 1957).

Brainne, Ch., *La Nouvelle Calédonie. Voyages, Missions, Moeurs, Colonisation*, t. I, (Paris, 1854).

Guiart, J., "Espiritu Santo (Nouvelles Hébrides", *L'Homme, Cahiers d'Ethnologie, de Géographie et de Linguistique*, NS, No. 2 (Paris, 1958).

——, "Maurice Leenhardt, Missionnaire et Sociologue", *Le Monde non chrétien*, NS, No. 33, (Paris, 1955), pp. 52–71.

——, "Naissance et avortement d'un messianisme. Colonisation et décolonisation en Nouvelle Calédonie", *Archives de Sociologie des Religions*, No. 7, (Janvier–Juin 1959), pp. 3–44.

——, "L'Océanie. Histoire Universelle", *Encyclopédie de la Pléiade*, Vol. III, (Paris, 1958), pp. 1747–1799.

——, "Un siècle et demi de contacts culturels á Tanna, Nouvelles Hébrides", *Publications de la Société des Océanistes*, No. 5, (Paris, 1956).

Hanneman, E. F., "Le culte du cargo en Nouvelle Guinée", *Le Monde non chrétien*, NS, No. 8, (Paris, 1948), pp. 937–962.

Inselmann, R., *Changing Missionary Methods in Lutheran Missions in New Guinea*, Thesis submitted in partial fulfilment of the requirements for the degree of Bachelor of Divinity (Wartburg Seminary, Dubuque, Iowa, 1948, mimeograph).

——, *Letub, the Cult of the Secrets of Wealth*, Thesis submitted in candidacy for the degree of Master of Arts (Faculty of the Kennedy School of Missions, Hartford Seminary Foundation, 1944, mimeograph).

Leenhardt, M., *De la mort à la vie. L'Evangile en Nouvelle Calédonie* (Paris, 1953).

——, "Kapéa", *Le Monde non chrétien*, NS, No. 25, (Paris, 1953), pp. 77–91.

——, et J. Guiart, "Notes de sociologie religieuse sur la région de Canala (Nouvelle Calédonie)", *Cahiers Internationaux de Sociologie*, NS, Vol. XXIV, 5e année (Paris, 1958), pp. 18–33.

---

[1] *Cf.* J. D. Freeman, "The Joe Gimlet or Siovili Cult. An Episode in the Religious History of Early Samoa", in *Anthropology in the South Seas. Essays presented to H. O. Skinner* (New Plymouth, N.Z., 1959), pp. 185–200.

Leenhardt, R. H., *Au vent de la Grande Terre* (Paris, 1957).

——, "La première mission en Nouvelle Calédonie, d'après le journal de Taunga", *Le Monde non chrétien*, NS, No. 28, (Paris, 1953), pp. 430–443.

Murray, A. W., *Wonders in the Western Isles, being a narrative of the commencement and progress of Mission Work in Western Polynesia*, (London, 1874).

Parsonson, G. S., "La Mission Presbytérienne des Nouvelles Hébrides. Son histoire et son rôle politique et social", *Journal de la Société des Océanistes*, T. XII, No. 12, (Décembre 1956), pp. 107–137.

Paton, Frank H. L., *Lomai of Lenakel. A Hero of the New Hebrides. A fresh chapter in the triumph of the Gospel* (London, 1903).

Watt, Agnes C. P., *Twenty-Five Years of Mission Life on Tanna, New Hebrides* (London, 1896).

Williams, Th., and J. Calvert, *Fiji and the Fijians* (New York, 1859).

# "CARGO-CULTS" AND COSMIC REGENERATION

Many works have shed light on the social-political context of "cargo-cults". The historical-religious interpretation of these micro-religions is however scarcely begun. Yet it is only in the perspective of the history of religions that all these prophetic phenomena can be understood. It is impossible either to grasp the full significance of "cargo-cults" or to appreciate their extraordinary success without taking into account a mythical-ritual theme which plays a fundamental role in Melanesian religions: the annual return of the dead and the cosmic renewal which this implies.[1] The Cosmos has to be regenerated annually, and at the ceremonies of the New Year – through which regeneration is achieved – the dead are present. This complex mythical ritual is further prolonged and fulfilled in the myth of the Great Year, that is, in the complete renewal of the Cosmos through the destruction of all existing forms, a regression to Chaos, followed by a new Creation. To give an example, the prophet Tokeriu of Milne Bay (New Guinea) announced, in 1893, a *true* New Year and a *true* festival of the dead, which would inaugurate a new age of abundance. But before this, a terrifying cataclysm – volcanic eruptions, earthquakes, floods – would annihilate all unbelievers, that is all who had not joined the cult. After this catastrophe of cosmic proportions – in which one may see pictured the end of the world – the winds will suddenly change and bring good weather. Gardens will be filled with taro and yams, the trees will bend under their fruit, and the dead will arrive by boat to visit the living; their arrival will inaugurate an era of plenty and beatitude. Members of the cult should abstain from using articles of European origin.[2]

In 1929–30 the myth of the Golden Age spread among the Baining of New Britain. An earthquake was to destroy all Europeans and all the

---

[1] Credit for discerning the mythical-ritual scenario in the Melanesian "cargo-cults" belongs to V. Lanternari; see his "Origini storiche dei culti profetici melanesiani," *Studi e Materiali di Storia delle Religioni*, XXVII (1956), pp. 31–86, especially pp. 45 ff. See also C. Guariglia, "Profetismus und Heilserwartungsbewegungen bei den niedrigen Kulturen", *Numen*, V (1958), pp. 180–98.

[2] *Cf.* Charles W. Abel, *Savage Life in New Guinea* (London, 1902), pp. 104–128, summarized by Lanternari, *op. cit.*, p. 45, and P. Worsley, *The Trumpet Shall Sound* (New York: Schocken Books, 1968), pp. 51 ff.

sceptics among the natives, that is to say, all who had not joined the cult; the mountains would crumble into the valleys to give place to a vast plain covered with gardens and orchards that would bear of their own accord without need to tend them; the dead would revive, even including the pigs and the dogs that had died.[3] The prophet Ronovuro, of the island of Espiritu Santo, in 1923 predicted a flood to be followed by the return of the dead in cargo ships loaded with rice and other provisions.[4] In the valley of Markham (in the district of Marobe) in New Guinea, a native named Marafi in 1933 declared that Satan had paid him a visit and had led him into the bowels of the earth to meet the spirits of the dead who made their dwelling there. The latter told him that they were eager to return to earth, but that Satan prevented them. They added that if Marafi should succeed in convincing the villagers that Satan was the Supreme Being, they would be able to return to earth. It is remarkable that Marafi had drawn the logical conclusion of an inevitable revolt against the religious and political usurpation of the Whites: the true god of the prophetic religion had to be the anti-God of the Whites, Satan. There is no doubt that we have here a symbolic expression of Black-White antagonism, but there is also condemnation of the actual historical and religious situation, in that the Christianity of the Whites is out of tune with the spirit of the Gospel. Still more significant is the prophecy that the return of the dead will be preceded by a cosmic cataclysm: an earthquake will overturn everything, and then immediately a rain of kerosene flames will consume houses, gardens, and all living beings. Also Marafi advised the construction, at the first sign of the cataclysm, that is, at the first earth tremor, of a huge house large enough to shelter entire communities. The next day it would be found that the dead had already arrived, loaded with gifts: preserved meat, tobacco, rice, clothing, lamps, guns. There would be no need for the people ever again to work in the gardens.[5]

The prophecy of earthquakes and darkness to precede the return of the dead is a widely diffused theme in Melanesian "cargo-cults".[6] A myth famous in the Dutch East Indies predicts the return of the hero Mansren to inaugurate the Golden Age: in the place where he lives now (in Indonesia, but in some versions of the story, in Singapore or in Holland), Mansren will plant a tree whose tip will reach to Heaven (we have here an image of the *axis mundi*); then the tree will bend over to the island of Miok Wundi, Mansren's place of birth, and down its trunk will run a miraculous child, Konor. The arrival of this *puer aeternus* will mark the beginning of the Golden Age: the old will recover their youth, the sick will be healed, and the dead will return to Earth. There will be an abundance of food, of

---

[3]   P. Worsley, *op. cit.*, p. 90.

[4]   V. Lanternari, "Origini storiche dei culti profetici melanesiani," p. 47.

[5]   P. Worsley, p. 102.

[6]   See several examples in Worsley, pp. 116, 184, 199, 214, etc.

women, of clothing and of arms. No one will have to work any more or pay taxes.[7]

In recent versions of the myth, the arrival of Mansren and of the *puer aeternus* will radically modify not only the social situation, as concerning men's mode of existence, but the very structure of the Cosmos. Yams, potatoes, and the other roots will grow on trees while coconuts and other fruit will grow as roots. Fish will live on land and land animals in the sea. These are so many symbolic images of a total reversal of the forms and the laws of the present world: what is below will be found above, and so on. The entire Cosmos will be made anew: Heaven and Earth will be dissolved and a new Heaven and a new Earth will be created in their stead.[8]

The celebrated John Frum prophesied that Tanna, in the New Hebrides, would be flattened out following a cataclysm: the volcanoes would cast the mountains down into the valleys in such a way as to create a fertile plain. (The crumbling of mountains and the flattening of the Earth is an Apocalyptic theme particularly common in India and in the Near East). Immediately the old will recover their youth, sickness will be banished, garden work will become unnecessary, the Whites will depart, and John Frum will found schools to replace those of the missionaries.[9]

In a wild region of New Guinea, discovered barely twenty years ago, the millenarist myth has taken still more dramatic forms. There will be a Great Night, after which Jesus will arrive with the Ancestors and with a supply of merchandise. On receiving word of their arrival the natives are to erect bamboo poles, symbolizing telephone poles. They are also to raise a long notched pole by means of which Jesus may descend to Earth and they in turn may climb into Heaven. (We find here again the theme of the *axis mundi*). Graves were to be made meticulously clean, and there was to be care to destroy all personal property including arms. It was prophesied at the same time that black skins would turn white, and that all the property of the Whites would revert to the Blacks. After the aerial warfare between the Japanese and the Allies, the natives took to believing that a certain number of the Ancestors would arrive by plane.[10]

In all the Melanesian "cargo-cults", the period of waiting for the catastrophe which will precede the Golden Age is marked by a series of actions expressing an absolute detachment from ordinary values and behavior. Pigs

[7]  On the myth of Mansren, *cf.* F. C. Kamma, "Messianic Movements in Western New Guinea", *International Review of Missions*, vol. 41 (1952), pp. 148–160; P. Worsley, *op. cit.* pp. 126 ff.
[8]  On recent forms of the myth of Mansren, *cf.* P. Worsley, pp. 136–37.
[9]  On the John Frum movement see Jean Guiart, "The John Frum Movement in Tanna", *Oceania*, XXII (1951), pp. 165–77; V. Lanternari, p. 44; P. Worsley, pp. 152 ff.
[10]  R. M. Berndt, "A Cargo Movement in the East Central Highlands on New Guinea", *Oceania*, XXIII (1952–53), pp. 40–65, 137–58, pp. 53 ff., 60 ff.; summarized in Worsley, pp. 199 ff.

and cows are slaughtered in a holocaust; all savings are spent in order to
have done with European money, and money is even thrown into the sea;[11]
depôts are built for the storing of provisions, cemeteries are put in order and
decked with flowers and new pathways are made;[12] then all work ceases and
the people await the dead around banquet tables.[13] In the John Frum movement, a certain license is tolerated on the occasion of collective festivals;
Friday, the day on which the Golden Age is to begin, is a holy day, and
Saturday is spent in dancing and drinking kava. The young men and the
young women live in a common house; in the daytime they bathe together
and they pass the night in dancing.[14]

Apart from syncretic and Christian elements, all the Melanesian micro-
religions share the same central myth: the arrival of the dead is taken as the
sign of cosmic renewal. Now we know that this derives from a fundamental
religious idea of the Melanesians. The "cargo-cults" have simply taken this
traditional religious theme (the idea that the Cosmos is periodically renewed
or more exactly, that it is symbolically recreated each year), and have
amplified it, charging it with new values and with a prophetic and millenarist
intensity. Their New Year's day is a reflection of their cosmology: a new
world has just been born, a world fresh, pure, and rich, its potentialities not
yet worn down by time, in other words, the World as it was on the first day
of Creation. This idea, which is extremely widespread, betrays the desire of
the religious man to free himself from the burden of the past, to escape the
hand of Time, and to begin life again *ab ovo*.

In Melanesia, the great agrarian festival of the New Year consists of the
following elements: the arrival of the dead, the ban on work, offerings to
the dead on platforms, that is, a banquet offered to the spirits, and finally a
collective festival of an orgiastic type.[15] In this great New Year's festival
scenario it is easy to recognize the most characteristic elements of the "cargo-
cults": the waiting for the dead, the enormous holocaust of domestic animals,
the offerings to the spirits, the orgiastic rejoicing, the refusal to work.

Europeans have always been struck by the massive destruction of property
and by the absolute inaction, but it has been difficult for Westerners to grasp
the ritual significance of this behavior. They have not realized that the
natives had always been obliged to cease work while waiting for the dead.
In the "cargo-cults", however, it was not simply the dead returning for the
first day of the New Year; what has been awaited has been the *inauguration*

---

[11] On the John Frum Movement, see Worsley, p. 154; on the prophetic cult of the island
of Rambutjon, ibid., p. 188; etc.
[12] Cf. P. Worsley, *op. cit.*, p. 118.
[13] See, inter alia, Worsley, *op. cit.*, p. 88 ff.
[14] Cf. Jean Guiart, "John Frum Movement", pp. 167 ff.; P. Worsley, pp. 155 ff.
[15] Cf. V. Lanternari, "Origini storiche dei culti profetici melanesiani," p. 46; *id.*,
"L'annua festa 'Milamala' dei Trobriandesi: interpretazione psicologica e funzionale,"
*Rivista di Antropologia*, XLII (1955), pp. 3–24.

of a new cosmic era, the beginning of a Great Year. The dead were to return definitively, never to leave the living again. The abolition of death, of old age and of sickness would do away with any difference between the dead and the living. This radical renewal of the World signifies the establishment of Paradise. For this reason it will be preceded, as we have seen, by terrible cataclysms: earthquakes, floods, darkness, the raining of fire, etc. This time there will be a total destruction of the old world in order to make way for a new cosmogony and the establishment of a new mode of life, the life of Paradise.

If so many "cargo-cults" have assimilated Christian millenarist ideas, it is because the natives have rediscovered in Christianity their old traditional eschatological myth. The resurrection of the dead proclaimed by Christianity was to them a familiar idea. If the natives came to feel disappointed in the missionaries, if the majority of the "cargo-cults" ultimately turned anti-Christian, it was not on account of anything in Christianity itself, but because the missionaries and their converts did not appear to conduct themselves as true Christians. The disillusionments that the natives suffered in their encounter with official Christianity were many and tragic. For what attracted the natives to Christianity the most powerfully was the preaching of the coming renewal of the World, the imminent arrival of Christ and the resurrection of the dead; it was the prophetic and eschatological aspects of the Christian religion that awakened in them the most profound echo. But it was precisely these aspects of Christianity that the missionaries seemed in practice to ignore or not to take seriously. The millenarist movements became savagely anti-Christian when their leaders realized that the missionaries, who had indirectly inspired them, did not really believe in the arrival of the ships of the dead bearing gifts, that in effect they did not believe in the imminence of the Kingdom, the resurrection of the dead, and the establishment of Paradise.

MIRCEA ELIADE
*University of Chicago*

# NYASALAND AND THE MILLENNIUM

On 9 July, 1958, some ten thousand enthusiastic Africans, crying "Kwacha! Kwacha! Africa! Africa! Freedom! Freedom!", swarmed into Blantyre airport, Nyasaland, to welcome back home a small, dapper man who, during forty-three years abroad, had almost forgotten his native language. He was Dr. Hastings Kamuzu Banda, a graduate of both Chicago University and Edinburgh. After a decade of agitation from London against the inclusion of Nyasaland in a federation with Northern and Southern Rhodesia, he was going back to his own people to carry on the fight at the centre of conflict. The excitement and expectations which greeted his return might well be described by journalists, more concerned with evocation than exactitude, as "millennial".[1]

Yet would it be altogether fanficul to suggest that, in the welcoming crowd, there were Africans for whom Dr. Banda's return to Nyasaland was "millennial" in much more than the loose, journalistic sense? By 1958, after all, Nyasaland had experienced nearly a century of Christian missionary activity, and the concepts of the faith, both in unadulterated, Christian forms and in the guise of corruptions engendered by the clash of cultures, African and European, were familiar in many parts of Nyasaland. Furthermore, from the 1890s onwards, forms of independent African religio-political expression had grown up which created millennial and messianic associations that could easily be attached to such an outstanding event in the history of Nyasaland as the return of Dr. Banda.

Perhaps it is best to begin the story of the millennial tradition in Nyasaland *in medias res* with three stories that were told to the author by one of the leading African politicians of modern Nyasaland. The first concerns Dr. James Emman Kwegyir Aggrey, the Gold Coast African who spent over twenty years in America, studying at Columbia, teaching at Livingstone College, Salisbury, North Carolina, and increasing his attachment to the

---

[1] A more restrained statement was provided by the London *Observer* correspondent: "Some of those who watched his reception at the Blantyre airport by thousands of Nyasalanders beside themselves with joy discovered in the event some resemblance to a Second Coming." (Cyril Dunn, *Central African Witness*, London, 1959, p. 107.) *Cf. East Africa and Rhodesia* (London), January 1, 1959, p. 558, and May 7, 1959, p. 1051, *Manchester Guardian*, December 24, 1959, p. 7.

African Methodist Episcopal Zion Church. In 1921, Aggrey visited South and Central Africa as a member of the Phelps-Stokes Commission on African Education. As he went through South Africa, notes his biographer, he

was supposed to be the herald of some invading band of Negroes – they (the Africans) thought all Americans were Negroes – who would drive the whites of South Africa into the sea. Men came to Umtata on horseback, with empty sacks for saddle cloths. "He will order the merchants to sell their goods cheaply ... he may even compel them to give their goods away for nothing." [2]

A similar mood of expectation awaited Aggrey when he went up to Nyasaland, where the image of America as a land peopled almost entirely with Negroes was also widespread amongst Africans. Aggrey was the most successful African – in the European sense of values – that many of them had ever seen; hundreds flocked to hear him speak. His arrival in Nyasaland was seen by many as the prelude to an American Negro invasion, in which all wrongs would be righted and the Europeans driven out of the country. One version of this tale had it that the Negroes would come in aeroplanes and drop bombs which would hit only white people.

The second story takes up the aeroplane theme. In the 1930s, the first important flights, commercial and official, took place over Nyasaland.[3] Once again they were connected with the arrival of American Negro liberators. African songs began to spring up about them:

> ... Tungukwonda-taruta
> Timguya ku Amirika
> Kukapanga ndege
> Kusambizga amitundu ...

> (... Were pleased that
> We went to America
> To learn the making of aeroplanes
> So as to "fix up" all foreigners ...)

The third story harked back to the abortive Nyasaland Native Rising of 1915, in which an African, John Chilembwe, who had been educated at a Negro American Baptist seminary and had returned home to found his own independent church, attempted to overthrow British power in the Protectorate. The author, who at that time was just finishing a study of Chilembwe's movement,[4] was asked if he believed John Chilembwe was dead? What

[2] Edwin W. Smith, *Aggrey of Africa* (London, 1929), p. 181. Cf. p. 220: Aggrey tried, in Northern Rhodesia, to discredit the rumour that American Negroes were coming to expel the whites.
[3] It must be pointed out, however, that in reporting an aeroplane which dropped a message in a duster over most of the tea estates "going up the Ruo valley" on 1 January, 1932, the *Nyasaland Times,* 15 January, 1932, reported that the "more blasé" Nyasas received it with studied indifference.
[4] George Shepperson and Thomas Price, *Independent African. John Chilembwe and*

evidence had he that Chilembwe's body was ever found after he was said to have been shot by the British? The questions were evidence of a widespread African belief that John Chilembwe was never killed or that he would rise again to expel the British from Nyasaland. At the time of Aggrey's visit, the rumour got abroad that a telegram had been received from America to say that Chilembwe was about to come back. Whether the figure of Aggrey was confused with a renewed and returning Chilembwe it is difficult to say: but it is not impossible.

These three stories suggest parallels with the Cargo cults of Melanesia.[5] There are the same American Negro liberators. There is a similar introduction of cornucopian "cargo" from outside, though in the Nyasaland instances the aeroplane replaces the ship. There is the same fascination with the technical symbols of white civilization, aeroplanes, telegrams and the like.

And, although there is nothing apparently Christian about these millennial expectations of certain groups in Nyasaland in the 1920s and 1930s, the routine elements of the millennial hope are present in them: the deliverer from outside; the battle against the forces of evil, the Europeans; the final, new age. Like so many similar movements in other parts of the world, the expectations take a dramatic premillennial form: the saviour or delivering agency comes before and not – as in the case of postmillennialism – after the battle against the forces of evil. Premillennialism always means a deep distrust of the orthodox forces of reform open to a society; and the prevalence of this form of millenarianism in Nyasaland, both before and after the 1920s–1930s, is in itself a commentary on the state of race relations there.

If there was nothing immediately Christian about this Nyasaland millennialism of the 1920s and 1930s how far may it be said to have been of independent growth; and how much of it was a new form of traditional tribal messianic hopes or an offspring, apparently unrelated in features but none the less kindred, of the Christian millenarian concept which the European missionaries had introduced? It must be said at once that there was little of independent growth about the Nyasaland millennialism of the '20s and '30s. Its form and content are clearly related to the African reaction to European influences since at least the 1880s.

What is much more in question is its relationship to what may be termed "tribal millenarianism". Clearly, in societies whose universe was bounded by a narrow tribal horizon,[6] there would seem to be little room for the wide-ranging chronological schema which characterize Judaic and Christian mil-

---

the Origins, Setting and Significance of the Nyasaland Native Rising of 1915 (Edinburgh, 1958), to which reference should be made, through the index, for statements, etc., which are not documented in this essay.

[5] For which, in general, see Peter Worsley, The Trumpet Shall Sound (New York: Schocken Books, 1968).

[6] For an example of the historical sense of a Central African people, see Ian Cunnison, History on the Luapula (Cape Town, 1951).

lenarianism. Nevertheless, it ought not to be automatically assumed that all tribal horizons in Nyasaland were necessarily narrow before the coming of British power in the second half of the 19th century. Leaving aside the question of attenuated Christian influences coming up the Zambezi from Portuguese East Africa, throughout the 18th century what is now called Nyasaland was probed and plundered by the Arab slave trade and Africans knew of the existence of the far-off East Coast and perhaps of other continents. While it is unlikely that the Arabs introduced much serious Islamic theology, the possibility ought not to be ruled out that, in the pre-European days, a few Nyasaland Africans picked up some ideas of Islamic eschatology. Furthermore, the scanty knowledge of Nyasaland tribal history as it exists at the moment provides at least one example of something akin to messianic expectation: the last Malawi hero, chief Kankhomba who, when overwhelmed by the Yao, retreated to Soche Hill. He, it is believed, is still waiting there in a cave to come again when his people most need him. In European times, too, as the instance of Chanjiri (the Chikunda prophetess of 1907 [7] who gave out that at the end of the year the white men would have to leave the country and no more tax need be paid) seems to show, traditional types of prophets existed for Nyasaland as for other parts of Central and East Africa. But "tribal millenarianism" and the extent and practice of tribal prophets [8] are subjects which still await detailed investigation for Nyasaland. It is probable that, because of the scanty character of records, little will ever be known about them. Yet the possibility that they played some part in African life in Nyasaland before the coming of the Europeans and that this may have had some influence on millennial-style and messianic movements in the period of European influence ought not to be lightly dismissed.

That Islamic millenarianism seems to have given some colour – and perhaps content – to these movements is suggested by tantalizing notes made during the 1914–18 War, when Africans of Nyasaland were disturbed by a variety of religio-political movements, all critical of European rule. In July of 1915, an Anglican missionary reported "much talk of the coming of

[7] *Nyasaland Annual Reports, 1907–8* (Cd. 3729–38, No. 574), p. 22; *Zambesi Industrial Mission Occasional Paper* (London), July–September, 1909, p. 12.
[8] *Cf.* Edwin W. Smith and Andrew Murray Dale, *The Ila-Speaking Peoples of Northern Rhodesia* (London, 1920), II, pp. 140–152; Cullen Gouldsbury and Hubert Sheen, *The Great Plateau of Northern Rhodesia* (London, 1911), p. 83; *The Last Journals of David Livingstone* (London, 1874), ed. Horace Waller, I, pp. 153–4; *Livingstonia News*, 1910, III, p. 4; G. W. B. Huntingford and C. R. V. Bell, *East African Background* (London, 1950), p. 19; B. Bernardi, *The Mugwe, A Failing Prophet: A Study of a Religious and Public Dignitary of the Meru of Kenya* (London, 1959); Georgina A. Gollock, *Sons of Africa* (London, 1928), p. 218. Solomon T. Plaatje, *Native Life in South Africa* (London, n.d.), p. 255; Edwin W. Smith, *African Beliefs and Christian Faith* (London, 1943), pp. 109–10. *Cf.* also J. H. Driberg, "Yakañ", *Journal of the Royal Anthropological Institute* (London), LXI, 1931, p. 420, "... while the cult is directed against aliens and any form of alien domination, it is not essentially anti-European, but is quite catholic in its operation."

Mzilima (a sort of Mohammedan messiah-mahdi)";[9] and in 1916, Count Falkenstein, commander of the German forces on the Nyasaland borders, commented on a "certain Mwalimu Isa who exercised great influence on the large Mohammedan population living on both sides of the British Portuguese border near Lake Nyasa."[10]

Yet, when allowance has been made for possible tribal and Islamic millenarian influences in Nyasaland, the greatest force in stimulating millenarianism there has been Christianity and the agencies by which it was developed.

Of all these agencies none was greater than one single individual. This was Joseph Booth, a passionately sincere fundamentalist Baptist who, from 1892 when he first arrived in Nyasaland to his deportation between 1902 and 1904, introduced groups of Africans who sought his allegiance to the millennial concepts of the Seventh-day Adventists and the Watch Tower movement. Booth travelled with bewildering frequency between Australia, New Zealand, Nyasaland, South Africa, the United States and Great Britain and sampled the fundamentalist eschatology which was more prevalent than is commonly imagined amongst sections of the English-speaking lower-middle and working-class in the forty years before the outbreak of the 1914 War. It might be said that he brought many Central African groups, Nyasaland and Rhodesian, within the orbit of an Anglo-American "international" of lower-middle and working-class millenarianism: an "international" which bears comparison with the more famous International and which, like it, was characterized by continual sectarianism.

A leading force in this "international" was the Watch Tower movement, the moving spirit of which was Pastor Charles Taze Russell of Alleghany, Pennsylvania, whose doctrines, in a modified form, are the basis for present-day Jehovah's Witnesses' teaching. Russell's millenarian ideas, which Booth introduced through African intermediaries into Nyasaland about 1908, might almost have been especially shaped to fit the dissatisfactions with European rule which some Africans were feeling by this time. Russell claimed that Christ had returned invisibly to earth in 1874, but that there would be no *kairos*, "no perfect fruit before October 1914 – the full end of 'Gentile Times' ... The time of trouble or 'day of wrath' which began in October 1874 ... will cease about 1915."[11] Africans in Nyasaland who were critical of European influences could appreciate the ascription of "time of trouble" to the 1874 period, for that symbol of the European regime, the first effective Christian mission, the Free Church of Scotland's Livingstonia, made its plans

[9]  *Nyasaland Diocesan Chronicle*, July, 1915, p. 9.
[10]  *Times* (London), 14 January, 1916, p. 7.
[11]  *Studies in the Scriptures, IV, The Battle of Armageddon* (Brooklyn, N.Y., 1897), pp. 604, 622, quoted in Milton Stacey Czatt, *The International Bible Students. Jehovah's Witnesses* (Scottdale, Pa., 1933), p. 8. See also Royston Pike, *Jehovah's Witnesses* (London, 1954), pp. 57–66.

in 1874 and, in 1875, started work in Nyasaland. It was Africans, lapsed communicants, of this Mission who provided the basis for Nyasaland's first modern millenarian movement and one which, by its creation of a cadre of African Watch Tower preachers, was to have considerable consequences for the development of similar movements in neighbouring territories.

Russell, it must be noted, did not say that the world would end in 1914–1915 – indeed, it is often difficult to know exactly what he did mean – but he made it very clear that these years were to be especially important for the emergence of the Millennium. For many of the Central African followers of his teaching this was tantamount to saying that the new order, devoid of European control, would start, albeit with cosmic cataclysms, at this time. Thus, between 1908 and 1915, groups of Nyasaland Africans lived in a state of tension and expectation which, because their hopes were to prove abortive in 1914–15, often sought new forms, either by changes in Watch Tower doctrine or by the assumption of new kinds of expectations, after these years had passed.

In less than a year, from September 1908 to June 1909, a sober European missionary witness claimed that 10,000 Africans,[12] around the Livingstonia mission area in Nyasaland, had been baptized into the new millennial faith of the Watch Tower movement. The baptizer-in-chief was Elliott (sometimes called Kenan) Kamwana. Kamwana was a young Tonga, a tribe whose domination by the militant Ngoni had been stopped by the *Pax Britannica* and who had then gone forward to accustom themselves to the ways of the white man's civilization much faster than their former masters. Kamwana had broken with the Scottish Livingstonia mission and then, like hundreds of other members of his tribe, had gone down into South Africa to seek his fortune in the mines. In 1907, he met Joseph Booth at Cape Town. Kamwana's rebellious disposition found excellent support in the new Watch Tower doctrine which Booth, after a visit to Pastor Russell in Pennsylvania, had brought back to South Africa, where he had been living after his deportation from Nyasaland for the effects of his religio-radical teaching on Africans. Armed with the new doctrine, Kamwana went back home; preached to vast crowds of Africans to the west of Lake Nyasa that the new age [13] was at hand, when Africans would supplant Europeans, and taxes would be abolished; and was deported by the Government after the end of the 1914–

---

[12]  *Tenth Foreign Mission Report. United Free Church of Scotland* (Edinburgh, 1910), p. 9; *Missionary Record of the United Free Church of Scotland*, IX, p. 321.

[13]  A succinct summary of Kamwana's tenets was given in answer to a Parliamentary question by the first British Labour Member, Keir Hardie, about official treatment of him: "That in October, 1914, the Second Advent will take place, that Christ will abolish all the present forms of government, that there will be no more taxation, that all the white population will disappear from Nyasaland and that the country will be placed in the hands of the natives who will govern themselves". (*Parliamentary Debates*, London, X, 1909, pp. 1287–90.)

1918 War, by which time officaldom, convinced that the world would not end as Kamwana, following Russell, had prophesied, felt that he might safely be allowed to return. The loss of the leader, however, was not the end of the Watch Tower movement in Nyasaland: indeed, a dispersal of many adherents into neighbouring territories ensued and the multifarious movement known as "Chitawala" in the Rhodesias and as "Kitawala" in the Congo and Portuguese territories – in both terms "tawala" being an African rendering of "tower" – had begun.

The Lakeside Tonga of Nyasaland, amongst whom this movement began, are one of the most unstudied tribes of Africa,[14] though, in addition to Kamwana they have given to the Central and South African political scene numerous important African religious and political leaders. Until more is known about them in the context of the second half of the last decade of the 19th century many elements in the social pattern of Kamwana's Watch Tower movement will remain unexplained.

In particular, the role which the Scottish Free Church Livingstonia missionaries played in preparing the background for the movement will not be easy to perceive. But that they had something to do with creating at least the formal conditions for it is clear. From 1895 onwards[15] they had encouraged the spirit of revivalism amongst the Lakeside Tonga and other African peoples of their area. They held mass Communion services: 4000 participants, for example, in 1904.[16] Although the following description of one of their revival meetings is taken from a report of 1911, it might also be applied to the whole crescendo of revivals, reaching its peak between 1908 and 1911 which they created in the region of Kamwana's movement. This description shows something of the milieu to which Kamwana returned in 1908 and suggests why so many of its African members had – to use the old but still very appropriate 18th century designation of the spirit of revival – the "enthusiasm" to follow him:

Great audiences assembled everywhere. The response to teaching was immediate and often with sobs and tears . . . a strong tendency to expect the blessings of God through spasms . . . Silly rumours were spread by ignorant people that fire was to come down from heaven to burn up all who concealed their sins. Exaggerated desires for wild physical emotions were evident . . . a youth rose and began to pray with a tremor in his voice and I (the Livingstonia missionary, Donald Fraser, is speaking) ordered the man to stop at once . . . Soon two or three began to pray at the same time . . . I stopped them, forbidding more than one at a time to pray. But during the struggle of these few minutes with the force of disorder and emo-

---

[14]   Dr. J. Van Velsen's study in *African Studies,* XVIII, 3 (1959) pp. 106–117, suggests that the Tonga are at last receiving the attention they deserve.

[15]   *Cf.* Raoul Allier, *La Psychologie de la Conversion chez les Peuples Non-Civilisés* (Paris, 1925), I, pp. 559–60; *Missionary Record of the United Free Church of Scotland,* 1902, p. 357; 1906, p. 448, photograph; 1909, p. 450, photograph; 1910, pp. 168, 409; 1911, p. 30. See also Rev. Chas. Inwood, *An African Pentecost* (London, 1911).

[16]   *Missionary Record, op. cit.,* 1904, p. 214.

tion. one felt as if we were passing through a powder magazine, and some were trying to light matches.[17]

It is a report which reads like the description of a Wesleyan meeting among the emerging proletariat of 18th century Britain and one is tempted to discuss the Kamwana movement – many of whose Tonga members were, like so many of Wesley's followers, people who had been rudely forced from an agrarian to an industrial way of life through their migrant service in the South African mines – in the light of the interpretations which historians have made of the excellently documented Wesleyan movement. Such an approach would be useful: but, until much more is known of the social changes at work amongst the Nyasaland Tonga in the first decade of the 19th century, it must be employed with care, otherwise it might lead to distortion.

If it is to the survival of frustrated millennial expectations akin to the Kamwana movement in its hey-day of 1908–9 that much of the enthusiasm which greeted Dr. Aggrey when he visited the Lakeside Tonga area in 1921 may be attributed, the use of American Negroes as the militant introducers of the new age remains to be explained. Kamwana added militant elements to the "Millennial Dawn" ideas of Pastor Russell when he applied them to his own local conditions but his eschatological thinking was, so far as can be gathered, within the framework of Christian fundamentalist concepts of the Last Things. He promised no American Negroes or non-Christian agencies for his deliverers.

The part played by American Negroes in the millennial ideology of groups of Nyasaland Africans has complicated origins. Briefly, four elements may be singled out in these. First, there is the fact that the leader of the multi-tribal Nyasaland Native Rising of 1915, John Chilembwe, spent from two to three years in America between 1897 and 1900 receiving education in a racially conscious Negro theological seminary in Virginia. Chilembwe's return, dressed in the clerical garb of a Negro American *evolué* of the turn of the century, stimulated interest in the coloured people of the United States amongst Nyasaland Africans. His correspondence with militant Negro Americans and the reflection of their ideas in his preaching to his independent African congregation added a kind of religious pan-Africanism to their concept of the Negro in America and his interest in Africa. After Chilembwe, before the Nyasaland millennial year of 1915, four other Africans from Nyasaland went to America and lived in a Negro American milieu. In 1906, Matthew and Fred Njilima followed a Negro American missionary, who had assisted Chilembwe at his mission station, to the United States. In the same year, Dr. Daniel S. Malekebu, who, in 1926, with the backing of American

17 *Ibid.*, 1911, pp. 410–11. *Cf.* Donald Fraser, "An African Panic", *Southern Workman* (Hampton), XXXVIII, 10 (October, 1909), pp. 568–9.

Negro Baptists, was allowed to open up again Chilembwe's old mission station which had been closed by the authorities, pursued the same course and received medical training in a Negro American college. And then, in 1915, a pupil from Kamwana's old school, Livingstonia, left home on the long trail that was to lead him to America. He was Hastings Kamuzu Banda. Thus, from Chilembwe in 1897 to Banda in 1915, five Nyasaland Africans, at least, had gone to an American Negro environment and had conveyed, in person and by correspondence, many of its aspirations, at a critical time in United States race relations, to their kinsmen in Nyasaland.

The second element in the growth of the idea of the Negro American in Nyasaland which should be noticed is the presence there of a number of coloured Americans. The first Seventh-day Adventist missionary in Nyasaland (indirectly the result of Joseph Booth's influence) was Thomas Branch who arrived in April, 1901. Branch was, from all accounts, a quiet and conservative man: but he stood for a denomination with a markedly millennial cast of thought.[18] In the same year, two other Negro Americans, L. N. Cheek and Emma B. DeLany came to assist John Chilembwe in the building up of his mission. Neither held pronounced millennial beliefs, being Baptists of a not unduly "enthusiastic" character. But Cheek at least was an outspoken critic of imperialism. In western-style education, all three of these American Negroes were well above the local standard. They seemed to many Africans persons of power and position, from whom help, when necessary, could be readily expected. That there were so few of them added to the speculation of a people, at that time largely untutored in western ways of thought, about their life in America and what they might do to help Africa.

A third element which must not be overlooked in the fascination of liberatory American Negroes for Nyasaland Africans is the presence in South Africa from the 1890s onwards of a much larger number of coloured Americans who had come to assist the formation of the independent African churches. Although many of these were from orthodox bodies such as the Negro American African Methodist Episcopal Church, others, in the new century, came from such millennial and radical groups as the Church of God and the Saints of Christ.[19] In the year that Aggrey was going to Nyasaland, an offspring of this Negro American denomination, Enoch Mgijima and the "Israelites", charged the guns of the civil power at Bulhoek commonage in

[18] Although, for a while, the term "Adventist" had something of the significance of "Watch Tower" for Nyasaland Europeans, the Seventh-day Adventists have, on the whole, as an organized denomination, exercised a conservative force in the Protectorate: see *Independent African, op. cit.,* 327–30 and *Nyasaland Times,* 13 September, 1929, p. 2.

[19] Elmer T. Clark, *The Small Sects in America* (New York, 1957), pp. 151–53; *Interim and final reports . . . relative to "Israelites" at Bulhoek and other occurences in May, 1921* (Cape Town, 1921, A. 4–'21), pp. 1–2.

South Africa and suffered 163 killed and 129 wounded.[20] In the same year, the myth of the liberatory Negro American had reached such a pitch in South Africa that in the Transkei, one Wellington Butelezi, could pose as an American Negro, tell his followers that all Americans were Negroes and that they were coming soon in aeroplanes to free the Bantu from European power and taxes.[21] While it is clear that the use of the Negro American – with or without aeroplanes – as a millennial agent has its own independent origins amongst Nyasaland Africans, it could not but be strengthened by the growth of a similar myth in South Africa, for in the first two decades of the 20th century, Nyasaland African labour migration to and from South Africa reached alarming proportions. Migrant labourers would take back to Nyasaland these ideas which would lose nothing of the mythical in the thousand-mile trek.

This Nyasaland labourers' connection with South Africa suggests a fourth element in the Negro American role in some Central African millennial movements: the influence of Marcus Garvey's Universal Negro Improvement Association. That there was some organizational connection between the Garvey movement and certain Nyasaland Africans seems clear from the fact that Isa MacDonald Lawrence of Chiradzulu, the district in which the Chilembwe Rising of 1915 was planned, was sentenced to three years' hard labour for importing into Nyasaland six copies of Garvey's publication, *The Negro World*, with which Lawrence himself had corresponded. He seems to have been interested in Garveyism from 1922 onwards.[22] It may be that Lawrence had first heard of this pioneering *négritude* movement in 1920, for this was a peak year of Garvey's influence: he sent a delegation to Liberia to sound out the possibilities for mass Negro emigration and, above all, the great conference of his Association in New York at this time had issued its resounding "Declaration of Rights of the Negro Peoples of the World", with its militant emphasis on "Africa for the Africans". The significance of these happenings was felt in several parts of Africa. In the Congo – a region that had been influenced by emigrant Nyasas and could, in its turn, influence them – the movements which centred on the millenarian Simon Kimbangu appear to have been touched in some way by Garveyism.[23] After Kimbangu's trial and sentence to death in 1921 the rumour spread that Negroes were coming from America to deliver the Congo natives from bondage.[24] Even before this, the belief had appeared that a ship would come up the Congo

---

[20]   *Interim and Final Reports, op. cit.;* Edward Roux, *Time Longer Than Rope* (London, pp. 143–8.

[21]   *Ibid.,* pp. 148–9.

[22]   *Nyasaland Times,* 24 September, 1926, p. 3. At Lawrence's trial, the Judge claimed that he was a brother-in-law of Dr. D. S. Malekebu who had been allowed to re-open Chilembwe's old mission in the Chiradzulu district in 1926.

[23]   Efraim Andersson, *Messianic Popular Movements in the Lower Congo* (Uppsala, 1958), pp. 250–56.

[24]   *Ibid.,* p. 71.

at Manyanga, after which all the whites would leave. It has been claimed
that the origins of this idea lay in Garvey's Black Star Line which he formed
to take New World Negroes back to Africa.[25] Such ideas may have made
their way into Nyasaland through labour migration to and from South Africa
and the Congo. But whatever their points of origin and with whatever degree
of exactitude they may have been held, Garvey-ite ideas added some element
in the crisis years of the early 1920s to the concept of Negro Americans, in
ships or aeroplanes, as millennial-style deliverers in Nyasaland.

Indeed, one of the most fascinating things for the historian is the attempt
to trace the spread and transformation of millennial ideas and imagery across
Central Africa. The way, for example, in which the "Back-to-Africa" ideas
of American Negro groups in the post-Civil War period have reached Africa
and then have been transformed into part of the millennial mechanisms of
African cults indicates the complexities of the process.[26] In a similar fashion,
the development of the ideas of Pastor Charles Taze Russell, after their
introduction into South and Central Africa by Joseph Booth's native agencies, demonstrates interesting patterns of selective borrowing.

From Nyasaland,[27] after the failure of the Kamwana movement in 1909,
variants of the Watch Tower pattern spread into neighbouring territories
(Northern [28] and Southern Rhodesia,[29] Angola,[30] Tanganyika [31] and the

---

[25]   *Ibid.*, p. 254.

[26]   It should be noted that these ideas reached South and Central Africa over two
decades, at least, before the Garvey movement. A useful starting point is 1898 when
Henry M. Turner, American Negro bishop of the African Methodist Episcopal Church,
toured South Africa to assist the newly formed "Ethiopian" independent African church
movement. Turner was a passionate exponent of the "Back-to-Africa" dream. *Cf.* also
the experience of the Negro American Presbyterian missionary, William Henry Shep-
pard, in the Belgian Congo in the 1890s: his command of the vernacular was such that
it "persuaded the Bakuba that his body contained the spirit of some member of the
tribe who was trying to return to them after death. Thus he received a royal welcome."
See Ruth Slade, *English-Speaking Missions in the Congo Independent State, 1878–1908*
(Brussels, 1959), pp. 105–6.

[27]   Despite some statements that the Watch Tower doctrine was first introduced into
Nyasaland in 1906 (e.g. *Report ... on Tanganyika ... 1923,* Colonial No. 2, London,
1924, p. 22; *Congo* (Brussels), I, 5, July, 1931, p. 711), it seems more likely that it
was not effectively established there until 1908: see *Independent African, op. cit.,* pp.
153–55.

[28]   R. L. Buell, *The Native Problem in Africa* (New York, 1928), I, p. 243; Katesa
Schlosser, *Propheten in Afrika* (Braunschweig, 1949), pp. 235–9; *Report of a Commission to inquire into the disturbances on the Copperbelt, Northern Rhodesia* (London,
October, 1935, Cmd. 5009); Griffith Quick, "Some aspects of the African Watch Tower
movement in Northern Rhodesia", *International Review of Missions* (London), XXIX,
April, 1940; "Kitawala", *Bulletin de Jurisdictions et du Droit Coutumier Congolais,*
10 (Elisabethville July–August, 1944), pp. 234–5; Ian Cunnison, "A Watch Tower As-
sembly in Central Africa", *International Review of Missions,* XL (London, October
1950) and "Jehovah's Witnesses at Work. Expansion in Central Africa", *The Times
British Colonies Review* (London First Quarter, 1958); L. H. Gann, *The Birth of a
Plural Society* (Manchester, 1958), pp. 187–8; George Shepperson, "The Literature of
British Central Africa", *Rhodes-Livingstone Journal,* XXIII (June 1958), pp. 40–43;
Peter Fraenkel, *Wayaleshi* (London, 1959), pp. 124–130. See also *Nyasaland Times,*

Belgian Congo[32]), adapting themselves to the particular social needs of different groups. Four main types of Watch Tower influences on these African groups may be noted. First, there are those Africans who maintain clear organizational links with Jehovah's Witnesses (formerly the International Bible Students) in the United States, who study the orthodox literature of the American movement and are represented at its conventions. These groups are mainly passive and accept the main tenets of the Russellite teaching to wait patiently for the End. For such Africans participation in the world-wide organization of the Witnesses seems to satisfy a need for political responsibility which has sometimes been denied them at home. They are particularly strong in Northern Rhodesia (over 20,000 members in 1953[33]). Elsewhere, Government ban (as in the Congo) on the membership of the Witnesses encourages the formation of secret organizations, which the American parent body can in no way control. This draws attention to the second Watch Tower influence in Central Africa: the formation of independent groups.[34] Such groups began to emerge very rapidly in Nyasaland after the official proscription of the Kamwana movement. Increasingly, the American leadership found them difficult to discipline.[35] Because of this, they soon began to draw apart from the official doctrines of the movement and often refused to wait passively for the End but entered into combat with the secular authorities. An interesting example of this process is the Ba

---

31 May and 28 June, 1932, pp. 3 and 2 respectively for the case of Joseph Sibakwe, a Watch Tower preacher. Sibakwe also preached the liberatory role of the Negro American in Northern Rhodesia.

[29] Although the *Nyasaland Times,* 31 May, 1932, p. 3, reported that the Watch Tower movement was rampant in Southern Rhodesia "three or four years ago", attention on its activities in Central Africa has concentrated on Northern Rhodesia and Nyasaland. *The Public Records of Southern Rhodesia, 1890–1923* (Cape Town, 1956) pp. 68a and 170a, suggests that material is available for a Watch Tower study concentrated especially on Southern Rhodesia.

[30] Andersson, *op. cit.,* p. 249; F. Clement C. Egerton, *Angola in Perspective* (London, 1957), p. 172. Owing to the problems of investigating African movements in Portuguese territories, such references remain tantalizing in the extreme.

[31] *Report ... Tanganyika ... 1923, op. cit.,* p. 22.

[32] The bibliography in Andersson, *op. cit.,* is probably the most comprehensive introduction to Watch Tower in the Congo.

[33] Cunnison, "Jehovah's Witnesses", *op. cit.,* p. 13.

[34] Because of the confusion which has often existed between African Watch Tower groups which owed allegiance to the American body and those which did not, the Watchtower Bible and Tract Society in 1948 issued a pamphlet, *The Watchtower Story* (New York) which attempted to draw the distinction. Unfortunately the distinction is not always preserved in press and other reports. For example, *East Africa and Rhodesia* (London, 12 November 1953), reports a march of 140 Jehovah's Witnesses on the Nyasaland Lilongwe boma in the crisis year of 1953 which was dispersed by baton charge after the Riot Act was read. But it is not clear whether this was an independent Watch Tower group or not.

[35] *E.g. The Watchtower,* XXXII, 2 (New York, 1911), William W. Johnston, "The Harvest Work in Africa".

Mulonda or "Watchman" movement of Northern Rhodesia.[36] These groups demonstrate what, after a long period of misrepresentation, is now being increasingly recognized: that the vague term "Watch Tower movement", as it has been applied to and is still used in Central Africa, represents two movements rather than one. Some would be inclined to broaden its scope and to say that it applies really to three: the third type being the influence of Russellite doctrines and techniques of proselytization on millenarian movements which have independent origins. The leading example of this process appears to be provided by the radical millenarianism of Lower Congo sects from the Kimbangu movement of the 1920s onwards, many of which have borrowed selectively from the Witnesses' teaching and techniques. A fourth instance of Watch Tower influence is its effect upon Central African movements which are not primarily millennial in their expectations. A leading example here is the John Chilembwe movement of 1915. Some of Chilembwe's Nyasaland followers were Watch Tower preachers. They may have added a dynamic of discontent against European rule to his movement but they in no sense assumed leadership. Yet because of their presence in his following Chilembwe has often mistakenly been dubbed a Watch Tower man.

To divide the so-called Watch Tower movement in Central Africa into two, three, perhaps four types, would undoubtedly draw from many local Europeans the response that this was unnecessary because "the African is unable to distinguish the finer points of doctrine". This, however, seems an untenable assumption. Historians, anthropologists and sociologists who wish to appreciate these various movements from the standpoints of their respective disciplines must be prepared to grapple with doctrinal differences much more than they have done in the past, because they are very real to African groups concerned.

One element in Central African millennial movements which deserves more study than, perhaps, it has received, is their role as "witch-finders". Witchfinding movements which seem to have nothing of the millennial in them – although it would be unwise to be too dogmatic about this – such

[36] The BaMulonda or "Watchman" movement exists in Northern Rhodesia, Nyasaland and Tanganyika. A local group in the Luapula Valley claims that the "Word" was brought to them by Elliott Kamwana Chirwa in 1947. He is the seventh Angel of God. The group is against the use of European medicine, permits polygamy, and employs a fantasy of Russellite teaching. It is not clear whether the movement was started by Elliott Kamwana after his release from detention or whether his name and career are used in a myth of origin. (It is perhaps worth mentioning that in 1954 I was informed by a Nyasaland African politician visiting Scotland that Kamwana was still alive and active.) I owe my knowledge of the movement to Mr. Robert Rotberg and the Rev. John V. Taylor of the Church Missionary Society who will, no doubt, discuss it in his forthcoming book on the Christian Churches in the Copper Belt of Northern Rhodesia. After I became aware of the existence of this movement, it was clear to me that the "independent Watch Tower" letter quoted in reference 60, page 498 of *Independent African, op. cit.*, came from this BaMulonda grouping.

as the *mcapi* movement of Nyasaland in the 1930s have been the subject of some study.[37] Witchfinding elements, however, easily enter into Central African millennial movements, particularly when they are of an anti-European character, since it is believed that the coming of the white man has led to an increase in witchcraft which must be cast out if the society concerned is to become healthy again. The Northern Rhodesian "Mwana Leza" (Son of God[38]) movement of 1925–27, led by a Tonga from Nyasaland, Tom Nyirenda,[39] who seems to have emerged from the wake of independent Watch Tower groups left by the failure of the Kamwana movement, is a good example of this. He is reported to have possessed a copy of Foxe's "Book of Martyrs", whose pictures of the drowning of witches he would show to his congregations with the question that if Europeans could drown their witches why should Africans not do the same?[40] (Nyirenda's movement seems to have had, also, the makings of a Cargo Cult, for it is claimed that he "promised that the Redeemer would arrive in an aeroplane one day laden with motor cycles and bales of calico."[41] The witchfinding element appears, too, in the most recent and spectacular of Northern Rhodesian and Nyasaland millennial movements, the so-called "Alice" movement, led by Lenshina Mulenga of Lubwa, who claims to have risen again after her "death" in 1953 to bring the promise that Christ, having gone up to Heaven on a white cloud, will come down from it at the Last on a black one. There is an annex to her main church, which has drawn away large numbers of Africans from the local Presbyterian mission, where "witchcraft charms discarded by Lenshina's followers (are) exhibited in fantastic heaps".[42] These episodes in Central African society seem similar to such events in European history as Savonarola's order to the Florentines to burn their vanities. Parallels of this sort are worth exploring.

Perhaps they indicate in these Central African millennial-style movements the "return-to-the-Golden-Age" theme which figures largely in kindred movements elsewhere. Yet it might be unwise to press the parallel too much here, for in some, if not all, of the millennial-style movements in Central Africa, there have always been strong elements which longed for the new

[37] Audrey I. Richards, "A modern movement of witchfinders", *Africa*, VIII (London, 1935); M. G. Marwick, "Another modern anti-witchcraft movement in East Central Africa", *Africa*, XX (1950), and "The social context of Cewa witch beliefs", *Africa*, XXII (1952).

[38] Not to be confused with the "Sons of God" movement under the leadership of Wilfred Good in Cholo, Nyasaland, in 1938. (*Nyasaland Protectorate. Annual Report of the Provincial Commissioners, 1938*, Zomba, p. 15.)

[39] His name is given as "Njendera" in *Nyasaland Times* 2 and 9 February, 1926.

[40] Kathaleen Stevens Rukavina, *Jungle Pathfinder: the Biography of Chirupula Stevenson* (London, 1951), p. 184.

[41] *Ibid.*, p. 184.

[42] Dunn, *op. cit.*, p. 36; Fraenkel, *op. cit.*, pp. 63–64. The Lenshina Mulenga movement might be profitably compared with the Chanjiri episode in Nyasaland in 1907. See note 7 above.

age, precisely because it would leave the African unhindered to adapt for his own purposes those aspects of European society which attracted him most. As Elliott Kamwana is reported to have cried out to his followers, "We shall build our own ships, make our own powder, make or import our own guns." [43]

It is, of course, true that in most millennial-style movements in colonial territories there is a political element. But in Nyasaland it seems to be a particular characteristic. The reasons for this are not yet completely clear, though some factors are readily apparent: its close contact with Scotttish missionaries, who came from a country with a markedly political consciousness; the influence on its emerging African politicians of the radical, fundamentalist missionary, Joseph Booth; the low level of its economy which made it peculiarly vulnerable to economic crisis and created its migratory labour cycle with neighbouring territories, especially South Africa; regional factors such as the political situation in Chiradzulu, from which the Chilembwe movement eventually emerged, from the time when the first Christian missionaries came to Nyasaland in the 1860s; and the development of the Lakeside Tonga, out of whom have sprung not only the Kamwana and kindred religious movements but primarily secular forces such as militant trade unionism and leading elements in the Nyasaland African Congress. Extracts from a letter which was published in the American *Watchtower* journal, for 1 September, 1914, a few weeks before the abortive Chilembwe Rising, by an African with a Tonga-sounding name, H. Simon Achirwa, exemplify these political characteristics in Nyasaland millennialism:–

Surely we are living in the time of the End, according to the Scriptures. We are seeing the clergy-people turning the Word of God into tables. They think they can stop the Christian people from sinning – as they call it – by whipping and by putting them in prison and by making them pay so much money. Can this stop people sinning? No: not at all! ... But we learn in the Bible that the Deliverer shall come ... People may remember that our Lord found the people of Israel doing wrong against the Word of God and they were proud. But we never see a single line in the Bible to say that he took every one of the Jews to the Roman Governor to be put in prison ... [44]

At a time when Dr. Hastings K. Banda and the greater part of the leadership of the Nyasaland African Congress are in prison,[45] these words have a peculiarly contemporary ring. They suggest that the millennial associations which many found in his return after nearly half a century from home are not altogether fanciful, for, as this essay has tried to indicate, there is a unique millennial tradition in Nyasaland. But they also suggest that a pitch of African exasperation, rightly or wrongly, with European rule may soon be

[43]  *Livingstonia News*, 4 (August 1909), p. 58.
[44]  *The Watchtower*, XXXV, 17 (New York, 1914).
[45]  These words were written on 20 December, 1959.

reached there. What effect this may have on the millenarian note which has often accompanied African reactions to European rule in Nyasaland in the past is not easily prophesied. Will it survive as part of a mood of passive resignation to apparently unchangeable conditions? Or will it add militancy to new political formations which will arise to challenge European hegemony – some of it, perhaps, even going over to the secular millenarianism that comes from Soviet Russia and China? One thing is certain: a new chapter in the story of pursuit of the millennium is opening in Nyasaland to-day.

GEORGE SHEPPERSON
*Edinburgh University*

# THE RAS TAFARI MOVEMENT IN JAMAICA IN ITS MILLENNIAL ASPECT

Ras Tafari, an offshoot of Jamaica-born Marcus Garvey's Universal Negro Improvement Association of the 1920s, began to take shape about 1930. Its basic doctrines are: first, black men, reincarnations of the ancient Israelites, were exiled to the West Indies because of their transgressions; second, the wicked white man is inferior to the black man; third, the Jamaican situation is a hopeless Hell; fourth, Ethiopia is Heaven; fifth, Haile Selassie is the Living God; sixth, the invincible Emperor of Abyssinia will soon arrange for expatriated persons of African descent to return to the Homeland; and seventh, in the near future black men will get revenge by compelling white men to serve them. Among the myths which are associated with these doctrines is the belief that £23,000,000 are available for the repatriation of black men to their Homeland.[1] In the early 1950s, the date for their departure had not been definitely set, but some Ras Tafarians expected to leave "any day now." Others expected repatriation to occur within three or four years, but one cultist's estimate was twenty years.

As an escapist-adjustive type of activity, this back-to-Africa cult has provided opportunities for lower class Jamaicans to denounce "the white man", Jamaican politicians, business men, teachers, the police and clergymen. Despite the hostility of the Ras Tafarians toward ministers and their congregations, the cult may be regarded as a pseudo-religious movement. Passages of the Bible are read or quoted at meetings and interpreted in ways which give support to Rastafarian doctrines, and many of the cult's songs are adaptations of Methodist or Baptist hymns. For many members who live in the economically depressed areas of West Kingston, the movement can be regarded as a functional equivalent of orthodox and revivalist religions, political parties, and a variety of social organizations.[2]

[1] When a delegation of Ras Tafarians suggested to the Premier on August 21, 1960 that the £20,000,000 given by the British Government for the emancipation of slaves be applied to the cost of emigration of Jamaicans of African descent desiring to go to Africa, Mr. Norman Manley explained that the money mentioned by the delegation was paid to slave owners by Britain for freeing their slaves and was not available now. *Trinidad Guardian,* August 22, 1960.

[2] See George E. Simpson, "Political Cultism in West Kingston, Jamaica," *Social and Economic Studies,* 4 (June, 1955), pp. 145–148. This study is based on field work done in May-December, 1953 with support of a grant from the American Philosophical Society.

According to the millennial dream of this movement, Africa is the promised land, a heaven ruled by the Living God. In Africa, the black man will get revenge. "We understand what the white man has done to us and we are going to do unto them as they have done unto us. In Ethiopia, the white man will have to serve us." In support of this belief Isaiah 14 is often quoted: ". . . and the house of Israel shall possess them [the strangers] in the land of the Lord for servants and handmaids; and they shall take them captives, whose captives they were; and they shall rule over their oppressors." Instead of the other-worldliness of the established Christian churches and the revivalist cults of Jamaica, the Rastafarians for thirty years have projected their hopes into the other-world of Ethiopia.

From time to time an African citizen visiting Jamaica has told Ras Tafarians that unskilled persons will not be welcome in the new nations of Africa. The most recent pronouncement of this type was made to a mass meeting in Jamaica on August 13, 1960 by Mr. Francis Cann, third secretary to the Ghana Mission in the United States. Mr. Cann said it would be unfair to add the problems which would be occasioned by mass immigration from the West Indies to the problems now faced by the members of the Negro race resident in African countries. Although Mr. Cann was given "a tremendous ovation" upon his arrival at the meeting, he departed "against a background of sullenness, resentment and suspicion on the part of the African migratory element." [3]

For years the Ras Tafari movement has attracted many types within the Jamaican lower class.[4] A recent study reveals a number of cleavages among the brethren: "those who belong to Locals of the Ethiopian World Federation Inc., and those who do not; those who grow their beards and long hair, those who also plait their locks, and those who do neither; those who have adopted the Niyabingi ethos [of violence] and those who have not; those totally alienated from Jamaican society, and those who are not; those with a definite Marxist framework of ideas, and those without. There are also important divisions between rural and urban brethren, between the young and the old, between those who regard a firm social organization as a necessary instrument for the achievement of their aims, and those who reject this idea totally; between the unemployed and the employed brethren; between those who are addicted to ganja [marihuana] and those opposed to it; between those for whom the Emperor has special importance as a spiritual force, and those who conceive of him in racial-political terms primarily." [5]

Indicative of the lack of unity in the Ras Tafari movement is the request during the last week of June, 1960 of a group calling itself "The United

[3] *Trinidad Guardian,* August 14, 1960.
[4] George E. Simpson, *op. cit.,* pp. 144–145.
[5] M. G. Smith, Roy Augier, and Rex Nettleford, *The Ras Tafari Movement in Kingston, Jamaica,* Institute of Social and Economic Research, University College of the West Indies (July, 1960), p. 28.

Rasses of Jamaica" that the Minister of Home Affairs provide by treaty for the establishment of a special area where its members could govern themselves.[6] The reply of the Minister was that the government had no intention of establishing a state within a state.

In December, 1959, the Rev. Claudius Henry, Rastafarian leader of the African Reform Coptic Church of God in Christ, The First Fruit of Prayer, God's Army Camp, urged his followers and sympathisers to sell their possessions, come to Kingston and board a ship that would sail to Ethiopia. Hundreds of Jamaicans followed his suggestion, and each person was given a card which was to transport him free to Africa. When the ship failed to appear, Mr. Henry blamed the Jamaican government for preventing its landing.

In 1955, it seemed ". . . conceivable that the verbal violence which characterizes the cult at present might lead to other kinds of violence."[7] In April, 1960, the Rev. Henry and fifteen of his followers were arrested after two raids on the headquarters of his church. Security officers seized revolvers, shotguns, dynamite, detonators, machetes, and a letter addressed to Fidel Castro. Tried on a treason charge in October, 1960, Henry and those arrested with him were given jail sentences ranging from three to ten years. On June 21, 1960, two soldiers of the Royal Hampshire Regiment were killed and three were injured during a security raid on a Ras Tafari camp. Three Rastafarians were then executed by the camp's officers for "challenging the authority of the men from abroad" and failing to push the anti-government movement "with the utmost vigor". Three days later one of the camp leaders was arrested and charged with the murders, and within a few days four others were captured. All five are United States citizens. The Jamaican government offered rewards for the capture of fifteen other American Negroes, who, it is alleged, arrived in Jamaica as tourists on a mission to overthrow the government. These men, at least two of whom are believed to have been born in Jamaica, are said to have trained one section of the cult in the use of firearms and insurrectionary tactics with the intention of establishing a Rastafarian state. On October 1, 1960, one Jamaican and three citizens of the United States, including Rev. Henry's son, were sentenced to death for the murder of the three Rastafarians. On November 8, 1960, two other Americans were sentenced to ten years in jail after pleading guilty to being accessories after the murder.

Some branches of the Ras Tafari movement have transferred the setting

---

[6] The inspiration for this proposal was the arrangement made with the Maroons in 1838. In that year, the Governor, Sir Edward Trelawney, drew up a treaty of peace and friendship between the government and the Maroons. The Maroons were given tax-free lands and were allowed to govern themselves. The treaty provided for trials by their own chiefs, but no chief could impose the death sentence.

[7] George E. Simpson, "The Ras Tafari Movement in Jamaica: A Study of Race and Class Conflict," *Social Forces*, 34 (Dec., 1955), p. 170.

of the millennial dream from Africa to Jamaica. The small group of Negro revolutionaries from the U.S.A. succeeded in finding some Rastafarians who were willing to translate their verbal violence into actual violence. Although the insurrection of June, 1960, failed, the possibility of further attempts to use this movement to bring about a totalitarian state remain.

Recent developments have been examined by a committee appointed by Dr. Arthur Lewis, Principal of the University College of the West Indies, after he received an appeal from representative Ras Tafarians for a study of the movement. Among other points which M. G. Smith, Roy Augier, and Rex Nettleford make in their report of July, 1960 are the following: first, since 1954 there has been a steady increase in criminality and violence within the movement; second, the Revivalist cult groups have lost ground steadily to expanding American Protestant missions (especially the Church of God movement financed originally from the United States) and to the Ras Tafari movement; third, drumming and dancing have been introduced into Ras Tafari meetings; and fourth, the belief in mass migration has been strengthened by the heavy migration to Britain in recent years and the report that Emperor Haile Selassie I has granted " '500 acres of very fertile and rich land . . . through the Ethiopian World Federation Inc., to the Black People of the West, who aided Ethiopia during her period of distress.' " [8]

Yinger has suggested that the term contraculture be used instead of subculture wherever "the normative system of a group contains as a primary element, a theme of conflict with the values of the total society, where personality variables [frustration, anxiety, feelings of role ambiguity, and resentment] are directly involved in the development and maintenance of the group's values and wherever its norms can be understood only by reference to the relationships of the group to a surrounding dominant culture." [9] This analytic distinction is quite useful in interpreting the values of the Ras Tafari movement. From the beginning, the normative system of the Rastafarians has constituted a contraculture.

The explanation which seems to fit the Ras Tafari case best is that of "deprivation", a variation of the frustration-aggression hypothesis. As Hogg points out, lower-class Jamaicans have always struggled against exploitation. Higher wages, civil and political rights and other gains have come slowly and against bitter opposition. Eruptions have occurred occasionally, but much of the hostility on the part of those who have sought social and economic advancement has been repressed. [10] For more than a century, Afro-Jamaican religious cults – Native Baptists, Revival (Pocomania, Revivalist,

---

[8] M. G. Smith, Roy Augier, and Rex Nettleford, *op. cit.*, pp. 15–19.

[9] J. Milton Yinger, "Contraculture and Subculture." *American Sociological Review*, 25 (1960), pp. 625–535.

[10] Donald Hogg, "The Convince Cult in Jamaica," in Sidney Mintz, ed., *Papers in Caribbean Anthropology*, Yale University Publications in Anthropology, no. 58 (1960), p. 21.

Revival Zion), Cumina, and Convince – have provided outlets to their devotees for the expression of repressed resentment.[11] Emotional release has come to members of these autonomous cult-groups through vigorous, and even violent, physical activity and through verbal aggression during spirit possession. For the past two or three decades the Ras Tafari movement must be listed as another outlet for pent-up emotions.

In the case of the Ras Tafarians, deprivation cannot be taken simply "in the sense of a lowering of subsistence levels and of status . . . because the less privileged groups. . . increased in numbers without a proportional increase in opportunities to filter off into new land or new industries or otherwise find new kinds of opportunity to maintain or improve their position." [12] Deprivation is a relative term. It does not always mean actual suffering or even a decline in one's status or level of living. Ras Tafari members do not live well, but many are not deprived in the sense that they have lost out entirely in recent years or even that they have lived less well than formerly. Members of the movement have watched Jamaica's growing middle class acquire new cars, new houses, and new appliances and they think it is impossible for them to obtain such goods. All members of the movement refuse to participate in rallies sponsored by the two leading political parties and they abstain from voting. They expect no real achievement from labor unions. With the exception of the section of the movement which seeks to take over political control in Jamaica, they insist that their only hope lies in returning to Africa.[13]

---

[11] P. D. Curtin, *Two Jamaicas,* Harvard University Press, 1955, pp. 32–34; George E. Simpson, "Jamaican Revivalist Cults," *Social and Economic Studies,* 5 (Dec., 1956), pp. 411 ff; Donald Hogg, *op. cit.*; J. G. Moore and G. E. Simpson, "A Comparative Study of Acculturation in Morant Bay and West Kingston, Jamaica," *Zaire* (Nov. 1957), 979–1019 and (Jan. 1958), 65–87.

[12] Sylvia L. Thrupp, above, p. 26.

[13] The report made in July, 1960, by M. G. Smith, Roy Augier, and Rex Nettleford, *op. cit.*, p. 38, contains the following recommendations:

(1) The Government of Jamaica should send a mission to African countries to arrange for immigration of Jamaicans. Representatives of the Ras Tafari brethren should be included in the mission.

(2) Preparations for the mission should be discussed immediately with representatives of the Ras Tafari brethren.

(3) The general public should recognize that the great majority of Ras Tafari brethren are peaceful citizens, willing to do an honest day's work.

(4) The police should complete their security enquiries rapidly, and cease to persecute peaceful Ras Tafari brethren.

(5) The building of low-rent houses should be accelerated, and provision made for self-help cooperative building.

(6) Government should acquire the principal areas where squatting is now taking place, and arrange for water, light, sewerage disposal and collection of rubbish.

(7) Civic centres should be built with facilities for technical classes, youth clubs, child clinics, etc. The churches and the U.C.W.I. should collaborate.

(8) The Ethiopian Orthodox Coptic Church should be invited to establish a branch in West Kingston.

Millennialism is only one of many ways of reacting to prolonged frustration. There is no inevitability about the appearance of a millennial movement in the face of actual or perceived deprivation.

GEORGE E. SIMPSON
*Oberlin College*

---

(9) Ras Tafari brethren should be assisted to establish cooperative workshops.

(10) Press and radio facilities should be accorded to leading members of the movement.

# THE FREE SPIRIT IN THE HUSSITE REVOLUTION

The Hussite Revolution owed a great deal to the heresy of the Free Spirit, without which, indeed, the revolution might not have taken place. Hussitism itself was not derived from Free-Spirit heresy, nor did the latter really become Hussite, but these labels do not tell the story, and when we leave off comparing doctrines, and study the flow of events, we find that at a definite stage in the Bohemian reformation, the destinies of Hussitism were determined first by the upsurge and development of a Free-Spirit party, then by the struggle against it. Here as in many other of its aspects, Hussitism demonstrates its true character as less a national than a genuinely European event, one that took place in Bohemia but required the collaboration of many extra-Bohemian elements.

If modern scholarship had produced an authoritative monograph on the Brethren of the Free Spirit, or if there were a coherent body of approved opinions about them, we could begin this discussion by summarizing the views of other scholars. Instead, lacking such a standard picture of the sect, we may take advantage of the fact that the medieval Church had its own reasons for desiring a reliable definition of Free-Spirit heresy, and offer a summary of the classic definition by the Council of Vienne, in 1311, in its decree against the Beghards.[1] The sect, we are told, believed (1) "that man in his present life can acquire such a degree of perfection as to render him wholly sinless"; (2) that in this condition "a man can freely grant his body whatever he likes"; (3) that "those who are in this degree of perfection and in this spirit of liberty are not subject to human obedience ... for, as they assert, where the spirit of the Lord is, there is liberty" [II Cor. iii, 17]; (4) that man can attain the same perfection of beatitude in the present as he will obtain in the blessed life to come; (5) that "every intelligent nature is naturally blessed in itself"; (6) that the perfect soul does not need to practice acts of virtue; (7) that "the carnal act is not a sin, since nature inclines one to it"; (8) that the members of the sect "should not stand up when the Body of Jesus Christ is elevated, nor show reverence to it," for "it would be a mark of imperfection in them if from the purity and loftiness of their con-

---

[1]  The Council's decree may be found in the Clementines, V, iii, 3, ed. E. Friedberg, *Corpus iuris canonici*, II (Leipzig, 1881), col. 1183 f.

templation they descended so far as to occupy their minds with the sacrament of the Eucharist or the passion of Christ's humanity." So the Council of Vienne: what we have is an accurate and logical presentation of the sect's basic doctrines, from the viewpoint of offended Catholicism.

The picture can be profitably filled in from sources closer to the heresy. Thus – to take an outstandingly valuable example – John of Brno (Brünn) offered the following description of the Cologne Beghards in the first half of the 14th century, when he was a member of them.[2] The new member was received into a kind of novitiate, in which the emphasis was on absolute, Christlike poverty and humility: he had to sell all his goods and turn the proceeds over to the sect, and when he first appeared before the brethren he was stripped of his clothing. He was then sent out to beg, with a companion to whom he owed absolute obedience; he was also required to spend time in church, and to wash the feet of wayfarers. (Other texts amplify this information: the first stage of Beghardism was a life of harsh asceticism and unquestioning obedience, a life indeed of evangelical poverty.[3]) But after completing this discipline, the Beghard then passed to the highest degree of liberty; having killed his own nature, he was "transmuted totally and physically so as to be made one with God, and God was totally and physically with him." Thus his one requirement was "to allow the divine nature and truth to work in him" – this was the highest liberty and it involved absolute indulgence of the promptings of the presumably new nature: he could, for example, take money from anyone, deceive anyone, have sexual intercourse with anyone, at any time he wished. The only danger was that he might submit to some restraint and hence "fall away from the freedom of the spirit, from the perpetual to the temporal." Thus:

They say that those who are in true liberty cannot be commanded by anyone, or excommunicated, or forbidden anything; neither the pope nor an archbishop nor anyone alive has authority over them, for they are free and do not come under the jurisdiction of any man; therefore they do not heed any statutes or mandates of the Church.

It is not hard, in all of this, to recognize the Eckhartian scheme, of degrees of *paupertas* culminating in the total liberty consequent on divine possession. The Beghard who begins by imitating the poverty of "Christ on the Cross"[4] ends by being deified through the Holy Spirit, at which point he is superior to Christ, at least in the latter's earthly existence.[5] Thus the perfect life is

---

[2]  The text is edited by W. Wattenbach, "Über die Secte der Brüder vom freien Geiste," *Sitzungsberichte der kön. preuss. Akademie der Wissenschaften* (Berlin, 1887), pp. 529–537.

[3]  *Cf. ibid.*, pp. 524–526.

[4]  *Ibid.*, p. 530: "Post hec me instruxit de austeritate ordinis in hunc modum: 'Verus observator paupertatis nichil habet proprium, set debet esse vacuus ab omnibus rebus temporalibus, sicut Christus in cruce.' "

[5]  *Cf.* the interrogation of John Hartmann in Erfurt in 1367 (*ibid.*, p. 541): "Inter-

achieved in two stages, of which the first – the cult of evangelical poverty –
is identical with the religious ideal of many other groups – Waldensians,
Franciscans, orthodox Beguines, etc. – both within and outside the Church.
The second stage, that of the Free Spirit proper, involves nothing less than
a total transformation of the individual's nature, so that the evangelical precepts are transcended: even the slightest restraint is intolerable to the Beghard
who must, at all costs, preserve his feeling of perfection, power, and liberty.
Here the two-stage scheme of mysticism can be perfected by the Joachimite
scheme, in which the Age of the Son is to be succeeded by the Age of the
Holy Spirit, with a regime of perfect liberty and sinlessness replacing the old
order of subjection and restraint. Through this doctrine the transformation
of the nature of the individual is identified with a secular – indeed a cosmic –
event, and the Beghard's individual repudiation of external authority takes
on the potentiality of an ideology of social revolution. At least some of the
Free-Spirit groups went this far.[6]

But it was in Hussite Bohemia that the Free-Spirit, fused with Joachim-
itism, reached its highest medieval development, as a doctrine actually
operative in the construction of a new social order, that of Taborite chiliasm.
The details of this episode cannot be traced here – I have studied them in
an earlier paper[7] – but some general comments will be in order. Although
offering no absolutely new doctrines, Taborite chiliasm is uniquely interesting
as a realization of doctrine, and above all, we may suggest, as a demonstra-
tion of the enormous potentialities of the two-stage road to perfection. Tabor
had begun with the first stage: it was a movement of the Waldensian type,
stressing apostolic poverty, moral purity, and suffering.[8] It also shared
apocalyptic ideas with other Hussite parties, and, it may be argued, the very
intensity of early Tabor's evangelical spirit necessarily developed, or perhaps
presupposed, a special mood of eschatological tension.[9] Finally, the university-trained leaders of early Tabor never lost sight of their place in the

rogatus an Christus fuisset liber spiritu, respondit quod non, quod probavit per ewange-
lium, quia Christus in passione sua dixit: 'Pater, si possibile est, transseat a me calix
iste; non tamen sicut ego volo set sicut tu.' Et addidit quod Christus in die parascheves,
postquam mortuus fuit in cruce, tunc primo veram libertatem fuerit assecutus, propter
quod et feria sexta a vulgaribus dicitur fritag."

[6]  The best non-Hussite example of a fusion of Free-Spirit and Joachimite elements is
that of the Brussels "Homines intelligentiae", the record of whose interrogation by the
inquisition, in 1411, is published by P. Fredericq, Corpus documentorum inquisitionis
haereticae pravitatis Neerlandicae, I (Ghent: J. Vuylsteke, 1889), 269 ff.

[7]  "Chiliasm and the Hussite Revolution," Church History, XXVI (1957), 43–71.

[8]  See ibid., p. 10f.

[9]  The very name "Tabor", taken from the Palestinian mountain where according to
tradition the transfiguration of Jesus took place, and where he was supposed to have
appeared to his disciples after his death, suggests the mood of the early Taborites (see
ibid., note 3). Amadeo Molnár draws attention to the eschatological significance of the
fact that the Taborite congregations were held on mountains, for in the Scriptures "the
fundamental events of revelation take place on mountains" ("Eschatologická naděje
české reformace," Od reformace k zítřku (Prague: Kalich, 1956), p. 29.

national reform; although sectarian in spirit, the Taborite congregations also sought to make their program that of the whole Hussite nation. But in the course of the autumn of 1419 an alliance of the Hussite conservatives with the Catholics frustrated this effort, and from November on, the Taborites were subject to violent persecution, aiming at their physical extermination. Only revolution could save them, but their evangelical ideology could hardly illuminate that path – indeed, in the early fifteenth century the path did not yet exist. At this point chiliasm came to the rescue, and Tabor passed into its second stage, through the efforts principally of the priest Martin Húska, a political genius and a man of extraordinary religious fervor; his doctrine was unmistakably that of the Free Spirit, derived perhaps from pre-existing Bohemian sectarianism, perhaps from recently arrived Beghards.[10]

In essence Martin and his associates preached the imminent advent of Christ, to be prepared and consummated in a period of terrible catastrophe, and to result in a new secular dispensation, the millennium. First Christ would come secretly, inaugurating the time of punishment and vengeance, when he would be imitated not "in his gentleness and mercy, but in zeal, rage, and just retribution." [11] The Taborites in this time were "angels, sent to lead the faithful out of all cities, villages, and castles"; the brethren, gathered together, were the Body of Christ – *the* Christian society *par excellence*, for everything remaining outside their congregations was doomed to destruction, a process in which the Taborites would play the part of God's army. Then, after the struggle, Christ would descend openly, in his own

---

[10] The most sympathetic and illuminating treatment of Martin is that of J. Macek, *Tábor v husitském revolučním hnutí*, II (Prague, 1955), 108ff., and *passim*. But to Macek Martin is above all a spokesman of the poor and the creator of his own ideas – Free-Spirit influence (or indeed any other external influence) is excluded, on the general principle that ideology stems from the social situation, not from other ideology (*ibid.*, p. 127ff.). It is of course important to bear this point in mind, in order not to make Martin a mere dispenser of other people's ideas, but according to any ordinary view of the circulation of ideas Martin must be deemed a disciple of the Free Spirit, and the main question becomes that of determining his sources. For the recently arrived Beghards, see below; for pre-existing Bohemian sectarianism of the Free-Spirit variety, among the German population, see *Staré letopisy české*, ed. F. Šimek (Prague, 1937), p. 29. Ernst Werner has recently sought to amplify the evidence by drawing attention to what he calls "a Taborite tract... of the year 1421", beginning "We, the Society of the Free Spirit Brotherhood of Christ..." See "Popular Ideologies in Late Medieval Europe: Taborite Chiliasm and Its Antecedents," *Comparative Studies in Society and History*, II (1960), 349. But according to F. M. Bartoš, who published the tract thirty years ago ("Hus a jeho strana v osvětlení nepřátelského pamfletu z r. 1412," *Reformační Sborník*, IV (1931), 3–8, the text on pp. 5–7), the work is an anti-Hussite parody of 1412. Bartoš's edition was not known to Werner, whose dating (in 1421) can hardly stand up to Bartoš's arguments for 1412. What the tract does show, however, is an awareness of the sect of Brethren of the Free Spirit among the Bohemians – otherwise the parody would had no force.

[11] The quotations in this paragraph are drawn from Laurence of Březová's "Hussite Chronicle", ed. J. Goll, *Fontes rerum bohemicarum*, V (Prague, 1893), 413 ff. For other sources see my article cited above.

person, to take up his kingdom and complete the annihilation of the evil. The New Age would begin:

> In this second advent of Christ before the Day of Judgement, all kings and princes and prelates of churches will cease to be, nor will there be in the kingdom thus renovated any tribute or exactors of tribute, because the sons of God will tread on the necks of kings, and all kingdoms under the heavens will be given to them . . .
>
> In this renovated kingdom there will be no sin, no scandal, no abomination, no falsehood, but all will be the chosen sons of God, and all the suffering of Christ and of his members will cease. . . .Women will give birth to their children without pain and without original sin, . . . and children born in that kingdom, if they are of the kingdom, will never die, because death will no longer be.
>
> The Law of Grace [*scil.*, the New Testament] will be voided in this world in the renovated kingdom, and will cease as to act and execution.
>
> Those elect still living will be brought back to the state of innocence of Adam in Paradise, like Enoch and Elijah, and they will be without any hunger or thirst, or any other spiritual or physical pain. And in holy marriage and with immaculate marriage-bed they will carnally generate sons and grandchildren here on earth and on the mountains, without pain or trouble, and without any original sin. Then there will be no need for baptism . . . [with water] because they will be baptised in the Holy Spirit, nor will there be the tangible sacrament of the holy Eucharist, because they will be fed in a new angelic mode – not in memory of Christ's passion, but of his victory.

Those who heeded these prophecies and joined the Taborite congregation had in fact to leave homes and families, and then turn over all their goods to the common funds: the path was precisely that of the Beghard initiate.[12] The full, individual enjoyment of spiritual liberty would follow in due course, in the New Age; meanwhile the Taborites lived in a collective emancipation, recognizing no authority over them, no moral or legal restraints in their dealings with the outsiders, and no traditional norms in their own behavior.[13]

[12]   John of Brno, on preparing to join the Beghards, was told not only to give up all his property and turn the proceeds over to the sect (these were "the poor"), but also to send his wife away – he was not bound to her at all. Just so the Taborite recruits "sold their property . . . and threw their money at the feet of the priests" (Laurence of Březová, p. 356); most often, it would seem, the wives and children came with the men (*loc. cit.*), but not always, and one spouse might simply leave the other behind: it was necessary for the Prague University masters explicitly to refute the Taborite view that this was permitted (see my "Chiliasm", p. 51). The Taborite common funds, and with these the whole episode of Taborite communism (*ibid.*, pp. 53–55, 59), might thus be interpreted as an analogue of the common life of the Beghard brotherhood, itself of course inspired by the common life of ordinary monasticism.

[13]   There are many sources; see my "Chiliasm", *passim*, and *cf.* the following report by Master John Příbram (*Život kněží táborských*, ed. J. Macek, *Ktož jsú boží bojovníci* (Prague, 1951), p. 265): the chiliast prophets "said that the elect of God would rule in the world for a thousand years with Christ, visibly and tangibly. And they preached that the elect of God who fled to the mountains would themselves possess all the goods of the destroyed evil ones and rule freely over all their estates and villages. And they said: you will have such an abundance of everything that silver, gold, and money will be only a nuisance to you. They also said and preached to the people: now you will not pay rents to your lords any more, nor be subject to them, but will freely and un-

Having seceded from the old order, physically and spiritually, and having full confidence in the advent of a perfect new order, the Taborites could readily solve their immediate problems in an unprecedented way: by setting up a new society. Thus a number of cities in South Bohemia saw the inauguration of communist regimes, half theocratic, half military, and the capital of the Taborite complex was located, in a brand-new settlement, which took the name of Tabor. The Taborite movement was converted into a Taborite society.

But the ideology of the movement – chiliasm – could not become the ideology of a society, and when Tabor began to come to terms with the facts of ordinary life in this world, she began to move away from the chiliast inspiration. Thus, almost as soon as the Taborites returned to South Bohemia, after the defense of Prague in the summer of 1420, we find evidence of what may be called a party of order, which promoted ideas and institutions of stability against the chiliast insistence on tension, enthusiasm, and total dynamism. In September of 1420 the Taborites elected a bishop, Nicholas of Pelhřimov, to regulate preaching and other affairs of the church, and in October, in flagrant contradiction of chiliast principles, Tabor began to collect seigneurial rents from the peasants of the domains she had conquered; at about the same time she began, tentatively at least, to abandon the chiliast principle of total warfare in favor of expedient negotiation.[14] It was probably in this period too that the Taborite city of Písek became the seat of the party of order, thus giving a physical expression to the split in the Taborite ranks.[15]

In passing from movement to society, moreover, the Taborites developed a new orientation to the problems of religious reform. The movement had lived in constant religious tension, and the ordinary institutions of society had not been allowed to develop in a way or to a degree that would have led to the dissolving of that tension. But now, even though the religious inspiration remained paramount, the social, political, and economic spheres of life were necessarily passing from mere aspects of religion into a self-subsistent institutional existence – in the end, indeed, Tabor the city could exist without the Taborite faith. The religious sphere, for its part, was correspondingly narrowed, and it too took on an institutional form; as we have seen, the Taborites elected a bishop and organized their clergy into the beginnings of a church. Inevitably then, the ideological interests of the Taborite theoreticians – those, at least, of the party of order – contracted from

---

disturbedly possess their villages, fishponds, meadows, forests, and all their domains . . ." *Cf.* also the first of the paragraphs cited above, p. 170.

[14] For Tabor's election of a bishop and collection of rents, see Laurence of Březová, p. 438. The new attitude towards warfare is indicated by Tabor's armistice with Lord Ulrich of Rožmberk, 18 November, 1420 (for an English translation of the text see F. Heymann, *John Žižka and the Hussite Revolution* (Princeton, 1955), pp. 485ff.): see the discussion by Macek, *Tábor*, II, 256ff.

[15] Macek, *Tábor*, II, 238, 258, and *passim*.

schemes of secular salvation into practical efforts to define and justify the doctrines of the Taborite church. In this effort there could be no place for the Free Spirit, for the new society was not that of the millennium, nor indeed did even the communist institutions succeed in preserving their preponderance against more usual social and economic arrangements. The new Taborite theological enterprise rather turned back to the common Hussitism of the Prague University reform movement – the kind of scholastic religious thought that by its nature was fitted to deal, from the religious point of view, with the problems of a stable society. At the same time the Taborites did not give up their Waldensianist radicalism, which made itself felt in the new period chiefly as a kind of congregational orientation towards all religious problems. Thus, on the one hand, the theoreticians of Tabor's party of order, led by Nicholas of Pelhřimov, could find common ground with the Prague University masters and hence could debate current issues with them; on the other hand, however, the debates could never end in agreement.

The immediate issue concerned the Taborite form of worship. From the very first, Hussite radicalism, including the Prague party of Master Jakoubek of Stříbro, had attacked the pompous and sumptuous décor of the Roman rite, and had also tended to emphasize the essential meaning of the mass – and particularly communion – as against its external trappings. In his treatise, De cerimoniis, of about 1415, Jakoubek had pointed out that in Catholic faith there were only four technically necessary elements of a valid consecration of the Eucharist: bread and wine, the words of consecration, a duly ordained priest, and the intention of consecrating; in case of necessity, he argued, the whole mass could be reduced to these four.[16] As disciples of Jakoubek, the priests of Tabor knew his arguments, and as adherents of a Waldensianist faith they had still other reasons for abandoning the full Roman rite, on principle and not merely in case of need; since, moreover, the Taborites had begun by holding their services in the field, without consecrated altars or churches, their practice joined their theory, and the result was a simplified form of worship radically different from even the reformed rite of Jakoubek's party. Holding to the principle "that in the New Testament Christ sufficiently established everything required for the salvation of every faithful man," the Taborites asked: "Why then should human institutions and ceremonies not described in the Law be observed by the faithful?"[17] The priests of Tabor neither shaved nor tonsured themselves, nor did they assume chasubles or other special vestments in celebrating mass;

---

[16]    De cerimoniis, ed. J. Sedlák, Studie a texty, II (Olomouc, 1915), 150. The treatise was used by Nicholas of Pelhřimov in his defense of a simplified mass, in December/ January 1420/21, even though one of his opponents was Jakoubek himself. See K. Höfler, ed., Geschichtschreiber der husitischen Bewegung in Böhmen, II, Fontes rerum austriacarum, Erste Abth., VI (Vienna, 1865), 488ff. Cf. also the "Taborite Confession" of 1431, ibid., p. 613.

[17]    Laurence of Březová, pp. 406f.

using as altar an ordinary table covered with a linen cloth, and as chalices ordinary goblets, they simply knelt and said the Lord's Prayer, after which one priest would get up and pronounce the words of consecration, loudly and in the vernacular, over the bread and wine, and would then give communion, in both kinds, to the other priests and to the people.[18] To this basic ceremony was added a highly-developed system of liturgical hymns, always in the vernacular, through which the congregation was involved in almost every step of the service;[19] the congregational character of the worship was further manifested in that service was held every day, that everyone was expected to take communion at every service, and that a great deal of attention was paid to evangelical preaching.[20] Thus the Taborites, unlike the Praguers, had rejected the Roman concept of the mass as an objectively valid *opus dei*, a sacrifice in favor of a communion service regarded as a congregational action.[20a] Conflict between the two liturgies was therefore inevitable, and it broke out so sharply as to threaten Hussite unity in the nonreligious field.[21] Responsible leaders of both sides worked to bring about an exchange of views, and Nicholas of Pelhřimov began his literary career by preparing a defense of the Taborite position.

But the situation was complicated by the fact that Free-Spirit chiliasm, however unattractive it had become to the university-trained priests of the party of order, had not by any means lost its grip on the Taborite people. Christ had not come, the millennium had not arrived, and the human animal still suffered the painful and inconvenient effects of original sin, but the chiliast vision retained its pathetic power and its adherents could still hope for its realization, provided only that Tabor could be kept in motion. And although the old fantastic prophecies no longer resonated with the realities of Taborite life, the Free Spirit had other potentialities, more suitable to the new social and political situation. Again it was Martin Húska who showed the way, this time as the propagator of a new form of Free-Spirit heresy, Pikartism, which centered on a new concept of the Eucharist. Our main narrative source, the "Hussite Chronicle" of Master Laurence of Březová, tells us that this heresy had been brought into Bohemia in 1418 by a group of immigrants, the *Picardi*, who said they had been expelled from their homes "because of the Law of God" and had decided to come to Bohemia because

---

[18] *Ibid.*, p. 406f., and *cf.* p. 529f. *Cf.* also, for the Taborite liturgy, the text edited by F. Palacký, *Urkundliche Beiträge zur Geschichte des Hussitenkriegs,* II (Prague, 1873), 522f.

[19] See Z. Nejedlý, *Dějiny husitského zpěvu* (New Edition), IV (Prague, 1955), 219ff., 249–366.

[20] *Ibid.*, p. 289f.

[20a] Thus, e.g., Nicholas of Pelhřimov wrote, in the Taborite Confession of 1431 (Höfler, II, 581 f.): "in ecclesia primitiva ... unus sacerdos conficiebat in omnium fidelium congregatione ... et alii praesentes in memoriam mortis Christi, *quae est unica et sufficiens oblatio,* sacramentum Eucharistiae ab illo sumebant" (emphasis added).

[21] See the account in Heymann, p. 186ff.

they had heard that "the greatest liberty of evangelical truth" was in existence there.[22] Since Martin's Pikartism involved Free-Spirit ideas, and since the name "Picardi" is most probably a variant of "Beghardi",[23] it is natural to guess that the immigrants of 1418 were actually Free-Spirit Beghards, perhaps indeed responsible for Martin's chiliasm as well as his Pikartism; but evidence of this is lacking.[24] What we do know, according to Master Laurence's account, is that Pikartism itself – the eucharistic heresy – had not penetrated the Taborite corpus of doctrine as of August 1420,[25] but rather reared its head at that time in non-Taborite regions, around Žatec, Plzeň, and Prague, under the leadership of a non-Taborite, the squire Sigmund of Řepan. And it is as a collaborator of Sigmund's that Martin Húska formulated the principles of his new sect: the two men seem to have shared in the authorship of an exegetical treatise on the sixth chapter of the Gospel of John.[26]

[22] Laurence of Březová, p. 431.

[23] There are references to "Pikardi" as heretics in the sermons of Berthold von Regensburg (d. 1272): A. Schönbach, "Studien zur Geschichte der altdeutschen Predigt," *Sitzungsberichte der phil.-hist. Klasse der kaiserlichen Akademie der Wissenschaften*, CXLVII (Vienna, 1904), 81, 107; H. Grundmann, *Religiöse Bewegungen im Mittelalter* (Berlin, 1935), p. 393 n. 83, supposes that this term is a form of "Beghardi". The latter did in fact vary in ways that point to "Picardi" – see, e.g., "frater bycharus" in the statement of John of Brno (Wattenbach, *op. cit.*, p. 533).

[24] In 1788 J. Dobrowský asserted that the "Picardi" of Laurence's account meant "Beghardi", and the point was repeated by F. Palacký, "O stycích a poměru sekty Waldenské k někdejším sektám v Čechách," *Radhost*, II (Prague, 1872), 453 (the article was originally published in 1868), although Palacký supposed that the name was merely abusive and that the heretics in question were Waldensians. R. Holinka, "Počátky táborského pikartství," *Bratislava*, VI (1932), 191, regards the *Picardi* as Beghards. On the other hand, Aeneas Sylvius Piccolomini, *Historia Bohemica*, ch.xli, refers to "Piccardus quidam ex Gallia Belgica" who came to Bohemia and founded the Pikart-Adamite sect; it is impossible to say whether he followed specific evidence or merely his own inference from the name "Picardi". There is in fact strong evidence for ties between Taborite Free-Spirit heresy and "Gallia Belgica" (see my "Chiliasm", p. 20f.), and it is quite possible that, entirely apart from their name, the *Picardi* of 1418 are to be regarded as having come from that region. Finally, it may be noted that in his refutation of the full corpus of Taborite "errors", John Příbram said that he was refuting the "perfidissima dogma tot articulorum quadam subita tempestate per perfidissimos picardos advenas et alios errectorum" ("Contra articulos picardorum," MS. Vienna Nationalbibliothek 4749, f. 37').

[25] The list of Taborite heresies read off by the Prague masters at the Prague-Tabor meeting of 10 December 1420 (see below) included a number of Pikart doctrines; Laurence of Březová, who gives us the list in its proper place in his chronicle, does *not* however use it in the account of Taborite history and doctrine that he inserted in the chronicle *ad* August 1420, even though he almost certainly wrote the account after the meeting had taken place. Instead, he uses an earlier formulation of Taborite heresies, in which the Pikart doctrines are lacking. Moreover, his discussion of Pikartism, also inserted *ad* August 1420 (pp. 429–431), has no reference whatever to Tabor or Taboritism. The picture he means to draw is thus perfectly clear, and I know of no sound reason to suppose that he drew a false picture.

[26] Peter Chelčický, writing about 1424/1425, says in his *Replika proti Mikuláši Biskupcovi* (ed. J. Annenkov and V. Jagič, *Sočinenija Petra Chel'čickago, Otdělenija russkago jazyka i slovesnosti, Imperatorskaja Akademija Nauk* (St. Petersburg, 1893),

They began by considering Jesus' words, "Who eats my flesh and drinks my blood remains in me and I in him" [Joh. vi, 58]; what did he mean? The flesh is to be understood as bread, for Jesus said [vi, 52], "The bread that I give is my flesh, for the life of the world," but neither flesh nor bread is to be understood in the ordinary physical way. The interpretation rests on Jesus' words [vi, 27], "Do not work for the food that perishes, but for that which endures unto eternal life," and on the prologue to John's Gospel [i, 14]: "The word has been made flesh and has dwelt in us." Putting all of this together, Martin and Sigmund asserted that "The word has brought about the deeds of God in the body, and the soul which does God's work is fed by them as the body is with bread; these deeds of the word of God are called bread, for they feed the one who follows them, and they are called the body, for they are done in the body, being one with the body." Jesus' ultimatum [vi, 54], "Unless you eat the flesh of the Son of Man and drink his blood, you will not have life in you," means: unless you do the deeds that the Son of Man did in the flesh, to the extent of your power, and unless you understand the power and reason of his deeds, you will not have eternal life; but if you do, you will be one with the Father and the Son.[27] Here the spiritual concept of communion links up with the Pikart denial of a Real Presence in the Eucharist, through an interpretation of still another passage in John vi [63-64]:[28] "But what if you see the Son of Man ascending to where he was before? It is the spirit that gives life; the flesh is of no use at all. The words that I have spoken to you are spirit and life." Hence the conclusion: "Since Christ ascended to heaven in his body and sits on the right hand of the Father, he is not here in the sacrament and does not give his holy body according to a Real Presence; but his faithful only enjoy his holy body in a certain spiritual way, now in the sacrament."

So much for the basic theory; its broader religious implications appear in the further development of Martin's doctrine, during the autumn of 1420. By the beginning of December he had begun to propagate not only the basic Pikart denial of a Real Presence, with its corollaries (e.g., refusal to kneel to the Host), but also the doctrine that "the Body and Blood of Christ are

---

p. 458): "Martinek prorok taborsky, a Zygmund z Řepan ten rozom wedu na šestu kapitolu swateho Jana . . ." ("Martin, the Taborite prophet, and Sigmund of Řepan apply this reasoning to the sixth chapter of St. John"); the least problematical interpretation of these words would be that the two men actually collaborated. The summary of the exegesis that follows is taken from Chelčický's account, pp. 457–459, except where otherwise indicated.

[27] Chelčický's account, summarized thus far, agrees entirely with the passages of Martin's exegesis summarized by John Příbram, *Život kněží táborských*, p. 292f., and we may confidently suppose that both summaries are accurate.

[28] The material that follows in this paragraph is drawn from Jakoubek of Stříbro's anti-Pikart tract, "Jhesus Christus dominus et salvator," MS. Vienna Nat. Bib. 4944, f. 252; Jakoubek does not identify those he is attacking, but there can be little doubt that he refers to the exegesis of John vi by Martin and Sigismund.

taken sacramentally in every food just as well as in the sacrament [of the altar], as long as the recipient is in a state of grace."[29] And by the end of January 1421 he had begun to teach that the laity should take the consecrated bread and divide it among themselves.[30] In short, Martin was propagating a Pikart communion-service in the form of a banquet or love-feast. Contemptuously rejecting all the other Hussite ceremonies, in which the priests put little pieces of the bread into the mouths of the faithful, and gave them little sips of wine,[31] Martin held that the true form of the rite was that exemplified in the miracle of the loaves and fishes, in which the people were seated and really fed.[32] Hence he prescribed that the people taking communion should meet, "be diligent in the word of God" – presumably by listening to sermons – and eat a full meal.[33] There was no need for a priest to consecrate – any good layman could do it;[34] moreover the consecrated food did not have to be only bread and wine, for Christ was spiritually present in all food at such a banquet.[35] And with this all-pervasiveness of

[29] The list of Taborite doctrines read off at the meeting of 10 December 1420 contains the Pikart tenets (Laurence of Březová, p. 459f.).

[30] *Ibid.,* p. 470f. That this was a newly-promulgated doctrine at this time is stated by Laurence and confirmed by Martin himself: "I have come to understand," he then wrote, "that great impropriety exists in the giving of the bread of the Lord's body ... As yet I have not publicly mentioned this to you [*i.e.,* the Taborite leadership]" (*ibid.,* p. 495). Nor is the doctrine in the list of 10 December.

[31] See Martin's two letters to Písek, summarized by Příbram in his *Život kněží táborských,* p. 290ff.; cf. Příbram's Latin version, Höfler, II, 828. The point is included in Martin's profession of faith made just before his death at the stake: in Latin, Höfler, II, 829f.; in Czech (more fully): "Vyznání o chlebu živém a věčném. (Martina Húsky)", *Jihočeský sborník historický,* I (1928), 8 (*cf.* R. Holinka, "Počátky táborského pikartství," *Bratislava,* VI (1932), 187 n. 4).

[32] Chelčický, *op. cit.,* pp. 457–459, for this paragraph, *passim.*

[33] *Cf.* Martin's own interesting discussion of this point, preserved by Příbram, *Život,* p. 293f.: "The first Christians were not allowed to have a physical altar – it was Pope Sixtus who first prescribed that altars be had. But the first Christians were not allowed to set up an idol on an altar [a reference to the late-medieval "archa" – a monstrance kept on the altar], but were rather supposed to eat together to satisfy their hunger, and have a kind of banquet ["a jako hody jměli"]. And it is from this that church dedication-festivals originated. Then the popes instituted great church-buildings, altars, and idols on the altars, which idols they called the Body of God and [holy] images." *Cf.* the Latin text, Höfler, II, 829.

[34] This point was not included in the list read at the meeting of 10 December, but it appears in other versions of the list, in particular that used by John Příbram in his "Contra articulos picardorum" (see J. Döllinger, *Beiträge zur Sektengeschichte des Mittelalters,* II (Munich, 1890), 692). *Cf.* also Příbram's "Ad occurendum homini insano," Vienna Nat. Bib. MS 4937, f. 149', 150'.

[35] This point appears in the list of 10 December, cited above; also in Příbram's "Ad occurendum", MS *cit.,* f. 148'; also in Jakoubek's "Jhesus Christus Dominus et Salvator',' MS *cit.,* f. 250'. And *cf.* Martin's first letter to Písek, summarized by Příbram in *Život,* p. 291: "The Lord's Supper should be eaten as Christ ate it with the disciples, to whom he gave the bread and wine along with other foods" (in Latin in Höfler, II, 828). Both the last sources also say that Martin held that the Lord's Supper should be eaten with leavened bread. Later, after the Pikart sect had been wiped out, and after the Taborite church had taken over the Pikart denial of a Real Presence, the doctrine that "in

the divine spirit, it was only natural that the laity could simply take the food in their own hands from the leader of the feast.[36] Psychologically, the correlate of the presence of the divine spirit was a spirit of mutual love among the participants; Martin said that the Lord's Supper was founded on love, as exemplified in Jesus' washing of the disciples' feet.[37] Such acts of love, presumably, were the deeds that, according to Pikart theory, constituted the true communion of the soul with God.

Seen against the whole background of Tabor's development, Martin's Pikartism is readily understood: accepting the fact that Taborite society would not respond to raw chiliasm, Martin matched the party of order in developing a new form of worship. But this form of worship was not a matter of liturgy, it was rather a reconstruction, *in parvo*, of the chiliast community of the deified elect, a translation of the chiliast vision into a new form. This fact becomes clear as we re-examine the chiliast sources. We have already seen that the chiliasts preached that the sacrament of the Eucharist would give way to a new, "angelic" type of holy meal, celebrating Christ's victory rather than commemorating his passion. And this meal, according to the chiliasts, would certainly not be a church service, for they preached that in the New Age "Paul's institution of gathering in the church will not be observed"[38] – evidently a reference to I Cor. xi, 17-34, Paul's criticism of the Corinthians' habit of taking the Eucharist in connection with a meal. The kind of meal that the chiliasts had in mind was indeed a transformation of the Eucharist: "they preached," we are told,[39] "that Christ will descend to earth and rule temporally, and that he will hold great feasts on the mountains; and there will come so great an abundance of the Holy Spirit in the hearts of the faithful that no one will be taught by another, but all will be taught by God." A chiliast letter makes the point somewhat differently, but more clearly:[40]

The Lord already stands at the gate ... Let us be very vigilant, for we do not know what hour the third angel will blow his trumpet. And at once the sun will blaze, the clouds will disappear, the darkness will vanish, blood will flow from wood, and He will reign who is not expected by those living on earth ... There-

---

quolibet ferculo erit et consumetur humanitas Christi" was regarded as *the* "opinio Picardorum": see Příbram's *Surge domine,* ed. J. Sedlák, *Tab. trakt. euch.,* p. 88.

[36] Příbram, *Život,* p. 292; Höfler, II, 829; Příbram, "Ad occurendum", f. 155'; Laurence of Březová, p. 470f.; Döllinger, p. 692.

[37] *Cf.* Příbram, *Život,* p. 293; Höfler, II, 829: Martin asserts that the Roman form of the Eucharist has led to the freezing of love, the killing of the faithful, and all other evils.

[38] Laurence of Březová, p. 416.

[39] *Staří letopisové čeští,* ed. F. Palacký, *Scriptores rerum bohemicarum,* III (Prague, 1829), 478f.

[40] Ed. F. M. Bartoš, "Z dějin chiliasmu r. 1420," *Do čtyř pražských artykulů* (Prague, 1925), p. 96f.

fore let us be ready for the Lord's coming, that we may go with him to the wedding.

And who is ready? Only he who remains in Christ and Christ in him. And he is in Christ who eats him. But to eat Christ's body is livingly to believe in him. And to drink his blood is to shed it with him for his Father. And he takes Christ's body who disseminates his gifts, and he eats his body who livingly listens to his word. And in this way we shall all be Christ's body . . .

And through this eating the just will shine like the sun in the kingdom of their Father, when he comes in clouds with his glory and great power, and sends as representatives his glorious angels to sweep out all scandals from his inheritance. And then evil will be abashed, lies will perish, injustice will disappear, every sin will vanish; and faith will flower, justice will grow, paradise will open to us, benevolence will be multiplied, and perfect love will abound.

Here as in no other source the essential identity of chiliasm and Pikartism is made plain. The chiliast expectation is there, along with the idea of Christ's banquet – the "wedding." [41] At the same time, in preparation for this event, the faithful eat Christ's body spiritually, exactly in the manner of Martin's Pikartism – indeed, it is hard to believe that the letter could have been written by anyone but Martin. And this spiritual eating is the path to deification and the glories of the millennium.

＊
＊ ＊

Thus the Taborites were offered two alternative paths of development, and the choice between them could not be deferred. It was in fact the Prague masters who made this clear, for they refused to debate questions of rites and liturgy with Nicholas of Pelhřimov until the Taborites had made up their mind whether or not they wished to stand by all of their heresies, including chiliast and Pikart doctrines. Although no clearcut answer to this challenge was ever given, the details of the great Prague-Taborite confrontation of 10 December 1420, at the Prague house of Lord Peter Zmrzlík, make it sufficently plain that Martin and those of his party who wished to take a stand for chiliasm and Pikartism were unable to do so; the meeting indeed ended with an exchange of Prague and Taborite opinions about the rite of mass, and since the exchange was continued in subsequent weeks, we may suppose that in effect the question of Tabor's destiny had been settled by the party of order.[42] Perhaps the most striking sign of this fact is the appearance

---

[41]   Cf. Laurence of Březová, p. 415: "At the end of this consummation of the age, Christ will descend from heaven and openly come in his own person to take up his kingdom in this world, and he will be seen by the actual eye. And he will prepare a great banquet and supper of the lamb as a nuptial feast for his spouse, the Church, here on the physical mountains."

[42]   For the meeting of 10 December, see Laurence of Březová, pp. 447–469; Heymann, op. cit., pp. 186–198, offers a good summary and analysis. For the exchange of opinions, with some of the tractates exchanged, see also Höfler, II, 488 ff.

of Wenceslas Koranda, a powerful and militant Taborite who never lost his sympathy for Martin, on the side of Nicholas of Pelhřimov and as a defender, against Prague, of Nicholas's, not Martin's, form of communion service.[43] And we may suppose, finally, that the power of John Žižka, a pillar of the party of order, helped swing the balance.[44]

Thus it was that when Martin began, after the meeting of 10 December, to preach the full program of the Pikart communion banquet, and perhaps even to organize such celebrations, he was imprisoned by Lord Ulrich Vavák, one of Tabor's allies.[45] Appealing to his Taborite opponents for at least the grace of a hearing, he was released, presumably at their request, but it would seem that he merely continued his work of agitation.[46] In fact it is likely that he pushed his Free-Spirit doctrine even further.[47] By the end of February 1421, Nicholas of Pelhřimov and his associates were prepared to force the issue to a conclusion: Nicholas himself wrote a defense of the Real Presence against the leader of the Pikarts in Tabor, Peter Kániš;[48] Nicholas and the

---

[43] On 3 January 1421, Koranda came to Prague, preached the Taborite rejection of vestments, etc., to the people, and deposited a book containing the arguments that he had delivered orally (Laurence, pp. 466–469). It is clear from Laurence's account that Koranda's arguments were the same as those offered by Nicholas of Pelhřimov at the meeting of 10 December, 1420 (Laurence, p. 463f.), and it is indeed obvious that Koranda was implementing the decision of the meeting, to pursue a further exchange of opinions in writing. Since the text of the Taborites' "first writing" in the controversy, as preserved by Nicholas of Pelhřimov in his "Chronicon" (Höfler, II, 488–501), also corresponds, often verbally, to Nicholas's statement at the December meeting, we may reasonably suppose that the book delivered by Koranda was nothing but this "first writing", and that it had been composed by Nicholas. Cf. Heymann, op. cit., p. 195; for contrary, but to my mind clearly incorrect views: i.e., that Koranda was the author of the Taborite treatise, see F. M. Bartoš, "Rozchod Prahy a Tábora r. 1420," Časopis českého musea, XCVIII (1924), 104, and J. Macek, Tábor, II, 299f.

[44] See Heymann, op. cit., p. 196f.; Macek, Tábor, II, 238 & passim.

[45] Laurence of Březová, p. 470f. That Martin began to organize Pikart banquets is my inference from the statement that he was imprisoned for preaching that the laity should take the consecrated bread in their own hands (see above, note 30). He himself claimed that he had not preached it publicly, nor is there compelling reason to think that he would have been imprisoned just for preaching – he had preached other, equally shocking things before. Hence I suppose that his objectionable activity consisted of actually organizing groups of his followers.

[46] At the end of February Nicholas of Pelhřimov and John of Jičín wrote that Martin had infected more than 400 of the brethren (see note 49 below).

[47] A Czech narrative, in MS "O" of the Old Czech Annalists (ed. Palacký, Staří letopisové čeští, p. 476), says that "Martin's party began to hear sermons secretly, in taverns, and to follow strange and unheard-of customs among themselves." What these customs were we do not know, but there is reason to think that the Pikarts at Tabor were practicing adult baptism (see note 54 below). In his letter from prison Martin claimed to have discovered new truths about communion, baptism, and preaching (Laurence, p. 495), and perhaps he began to propagate them after his release.

[48] The tract survives only in excerpts cited twenty years later by John Rokycana, in his Tractatus de existentia corporis Christi in sacramento altaris, ed. Z. Nejedlý, Prameny k synodám strany pražské a táborské v létech 1441–1444 (Prague, 1900), passim. Rokycana gives the background of the tract thus: "... dum quidam sacerdos Petrus dictus Caniss in civitate Thabor cum sibi adherentibus contra sacramentum altaris in

Taborite Master John of Jičín addressed a formal request for doctrinal support to the Prague leaders, John Příbram and Jakoubek of Stříbro; [49] and finally more than two hundred Pikarts were expelled from Tabor.[50]

We are told that at this point Martin debated his ideas with the Taborite leaders and actually made a public recantation.[51] In fact he does disappear from view for about three months, during which period the Pikarts followed a path of their own, moving into the third and last stage of Free-Spirit development in Hussite Bohemia. Laurence of Březová reports the following, about those expelled from Tabor: [52]

Wandering through forests and hills, some of them fell into such insanity that men and women threw off their clothes and went nude, saying that clothes had been adopted because of the sin of the first parents, but that they were in a state of innocence. From the same madness they supposed that they were not sinning if one of the brethren had intercourse with one of the sisters, and if the woman conceived, she said she had conceived of the Holy Spirit.

It is not clear how much of this was already part of Pikartism even before the expulsion from Tabor. We know that Martin claimed, in January 1421,

---

sentencia, quam fides docet ortodoxa, consurrexerant, iste Nicolaus contra eundem se exponebat, verbis, factis et scriptis suas doctrinas reprobando, cui dum resistebat, [cum] certis personis sibi adherentibus prefatus Caniss ignis voragini traditus est." (p. 150).

[49] Laurence of Březová tells us (p. 474f.) that on 28 February, 1421 a letter was brought to Prague written by Nicholas of Pelhřimov and John of Jičín, and addressed to the Prague Masters Jakoubek of Stříbro and John of Příbram. The letter told how, "by the doctrine of certain priests and especially of Martin," more than four hundred Taborite men and women had been infected by Pikartism; it mentioned the Pikarts' denial of a Real Presence and their contemptuous behavior towards the Eucharist (but it did not mention communion-banquets), and it asked the two masters for information to help fight such errors. Bartoš supposes that Jakoubek's tractate, "Jhesus Christus Dominus et Salvator," and Příbram's "Ad occurendum homini insano," were responses to this request (Literární činnost ... M. Jana Příbrama (Prague, 1928), p. 66. In my "Otraktátn Ad occurendum nomini insano", Československý časopis historický, VIII (1960), pp. 895–904 I offer additional evidence to support Bartoš's arguments.

[50] Laurence of Březová, p. 475, writes, ad February 1421: "Because of this heresy, alas, the brethren living in Hradiště, or Tabor [i.e., the city of Tabor], were divided into two parts, a Pikart and a Taborite; the more faithful part, the Taborite, expelled more than two hundred men and women infected with the Pikart heresy..." The Czech account cited in n. 47 above dates the "great division among the priests and turbulence among the people" as early as 1420, and suggests that the Pikart exodus was voluntary (p. 476).

[51] The source is the same Czech account, p. 476. J. Macek, Tábor, II, 321, rejects this statement, for, "in reality Martin abated nothing of his zeal or of his revolutionary program;" moreover he subsequently endured martyrdom. Actually, however, there is no evidence that Martin accompanied his erstwhile followers in the last stage of their development (see below), nor is there anything psychologically improbable in his having first recanted, then resumed, his Pikart doctrine: one has only to recall the case of Jerome of Prague. And the prominence of Peter Kániš both among the expelled Pikarts and among the first victims of the anti-Pikart holocaust, tends to confirm the hypothesis of Martin's withdrawal at this time.

[52] Laurence, p. 475.

to have discovered new truths about baptism,[53] and we also have reason to think that at least in the last period of their existence among the Taborites, the Pikarts believed that baptism with water was not necessary (it will be recalled that this was also a chiliast doctrine), and that in any case baptism should be restricted to adults – no doubt as a form of initiation into the sect; the basis of these ideas was the Free-Spirit tenet that "the children of holy parents [i.e. members of the sect] are conceived without original mortal sin." [54] None of this necessarily implies nudism or free love, and it is highly unlikely that the Pikarts practiced either as long as they were a fraction within the Taborite movement. In exile, however, they passed from expectation of the millennium to a conviction of its immediacy – the "seventh angel" had already emptied his bowl [55] (an event that in Apocalypse xvi, 17 is followed by a loud voice saying "It is all over!"). And they also regarded their deification as an accomplished fact: their Lord's Prayer began, "Our Father who art in us . . ." [56] Thus the Pikarts, or Adamites as they are now called, assumed a total liberty exactly like that of the fully-qualified Beghards; [57] like these they felt free to plunder and kill all non-members. If then we believe in reports of Free-Spirit nudism and free love elsewhere in

---

[53] *Ibid.*, p. 495.

[54] In his "Ad occurendum homini insano," Příbram attacks these beliefs, but it is not clear from his statements just what the baptismal doctrine under attack was; he may not have understood it. The pertinent passages follow (MS Vienna Nat. Bib., 4937, f. 156' seq.): "Est et alter homo de infelici opinione qui conatur afferre aut dicere quod sanctorum parentum filii concipiuntur sine peccato originali mortali, sed concipiuntur in peccato veniali . . ." (f. 156'). "Verumtamen dicit quod parvuli huiusmodi, eciam quantumcumque sanctorum parentum fuerunt, debent baptisari quamvis sint innocentes . . . ; tamen si sic decederunt non baptisati salvarentur" (f. 156'). ". . . dicit quod peccata . . . venialia spiritus sanctus non remittit nec baptismus delet" (f. 157). "Stultus ergo esest nimis qui dicentem salvatorem universaliter, Nisi quis hominum [*cf*. Joh. iii, 5], vellet restringere ad adultos tantum . . ." (f. 159–159'). "Sed ipsi dicunt: ubi apostoli baptizabant parvulos?" (f. 160'). "Stultus esset qui aquam materialem declinare vellet, dicendo non intelligere Christum de aqua materiali" (f. 159'). The doctrine that infants ought to be baptized, even though this was not necessary, I interpret as a mere concession to customary opinion.

[55] Laurence of Březová, p. 518. *Cf.* also (*loc. cit.*): "They held that the holy church had already been reformed ["opravenú", = "reparatum" in the Latin chiliast sources] and believed that they would live eternally here on earth." Compare the chiliast texts quoted above, p. 170: what the chiliasts had looked forward to, the Adamites regarded as fulfilled.

[56] Laurence, p. 517. *Cf.* also, p. 518: "They say that . . . God is not in heaven nor the Devil in hell, but rather God is in the good people and the Devil in the evil." Also, *ibid.*: "They called Jesus Christ their brother, but not fully so, because he died, and they held that the Holy Spirit never dies, and the Son of God must be of the Holy Spirit." They also believed, p. 519, that they could not be killed.

[57] The congruence of doctrines is beyond question: see the parallel citations given by R. Holinka, *Sektářství v Čechách před revolucí husitskou, Sborník filosofické fakulty University Komenského v Bratislavě*, VI (1929), 168f.; *cf.* also the Beghard texts published by Wattenbach, *op. cit., passim* – compare, e.g., the attitudes toward Jesus quoted in notes 5 and 56 above. In the face of such almost literal correspondences, Macek's position (note 10 above) must be rejected.

Europe we might just as well believe in similar reports about the Bohemian
Adamites: both practices would have been entirely consistent with the sect's
beliefs.[58] And we may suppose that the expulsion from Tabor removed all
factors tending to inhibit Free-Spirit libertarianism in the earlier period. Thus
Adamitism might be regarded as a kind of terminal point; while preserving
the doctrines of both chiliasm and Pikartism,[59] it found its true center of
gravity in the full and open cult of the deified self.

But the history of Adamitism as a significant fraction of the Hussite
spectrum was brief. Some time in mid-April John Žižka and the allied Lord
Ulrich Vavák attacked those expelled from Tabor and burnt fifty prisoners,
including Peter Kániš, at Klokoty; on 20 April another twenty-five met the
same fate. Strong remnants still existed, and on 21 October Žižka launched
another attack, killing many and consigning the rest to the flames – only one
was spared, to give testimony of the sect's doctrines.[60] Martin Húska, meanwhile, found his own, separate martyrdom: resuming his Pikart activities, he
was captured, along with a companion, at the beginning of June, and after a
long period of imprisonment, interrogation, and torture, the two were burnt
to death, on 21 August. Martin's final confession of faith survives; it is
entirely Pikart, with no trace of Adamitism.[61] But perhaps a clearer view of
his true faith is to be found in the following passage, reporting a conversation
between Martin and Peter Chelčický, perhaps in the spring of 1421: [62]

But Martin was not humble or at all willing to suffer for Christ ... And he declared to us his belief that there will be a new Kingdom of the Saints on earth,
and that the good will no longer suffer, and he said, "If Christians were always to
have to suffer so, I would not want to be a servant of God." That is what he said!

---

[58]   The question of whether or not to believe in Free-Spirit sex-orgies is too complicated
to be settled here. Macek regards the testimony about them as slanderous (e.g., *Tábor*,
II, 352), and others too have pointed out that nasty-minded inquisitors wishing to
discredit heretics naturally imagined that the necessarily secret heretical conventicles
could only have existed for the celebration of sex-orgies. More cogent is the argument
of H. Grundmann, "Der Typus des Ketzers in mittelalterlicher Anschauung," *Kultur-
und Universalgeschichte,* Walter Goetz Festschrift, (Leipzig & Berlin: B. G. Teubner,
1927), pp. 103–106: medieval thought operated with "types", and the type of the heretic
included the sex-orgy. Of course Grundmann concedes (p. 93) that the typical may
also be true, and I think that in the case of the Adamites it is, for several reasons, of
which perhaps the most solid is the consideration that the Hussite opponents of the
Adamites were not nasty-minded inquisitors but rather responsible reformers, dealing
with men and women who had once been their associates and whom they knew quite
well. One might also argue that the contempt for objective truth displayed, e.g., in the
Moscow trials (a parallel situation) is a modern invention; the medievals did not forget
that God was watching. But solution of this interesting problem requires a study of *all*
the medieval cases known.
[59]   We have already noted the chiliasm of the Adamites; that they also adhered to
Martin's Pikartism is stated explicitly (Laurence of Březová, p. 517 – this is the testimony of the lone Adamite survivor, mentioned just below).
[60]   Laurence, pp. 517–520.
[61]   See note 31 above for references to the texts.
[62]   Chelčický, *op. cit.,* p. 464f.

But although his memory was cultivated by some Taborites deep into the 1420's, Martin's dream of a New Age of joy and an end to suffering passed out of the realm of politics and into that of idle fancy. In the middle of the decade Nicholas of Pelhřimov wrote: [63]

We do not consider to be true that story which some tell, that a good age is coming, in which there will be no evil doers, and that they will not suffer at all but will be filled with ineffable joy. For all this will be in Heaven [in patria], but the things that are to happen here are uncertain.

Thus, having revived the Primitive Church, Tabor was condemned to repeat that Church's history.

\* \*

But Pikartism did not vanish with its adherents. The Free Spirit had been liquidated, the love-feasts ended, and the Pikart political threat overcome, but the eucharistic doctrine of the enemy remained to exert its attraction. There was a distinct incompatibility between the doctrine of a Real Presence and the Taborite form of congregational worship; that Nicholas of Pelhřimov, the chief theoretician of the latter, should have defended the former against Peter Kániš is evidence, chiefly, that Nicholas had yet to work out his own doctrinal position. Even his major antagonist, Master John Příbram, could see the path that he would have to take.[64] But Příbram did not see where the path would lead; he thought the choice was one simply between the orthodox mass and Pikartism, or as we might say today, between church and sect, but in fact Tabor *created* a third entity, a genuine type of reformation that combined ecclesiastical and sectarian elements. It is here that the true meaning of the story traced in these pages may be most clearly seen, for, given the common Hussite tradition of extreme emphasis on the Eucharist, each Hussite party necessarily expressed its basic concept of reform in its doctrine and form of communion. That Tabor eventually took over the Pikart doctrine of a spiritual presence was due to the fact that despite her societal stabilization, Tabor still bore the marks of her chiliast childhood.

To understand Taborite theory in this matter we must first consider that of Prague. Here as always, John Příbram throws the clearest light on Prague's essential orthodoxy: "the sacrifice [of the mass] is principally made for the whole Church, which accumulates benefits thereby; nor should anyone deem it a small thing to be the mediator and arbiter between God and all the people on behalf of whom the most welcome sacrifice is to be offered to

---

[63] Cited by F. Bartoš, "Táborské bratrstvo let 1425–1426 na soudě svého biskupa Mikuláše z Pelhřimova," *Časopis společnosti přátel starožitností českých*, XXIX (1921), 111 (I have altered the text slightly on the basis of the manuscript: MS Vienna Nat. Bib. 4520, f. 80).
[64] See Příbram's refutation of the Taborite simplified liturgy, Höfler, II, 541f.

God the Father." [65] Added to this general theory was the eucharistic fervor of which Jakoubek of Stříbro was the outstanding exponent; for example: [66]

Those to whom Christ gives this food he constrains and obliges to change their lives and henceforth be incorporated into him and his mystical body, so that they may dwell in Christ and Christ in them. Christians who do not practice frequenting this sacred supper are disposed and prone to every evil, but those who worthily come to it and eat this heavenly bread are made more capable of loving spiritual things and embracing the things of heaven. For they have a joyful mind and one filled with the joy of the Holy Spirit, and if adversity strikes them they are able to suffer and endure it.

Thus the mass, objectively valid for the welfare of the whole Church, provided the possibility of communion, objectively valid for the inner reform of all who took it – worthily, of course. All of this, quite obviously, required a doctrine of Real Presence, even if only in the Wyclifite form of Remanence.

Against this doctrine there stood that of the Pikarts, for whom, as we have seen, the Church meant themselves: *they* were the Body of Christ, and their eating of the communion-banquet was a means by which they acquired not – as Jakoubek put it – the "joy of the Holy Spirit," but the Holy Spirit itself. The doing of acts of love had a similar effect. And their aim was not to become better able to suffer and endure adversity, but rather to be liberated from suffering, to become perfect in the sense of becoming deified. Paradoxically, their denial of a Real Presence involved the assertion of a much more real spiritual presence, and it was Martin's belief that the corruption of this true communion through the pompous formalism of the Roman rite had more than anything else killed the spirit of love among the Christian people. [67]

As a society composed, physically, of those who had left the evil old world and given up everything in order to form a community of the elect, Tabor could hardly avoid taking over some elements of Pikartism. But as a stable, well-developed society of people increasingly occupied in the routine of normal life, Tabor, like Prague and European Christendom generally, was in fact a *corpus permixtum*, including both good and bad. Her theologians accepted the Wyclifite doctrine of the True Church as the community of the predestined, [68] and her religious thought realistically shrank away from the Pikart fantasy of a totally regenerated humanity, in favor of a puritanical struggle against the evil within herself. All went to church, where confession was typically public, and all took communion – those failing to do so were

[65] "Contra articulos picardorum," MS Vienna Nat. Bib. 4749, f. 60'.

[66] "Jhesus Christus dominus et salvator," MS Vienna Nat. Bib. 4944, f. 254.

[67] See the references in note 37 above.

[68] See, e.g., the tractate of John Němec of Žatec, *Cum spiritus veritatis summe odiens mendacium*, ed. J. Sedlák, *Táb. trakt, euch.*, p. 6: ". . . corpus misticum, quod est ecclesia predestinatorum."

liturgically mocked.[69] But this meant not that the evil were absent, only that the evil had to become good. Now one of the most striking objections of the Taborites to the Prague doctrine of a Real Presence was that such a Eucharist was available to all, both good and bad;[70] this objection fits in with the Taborite denial of Purgatory and of the cult of saints – the bad were present, but the religion made no comfortable provision for them.[71] Thus Tabor's communion-service was a collective act, expressing the congregation's will to solidarity with God and at the same time helping to make that solidarity real. All that was necessary to perfect the liturgy developed for this purpose was a concept of the Eucharist that would relate the sacrament, functionally, to the congregation's experience of valid communion. And this was provided by the Pikart idea of a spiritual presence, real in its power *as it is being taken* by the worthy communicant. With the extermination of the Pikart sect, this idea could be taken up into Taborite orthodoxy; by 1424 at the latest it was made binding on the Taborite clergy,[72] and for

---

[69] Just before communion the congregation sang the hymn. "Časy svými jistými," which included the verses: "We ridicule him who dares not take communion" (Nejedlý, *Dějiny husitského zpěvu*, IV (Prague, 1955), 289f.; *cf.* 202ff.).

[70] John Němec, *op. cit.*, p. 6, argued that if the consecrated bread were "ydemptice corpus Christi, tunc Christus cottidie fieret deus recens in ecclesiis infinitis, et a quocunque infideli posset manducari, quod tota ecclesia negat, asserens quod infidelis sumit tantum sacramentum, sed non rem sacramenti." Peter Chelčický, *op. cit.*, pp. 446f., 457, who quotes this and similar passages from Taborite eucharistic treatises, showing how they follow necessarily from a denial of the Real Presence, points out that they do not differ from the belief of the Pikarts, and refutes them by arguing that according to Jesus and Paul the evil as well as the good *can* eat the Body.

[71] Taborite religion has yet to be systematically studied; in support of the statement made in the text I offer one item selected from among many others: in the "Taborite Confession" of 1431, Nicholas of Pelhřimov, refuting the Praguers' adherence to the orthodox cult of the Virgin Mary, noted Mary's various epithets ("the Hope of Sinners", the "Queen of Heaven", etc.), and urged: "From this great exaltation of her it seems to the simple people, even to the greatest sinners among them, that no one will be damned, because the "Hope of Sinners" rules in heaven and works energetically for her clients". See B. Lydius, ed., *Waldensia*, I (Rotterdam, 1616), 234.

[72] For the text of the decrees of the Taborite Synod of Klatovy see F. M. Bartoš, "Klatovská synoda táborských kněží z 11. listopadu r. 1424," *Jihočeský sborník historický*, VIII (1935), 6f. The Synod operated with a distinction between ordinary bread, the living bread that descends from heaven, and the bread of the Lord's Supper, a distinction originally developed by John Němec of Žatec. According to his treatise, *Cum spiritus veritatis*...(ed. Sedlák, *Tab. trakt. euch.*), Christ has several "modes of being"; according to his divinity he is everywhere *essencialiter et potencialiter* (p. 9), and according to his humanity he has the following four modes: (1) *substancialiter et corporaliter* (i.e., in his physical body); (2) spiritually, with the saints here on earth, through his grace (p. 12); (3) *virtualiter aut potencialiter*, just as a king is *potencialiter* in his kingdom which he rules *actualiter*; (4) *sacramentaliter* (p. 13ff.). In the Eucharist Christ is present: *sacramentaliter* or "figuratively"; *potencialiter*, for the sacrament strengthens the faithful against the Devil; and *spiritualiter*, for through it he gives his spiritual gifts. Thus, through a rich abundance of thoroughly scholastic distinctions, John Němec is able to say that, "in the aforesaid mode", the bread and wine of the Eucharist are the Body and Blood of Christ, and thus refute the Pikart doctrine, "that the sacramental bread does not differ from ordinary bread" (p. 19). On the other

twenty years thereafter the issue of Taborite "Pikartism" formed the central subject of the institutionalized disputations between the Prague and Taborite theologians.[73] Of course if Tabor had really taken over Pikartism there could have been no debate; as Tabor herself had shown, the only answer to the Free Spirit was that of the sword and the stake.

HOWARD KAMINSKY
*University of Washington*

---

hand, he refutes transsubstantiation, with its "gross" view that "the material flesh of Christ" is in the sacrament (*loc. cit.*). He concludes (p. 20): "We hold the middle view . . ." All of this may seem tedious to the modern reader, but Němec's distinctions were of the greatest importance, for they and they alone enabled the Taborite party of order to take a necessary Pikart doctrine out of the unmanageable world of Free-Spirit sectarianism, and insert it into the rational world of a scholastic religion illuminating a stable society.

[73] For the most important texts, see Höfler, II, 589ff., and Nejedlý, *Prameny k synodám . . .*, *passim*.

## MILLENARIANISM IN A CIVIC SETTING:
## THE SAVONAROLA MOVEMENT IN FLORENCE *

The Savonarola movement was more than a religious revival. Born in a civic crisis, it embodied the political as well as the religious aspiration of the Florentines, and it drew upon the city's patriotic traditions. Savonarola combined religious prophecy with labor for a reformed and a revived republic. He attracted the support of men of varied social backgrounds and interests. Many of the leading Florentine thinkers and artists worked and wrote for the movement; many leading citizens guided its political destinies. They had been prominent under the Medici regime, they were active in the Savonarolan republic, and they remained in the forefront of public life after Savonarola had been put to death. At the same time, notwithstanding its continuity with the civic past, the movement had radical and millenarian elements which have been minimized or ignored in the major studies of Savonarola's life and work.[1] By giving these elements their full value we not only illuminate an obscure side of the Savonarola movement, we also broaden our view of the millenarian phenomenon. Here is a case of millenarianism that did not arise out of the protests of the poor and cannot be explained by economic crisis.[2] Its roots were as diverse as the make-up of the movement itself and its radicalism was linked to Florentine political tradition.

After the revolt against the regime of Piero de' Medici on November 8-9,

*  Part of the research upon which this article is based was financed by a grant from the Johnson Fund of the American Philosophical Society.
[1]  The need to study this aspect of Savonarola's thought, particularly in its relation to late medieval eschatology, was pointed out by Delio Cantimore, "Giuseppe Schnitzer: Savonarola, traduzione italiana di E. Rutili, Milano Treves 1931," *Annali della R. Scuola Normale Superiore di Pisa Lettere, Storia e Filosofia* 2.1 (1932), pp. 90–104, and by Giorgio Spini, "Introduzione al Savonarola," *Belfagor* 3.4 (1948), pp. 414–28. Of Savonarola's major biographers, Schnitzer goes farthest in trying to relate Savonarola to the cultural currents of the time, but he does not give much attention to the radical aspects of the movement. For a recent interpretation, considerably different from my own, see André Chastel, "L'Antéchrist à la Renaissance," *Atti del Congresso Internazionale di Studi Umanistici* ed. Enrico Castelli, *L'Umanesimo e il demoniaco nell'arte* (Rome, 1952), pp. 177–186.

[2]  For the most recent study that stresses the socio-economic and lower class origins of millenarian movements see Norman Cohn, *The Pursuit of the Millennium* (London, 1957).

1494, Savonarola urged the adoption of a popular government and made this the basic condition for the fulfilment of his prophecies to the Florentine people.[3] The voice from the pulpit was an inspiration, and the republic, which lasted beyond Savonarola's death until 1512, has always been associated with his name. But the uprising of 1494 was not a revolution inspired by an inflammatory preacher of an egalitarian millennium. Savonarola only turned his attention to social and political reform after the Florentines had risen against the Medici regime. Indeed, he had played little or no part in the uprising itself, and, although in his earlier days his enemies had dubbed him "the preacher of the desperate", he had never incited men to revolt or preached that the structure of the state or society should be changed. In his sermons of 1490, after he had returned to Florence to stay and had begun to preach in his new, sensational prophetic style, he had spoken of the Last Days and of universal conversion and religious reform; but this was to be a prelude to the Last Judgment, not to some brighter, earthly society.[4] In those days he was an apocalyptic prophet, but not a millenarian. In his sermons of 1491, Savonarola had condemned social injustice and political oppression, and he had made pointed remarks about tyrants, but he had dwelt little upon the possibilities of reforming human institutions, and he had urged his listeners to patience in bearing their suffering lot in this world. Relief, he said, would come in the next life. For Florence, his adopted city, he had no special praise or hope for a bright future. In fact, he singled her out for special destruction. In the days when God poured out the vials of His wrath she would no longer be called *Florentia* but "turpitude and blood and a cave of robbers." [5]

Savonarola had little to do with the troubles that had been mounting up for the regime of Piero de' Medici almost from the day of its inception. Piero Parenti, the most authoritative Florentine chronicler of those years, described the resentment that began to form against Piero when he succeeded his father, the Magnificent Lorenzo, as unoffical head of the city, in April, 1492.[6] Many were disappointed that Lorenzo's death brought no relaxation

---

[3]  On the revolt and the political aspects of the Savonarola period see Nicolai Rubinstein, "Politics and Constitution in Florence at the End of the Fifteenth Century," *Italian Renaissance Studies*, ed. E. F. Jacob (London, 1960), pp. 148–183. Professor Rubinstein's emphasis is different from mine, but I think it is accurate to say that we have come to the same conclusions about the role of Savonarola in the revolt and in the introduction of the first reforms.

[4]  Roberto Ridolfi, *Vita di Girolamo Savonarola*, 2 vols. (Rome, 1952) I, pp. 46–55. English translation by Cecil Grayson, (New York, 1959) without notes. By his new, more sensational style I mean Savonarola's prophesying, which he began, apparently, in his San Gimignano sermons of 1485. *Ibid*. I, p. 32.

[5]  Museo di San Marco (Florence) Ms. 480, fol. 57 v. Partly published in Pasquale Villari, *La storia di Girolamo Savonarola*, 2 vols, 2d ed. (Florence, 1926) I, append. xxx.

[6]  On Parenti and his chronicle, most of which is still unpublished, see Guido Pampaloni, "Piero di Marco Parenti e la sua 'Historia fiorentina'", *Archivio storico italiano*, Anno CXVII (1959), pp. 147–153, and Joseph Schnitzer in his edition of part of

of one-man rule, no return to the *vita civile* of old.[7] Piero further alienated many of the *ottomati* – or *primati*, as Parenti called the leading political men – by refusing to take their advice, by putting forward new young men for offices and honors in the place of the older supporters of his father, and by generally blocking the old avenues of *ottimati* influence in the state.[8] According to Parenti, Florence was soon tense with expectation, as everyone awaited some event that would lead to the recovery of *vera libertà*. One such occasion began as a squabble among the Franciscans of Santa Croce and turned into a general riot in that quarter of the city. Parenti describes how men of some of the leading families, of the Alberti, the Serristori, and the Corsi, among others, rode among the crowd inciting the populace to violence against the regime; but as yet Piero de' Medici was able to rally his supporters and suppress the riot.[9] Other outbursts resulted from the incitement of preachers, notably Fra Domenico da Ponzo and Fra Bernardino da Feltre, who aroused popular feeling against the Jews and provoked demonstrations against Piero's government for protecting them.[10]

During these same years Savonarola continued to direct his growing following in peaceful courses. After Lorenzo's death his relations with the government even improved.[11] In 1493 and 1494 he was involved in delicate maneuvers in Rome to free his convent from the Lombard Congregation and to establish a reformed Congregation of San Marco. In this Savonarola had to rely upon the good will and the support of Piero de' Medici, who put the diplomatic resources of the Florentine state at his disposal. Savonarola's letter to Piero on May 26, 1493, just on the eve of the papal order for the separation of San Marco from the Lombard Congregation, leaves no doubt that the friar was conscious of his debt to the ruler of Florence, and that he was committed to close cooperation with him.[12] In June, 1494, when Piero ordered some of the preachers of the city to suspend their preaching lest they exacerbate the dangerous public tension, he did not include Savonarola in the proscription.[13]

So far from creating the anti-Medicean revolt of November 1494, Savonarola was rather its creature, for it was the revolt that brought him to the

Parenti's chronicle, *Savonarola nach den Aufzeichnungen des Florentiners Piero Parenti* (Leipzig, 1910), pp. XXV–CLXII.

[7] Piero di Marco Parenti, *Diario fiorentino*, Biblioteca Nazionale di Firenze Ms. II.IV.169, fols. 128ff.

[8] "metteva innanzi gioveni e gentilotti favoriva questi contro all voglia di antichi principali et huomini di matura età." *Ibid*. f. 132v.

[9] *Ibid*. fols. 145–7.

[10] *Ibid*. fols, 143–4.

[11] Ridolfi, *Vita* I, 76–7.

[12] For a full account of the struggle for reform see Joseph Schnitzer, *Savonarola im Streite mit seinem Orden und seinem Kloster* (Munich, 1914). The letter to Piero is in Roberto Ridolfi, ed., *Le lettere di Girolamo Savonarola* (Florence, 1933), p. 30.

[13] Parenti, *Diario* f. 164.

political stage and provided him with his script. The overthrow of the Medici regime was the last in a chain of events forged by Piero himself. Having reversed his father's policy of friendship with France, Piero was blamed when Florentine merchants were driven out of that country,[14] and he was placed in further difficulties when Charles VIII of France invaded Italy in the late summer of 1494. When Charles stood upon the edge of Tuscany with his forces Piero lost his nerve, rushed to the king's camp, and purchased a reconciliation by surrendering the Florentine fortress towns and seaports. The Florentines were enraged. A number of *primati* convened to deliberate upon a course of action. They decided to send their own embassy to the French king and on November 5, the Council of One Hundred met "to make provisions as a free city," and to choose the ambassadors. Among the five chosen for the mission was Savonarola, a highly revered public figure, a prophet whose predictions of tribulations for Florence and for Italy were now coming true. At first, however, Savonarola refused to go, and he finally accepted with great reluctance and with special conditions: he gave notice that he did not intend to discuss with the king the status of private persons,[15] and that he would confine himself to pleading for Charles' benevolence toward the city.[16]

It seems, then, that while his preaching may have added to the excitement in Florence, Savonarola had no revolutionary intentions and even hesitated to involve himself in politics after the revolt against Piero had got underway; indeed, the revolt began with this assertion of independence by the *primati*.[17] Savonarola's refusal to discuss the status of private persons was an obvious attempt to dissociate himself from action against the man who had been his patron and his benefactor in the fight for Dominican reform. Similarly, in his sermons during those tumultuous days he interpreted the French invasion as an apocalyptic event, as God's scourge for Italy's sins, and as a confirmation of his own prophecies; he urged the Florentines to repentence and conversion, but not to rebellion. He continued to concern himself with the government of souls, but he did not yet concern himself with the rule of cities.[18]

Savonarola was out of Florence, on his mission to Charles, when the *coup* against Piero de' Medici was brought off. When Piero returned to Florence from his own mission to the French king he found that a hostile *Signoria* had barred him from the governmental palace and was raising the populace

---

[14] Parenti (ed. Schnitzer) p. 7.

[15] Piero, although effective ruler of the city, was – as were the Medici rulers before him – private citizen with no official status.

[16] Parenti (ed. Schnitzer), pp. 9–10.

[17] "This, rather than the popular rising, proved the decisive element in the revolution of November 9.", Rubinstein, "Politics and Constitution," p. 151.

[18] Girolamo Savonarola, *Prediche italiane ai fiorentini* 3 vols in 4, ed. F. Cognasso and R. Palmarocchi (Perugia-Florence, 1930–5) For the sermons of this crucial period see I, 1–65.

against him with the cry of *popolo e libertà*. Failing to rally his supporters, and with a price on his head offered by the Signoria, Piero fled on November 9.[19] Now the Florentines, with "a mixture of fear and wonder," [20] awaited Charles VIII, who entered the city on November 17. Charles had a double motive for anger in the city's recent opposition to his Italian venture and now in her uprising against his new ally, Piero de' Medici. Many tense moments arose during the king's sojourn, but the crisis passed with the signing of a treaty restoring the old Franco-Florentine friendship. Charles promised to restore Pisa and the fortress towns and the Florentines promised a subsidy, while successfully resisting the king's demands for the restoration of Piero to power in the city.[21]

Savonarola returned to Florence on November 11, two days after Piero's expulsion, and resumed his almost daily preaching. While he referred to Florence's new-found liberty,[22] and intervened with the French king to plead for the city,[23] he does not seem to have participated in the early deliberations for the revision of the government. The *primati* decided to abolish the councils that had served as the vehicles of Medici domination and to establish an interim board of twenty commissioners, the *Accoppiatori*, who would choose the *Signoria*, or executive body, until the electoral lists could be revised. Having met and decided on this course of action the *primati* then called for a *Parlamento*, the assembly of all the people traditionally gathered to pass on fundamental constitutional decisions. The *Parlamento* gathered on December 2, and performed as expected, ratifying the provisions placed before it by the leaders, who knew of old how to manipulate the assembly to their purposes.[24] Since the *Accoppiatori* were the same men who had organized the *coup* against Piero, the action of December 2 meant that this group retained its hold upon the State.

But this hold was jeopardized from the start. The leaders of November 8-9 were themselves divided by personal animosities and conflicting ambitions. Moreover, they were now threatened by the returning political exiles, those who had suffered under the previous regime and in whose eyes anyone who

[19]  Parenti (ed. Schnitzer) f. 194 r-v; Francesco Guicciardini, *Storie fiorentine dal 1378 al 1509*, ed. Roberto Palmarocchi, *Opere* Vol. 6 (Scrittori d'Italia Vol. 134; Bari, 1931), pp. 95-7; Luca Landucci, *Diario fiorentino dal 1450 al 1516*, ed. Iodoco Del Badia (Florence, 1883), p. 75.

[20]  Bartolommeo Cerretani, *Storia fiorentina*, Joseph Schnitzer ed., *Quellen und Forschungen zur Geschichte Savonarolas*, III (Munich, 1904), p. 21.

[21]  The treaty is published in *Archivio storico italiano*, I (1842), pp. 362-375.

[22]  For the sermons of this period see Savonarola, *Prediche italiane*, I, pp. 66-105.

[23]  See his own remarks on the role he played, Savonarola, *Prediche*, ed. G. Baccini, (Florence, 1889) p. 564.

[24]  "e signori facto sonare a parlamento colloro collegi scesono in ringhiera et quivi per loro notaio lecto il primo et ultimo contenuto d'essa riforma stato, senddo da ghonfaloni presse tutte le bochche di piaza, fu da tutta la moltitudine con alte voce conffermo." Cerretani, *Storia fiorentina*, pp. 29-30; Parenti, *Diario*, ff. 208v-210v (partly published in Schnitzer's edition of Parenti, pp. 19-22).

had supported the Medici despotism was tainted. Factions formed, each looking outside its own ranks for support. Meanwhile, protest was mounting against the restrictive provisions of December 2. This came, according to Parenti, from the "good citizens", who complained that they had fought for liberty only to preserve in power the same men who had been ruling before.[25] With the returning exiles calling for a purge of supporters of the old regime, with the "good citizens" chafing against oligarchy, and with the *popolo* clamoring for the blood of former Medici officials,[26] the leaders of November 8-9, who had thought to dominate the new republic, had cause enough for anxiety.

In this new crisis Savonarola began to turn his attention to political problems. In his sermon of December 7 he advised that a law be adopted to prevent the rise of a new despot,[27] and he said that the constitution needed revision, mentioning the constitution of Venice as a possible model.[28] From a careful study of his sermons we can see how both these ideas, of constitutional revision and of using Venice as a model, gradually gained the center of his attention. In the sermon of December 7, Savonarola referred to the need for reform, but he continued to insist that the spirit was more important than the form of any government, and he maintained that the remedy for civil discord was forgiveness and reform of spirit. The Venetian plan he mentioned as a possible choice, but he added that God might inspire his hearers with a better one.[29] During the next week Savonarola preached several times without alluding to this problem at all, while he continued to exhort the Florentines to repentance and conversion of life as the way to build God's new city. But on December 14 he returned to the subject of constitutional reform, saying that God had inspired him to instruct the Florentines in these matters. He now urged them to take the Venetian Grand Council as their model, but to refrain from borrowing the institution of the doge which he found unsuitable for Florence.[30] Whether, as many believed at the time, Savonarola had been persuaded by Paolo Antonio Soderini, one of the leaders of November 8-9, to put forward the Venetian plan,[31] or

[25] Rubinstein, "Politics and Constitution," p. 154. On the conflicts within the group of leaders see Parenti (ed. Schnitzer) p. 23. On the dissatisfaction of one of the group, Paolantonio Soderini, see Guicciardini, *Storie fiorentine*, pp. 106-7. On the popular reaction against what Parenti called the *falsa et fraudolenta Parlamento*, see Parenti, *Diario*, fols 210, 216; Guicciardini, *op. cit.*, pp. 107-8, Cerretani, *Storia fiorentina*, pp. 31-2.

[26] Landucci, *Diario fiorentino*, pp. 75-77; Ridolfi, *Vita*, I, p. 137.

[27] "...che nessuno più per l'avvenire possa farsi capo..." Savonarola, *Prediche italiane*, I, p. 115.

[28] *Ibid.* I, p. 117.

[29] ..."o come fanno e Veneziani, o come meglio Dio vi inspirerà." *loc. cit.*

[30] *Ibid.* I, p. 195.

[31] Guicciardini, *Storie fiorentine*, pp. 106-7; Iacopo Nardi, *Istorie della città di Firenze*, 2 vols. (Florence, 1838-41), I, p. 158; Rubinstein, "Politics and Constitution", pp. 151-161.

whether he took it up on his own is impossible to say, but clearly Savonarola at last realized there would be no religious reform in Florence without the establishment of a stable and peaceful republic. Here began the theme that was henceforward to be so important in Savonarola's preaching – that religious reform in Florence was bound up with a free republic. From this time the *governo populare* became an indispensable part of Savonarola's program, and from this time too Savonarola's hitherto largely moral influence developed into a popular movement with a set of political goals. Under mounting pressure more of the *ottimati* who had at first opposed the constitutional revision now embraced it. For them the proposal was sweetened by the promise of a general reconciliation of factions which Savonarola made an integral part of the reform.[32]

Most of the goals of the reforming group were realized in the succeeding months – sovereignty vested in a Great Council, revised procedures for choosing men for public offices, a Law of Appeal to safeguard judicial rights, the introduction of fiscal reforms. These measures were championed by Savonarola from the pulpit, while the *ottimati* who had allied with the reform group championed them in the councils of state.[33] But although the new republic was commonly called *governo popolare*, it was no democracy. While the scope of political participation was broadened by making room for new men, not all Florentines were eligible for membership in the Great Council or for holding office. The end for which Savonarola seems to have worked, and successfully, was the restoration of free republican institutions and a compromise between the *ottimati* who were in power and the lesser middle class which aspired to power.[34] The middle class hold on the State was broadened but preserved. In this Savonarola worked to reinforce not a radical but a traditional Florentine ideal of republican liberty, the ideal that Rudolf von Albertini has defined as the right to be a part of the state, not freedom from the State; but this was a right not generally conceded to all.[35]

---

[32] On the fear of the *ottimati* see Parenti (ed. Schnitzer), pp. 28–9; Cerretani, *Storia fiorentina*, pp. 31–2; Guicciardini, *Storie fiorentine*, pp. 106–7. On Savonarola's call for civic peace see *Prediche italiane*, I, p. 194.

[33] For the best analysis of the reforms see Nicolai Rubinstein, "I primi anni del Consiglio Maggiore di Firenze (1494–1499)", *Archivio storico italiano*, Anno 112 (1954), Pt. I, pp. 151–194; Pt. II, pp. 321–347. On the financial reforms see Louis Marks, "La crisi finanziaria a Firenze dal 1494 al 1502," *Ibid.* pp. 40–72.

[34] In his sermon of December 14, Savonarola said that in some way the artisans had to be given responsibility in the state. I take it he was referring to craftsmen and shopkeepers, members of the lesser gilds, as distinct from wage-earning proletarians. He proposed that while the major offices continued to be elective the minor ones be filled by lot. *Prediche italiane*, I, p. 195. In general this was the upshot of the electoral reforms. See Rubinstein, "I primi anni". Savonarola was almost violent in his opposition to the *Parlamento,* while his ready embrace of the Venetian plan seems to have been due to his liking for its more conservative rather than its democratic features.

[35] "Libertà wurde nicht als Freiheit vom Staate verstanden, sondern war das Recht, am Staate beteiligt zu sein, also gewissermassen Teil des Staates zu sein. Der Begriff

What is true of Savonarola's political awakening is also true of his millenarian vision: it was the product rather than the cause of the Florentine upheavals, and its features were shaped by Florentine requirements. As Savonarola emerged as a political leader his prophecy and his doctrine underwent fundamental transformations. Right up to the time of the Medici expulsion he had continued to foretell disaster for Florence as for the rest of Italy. His prophecy continued to be apocalyptic, his vision the imminent approach of the Last Days following the outpouring of God's wrath. After the revolt, however, and particularly after the French troops departed from Florence on November 28, without having sacked the city, Savonarola became much more optimistic about the future of Florence and about the possibility that Charles VIII might indeed be, as the prophecies circulating in Florence and elsewhere were saying he was, the new Charlemagne who would reform Christendom.[36] The events of these crucial days seem to have persuaded him that Florence was chosen to lead the way to reform. How to turn Florentine energies into spiritual enthusiasm – this had always been Savonarola's problem. The invasion, the revolt, and the ensuing constitutional crisis in Florence gave him his solution. Now he was able to see a connection between his prophetic mission, of which he had long been convinced, and Florentine affairs. Now he was able to see why God had sent him to Florence rather than elsewhere. The French invasion was the opening of the fifth age of the world, the age of Antichrist and of the universal conversion to Christianity. Both his own mission and the Florentine revolt, he now saw, were part of God's plan. Charles VIII was the new Cyrus come to scourge the church and establish the conditions for the New Era. In the reformed Church a Holy Pastor would appear, the infidel would be converted to Christianity, and the world would be united in one sheepfold under a single shepherd, then to repose in the joy of contemplating the Cross. Now, moreover, he was certain that Florence had a glorious future and that he himself had been divinely chosen to bring this message to this city.

---

des 'popolo' fasste die städtische Bürgerschaft zusammen und galt nicht etwa für alle Einwohner der Stadt." Rudolf von Albertini, *Das florentinische Staatsbewusstsein im Übergang von der Republik zum Prinzipat* (Bern, 1955), p. 21. For a definition of types of government in Florence see Marvin B. Becker, "Some Aspects of Oligarchical, Dictatorial and Popular Signorie in Florence, 1282–1382," *Comparative Studies in Society and History*, II. 4 (1960) pp. 421–39, and his "Some Economic Implications of the Conflict between Church and State in 'Trecento' Florence," *Mediaeval Studies*, Vol. XXI (1959) pp. 1–16. No such studies of the republic of 1494–1512 exist, to my knowledge.

[36] Some of the late 15th century prophecies published in Florence of this type are in: *Prophetia Caroli Imperatoris con altre prophetie de diversi santi huomini* (Florence, n.d.) Biblioteca Nazionale di Firenze Incunabulum Guicciardini 2-3-57; *Questo è il Judicio Generale chè tracta de la fine del mondo quand Jesu Christo venirà a iudicare li boni e li rei* (Florence, n.d.) Biblioteca Nazionale di Firenze Incunabulum Guicciardini 3-4-25.

... I announce this good news to the city, that Florence will be more glorious, richer, more powerful than she has ever been.

First, glorious in the sight of God as well as of men: and you, oh Florence, will be the reformation of all Italy, and from here the renewal will begin and spread all over, because this is the navel of Italy. Your counsel will reform all by the light and grace that God will give you. Second, oh Florence, you will have innumerable riches, and God will multiply all things for you. Third, you will spread your empire, and thus you will have power temporal and spiritual.[37]

Savonarola uttered this remarkable prophecy *for the first time* on December 9, four years after he came to Florence,[38] a month after the revolt, and during the same week in which he began to formulate his political program. It was a decisive abandonment of his former universal, ascetic apocalypticism for a millenarianism that was peculiarly directed to Florence and that held out the promise of wealth and power. Was this inspiration or charlatanry? Sincere belief or demagoguery? Scholars still ask these questions and they still answer them with partisan passion.[39] But we can believe that Savonarola was convinced of the prophetic origin of his message without accepting his own explanation of it.[40] While he was prepared, both by training and by temper, to believe in his own divine inspiration, we are more inclined to regard his vision as the product of his experiences and his hopes, and to look for the circumstances and the influences that help explain it. The events of November 1494 were crucial: they seemed to vindicate his earlier prophecies of the coming *flagello*; they drew him forward as a leader; finally, they gave him the confidence to promise that if his way were followed a New Era would dawn.

Not only did Savonarola draw inspiration from Florentine events; he also came to express Florentine aspirations and attitudes that had played no part in his earlier preaching. Indeed, his new millenarian vision took on the coloration of his surroundings so much that we ought to speak of the Florentine conquest of Savonarola rather than the other way round. By introducing the idea of Florentine leadership in the new age he brought his prophecy into line with civic tradition. The Florentines had long since come to think of themselves as a chosen people. A leit-motiv of their civic literature was the idea of Florentine superiority, a visible excellence that confirmed the city's destiny to leadership and lent moral strength to her undertakings in politics and culture. We may call it patriotic rhetoric or a political ideology or a civic myth; it was all of these, taking different forms in different circles

---

[37]  Savonarola, *Prediche italiane,* I, p. 145.
[38]  He came to Florence to stay in May or June, 1490. Ridolfi, *Vita,* I, p. 44.
[39]  For example, the fervent partisanship of Ridolfi's *Vita* and the bitter polemical tone of Warman Welliver's "La demagogia del Savonarola," *Il Ponte,* XII (1956) pp. 1194–1202.
[40]  For Savonarola's own account see his *Compendium Revelationum* in Gianfrancesco Pico della Mirandola, *Vita R.P. Fr. Hieronymi Savonarolae Ferrariensis,* ed. Jacques Quetif, 2 vols. (Paris, 1674), I, pp. 216–385).

and times. Among the humanists of the early fifteenth century, as Hans
Baron has shown, it took the form of an ideal, that of the city's historic role
as a champion of liberty, a role that seemed to justify Florentine ambitions
for primacy in central Italy.[41] Later, among the Neoplatonists of the Medici
circle, this concept of Florentine superiority took a different form: Marsilio
Ficino, Ugolino Verino and others celebrated the revival of philosophy, the
arts, and religion which made Florence the center of a new golden age.[42]

Between these varieties of civic myth and Savonarola's new vision there
were some obvious connections. When he explained that Florence was a
chosen city, the center of Italy,[43] where wit, culture, and piety abounded
more than elsewhere,[44] he was using images and themes already fashioned
by Florentine writers and thinkers. When he argued for a free republic as
best suited to the restless spirits of Florence he was borrowing from Florentine humanist historiography, as he acknowledged when he urged his listeners
to read Leonardo Bruni and the chroniclers of the city.[45]

Yet, while Savonarola absorbed these humanist ideas of Florentine superiority and leadership, he cast them in an eschatological, rather than in a
secular historical mold. Where Marsilio Ficino saw Florentine leadership as
the achievement of art and philosophy, Savonarola saw it as the sign of God's
election, and he envisioned the golden age as a reign of the spirit in which a
regenerated Florence would set the standard. There was nothing unusual or
anachronistic in such expectations, as we can see from the literature of
religious prophecy of fourteenth and fifteenth century Italy. Daniel, the
Book of Revelation, the Sibyls, Merlin and Joachim of Fiore continued to
be cited, commented upon, and reinterpreted in order to bring them to bear
upon current problems. Prophecies appeared under the names of St. Francis
of Assisi, Jacopone da Todi, St. Catherine of Siena. The *Revelations* of St.
Bridget of Sweden and the prophecies of St. Vincent of Ferrer were especially popular in Italy, while a host of new Italian prophets made their
appearance, among them, Fra Tomasuccio da Foligno, Fra Amadeo, Fra
Antonio da Rieti, and Fra Stoppa.[46] Behind the names and the various

[41]  Hans Baron, *The Crisis of the Early Italian Renaissance*, 2 vols. (Princeton, 1955).
[42]  Marsilio Ficino, Letter to Paul of Middelburg, September 12, 1492, *Opera* (Basel,
1561), p. 944; Ugolino Verino, *Flametta*, ed. Luciano Mencaraglia (Florence, 1940)
p. 96.
[43]  Savonarola, *Prediche italiane*, II, pp. 324–5.
[44]  *Ibid.* I, pp. 183, 4.
[45]  Savonarola, *Prediche sopra Ezechiele*, ed. Roberto Ridolfi, 2 vols (Rome, 1955–6),
I, p. 97. In his *Trattato circa il reggimento e governo della città di Firenze*, ed. Audin
de Rians (6th ed; Florence, 1847) p. 13 Savonarola appealed in a general way to the
evidence of "the chroniclers" of the city's history.
[46]  The literature of the subject is extensive but fragmentary; no systematic treatment
exists. In general see Johann von Döllinger, "Weissagungsglaube und Prophetentum in
christlichen Zeitalter", *Kleinere Schriften* (Stuttgart, 1890), pp. 451–557; Friedrich
Baethgen, *Der Engelpapst* (Halle, 1933); Alessandro d'Ancona, *Studi sulla litteratura
italiana dei primi secoli* (Ancona, 1884); Michele Faloci-Pulignani, *Le profezie del B.*

texts, however, there was no great variety of ideas. The themes were those that had long since been developed by, or in the name of, the visionaries of past times. Again and again we find the metaphors of the Book of Revelation, the animal symbolism of the Merlin and Daniel prophecies, the legends of Last Emperor and Angelic Pope, and the political chiliasm of the Joachimites of the 13th and 14th centuries.[47] Another important source of religious prophecy in the 15th century was astrology. The inaugural of the Great Year, when Jupiter would acceed to the house of Aries, would bring a momentous religious revolution, fulfilling the prophecies of the Book of Revelation.[48]

Nothing in the literature suggests that these prophecies were less seriously intended or believed in the 15th century than they had been in previous centuries. If they were used for propaganda there was nothing new in this; they had always been so used. The effectiveness of prophecy as propaganda depended upon the extent to which it was accepted as a true form of knowledge and as a living link between the revelation of the past and its fulfilment in the present and future. The wide diffusion and continued growth of prophecies, and the passionate tone of many of the texts, suggests that this acceptance was considerable.

Prophecy flourished in Florentine soil. During the Florentine war with Pope Gregory XI, from 1375–1378, an important addition to the pseudo-Joachimite *Prophecies of the Popes* was manufactured in the city, probably in Spiritual Franciscan circles.[49] In the same period the Florentine government gave free rein to the Fraticelli and other heretical preachers of Joachimite and pseudo-Joachimite millenarian ideas. Under Fraticelli influence the revolutionaries of 1378 – the Ciompi – came to think of themselves as *il popolo di Dio* and the heirs of the "true religion."[50] In succeeding years, the crisis in the Church brought on by the Papal Schism of 1378 and the looming threat of Milanese expansion southward focused Florentine attention on broader religious and civic, rather than narrower class problems, and new dimensions were added

*Tommasuccio da Foligno del 3 Ord. di S. Francesco,* (Foligno, 1887); Angelo Messini, "Profetismo e profezie ritmiche italiane d'ispirazione gioachimito-francescana nei secoli XIII, XIV, e XV", *Miscellanea Francescana,* XXXVII (1937), pp. 39–54; XXXIX (1939), pp. 109–130.

[47] For a typology of prophecies see Rupert Taylor, *The Political Prophecy in England* (New York; Columbia University Studies in English, 1911).

[48] On astrology and religious expectations in fifteenth century Italy see Benedetto Soldati, *La poesia astrologica nel Quattrocento* (Florence, 1906). On the origins of this theory in Italy see Nicolai Rubinstein, "Some Ideas on Municipal Progress and Decline in the Italy of the Communes," in *Fritz Saxl 1890–1948,* ed. D. J. Gordon, (London, 1957) p. 178 and note 2. Some of the contemporary texts containing prophetic themes mentioned here are: Biblioteca Nazionale di Firenze Mss. Magliabecchi VII, 1081, VIII, 1443 and XXXV, 116; Biblioteca Riccardiana (Florence) Ms. 1222 (4 vols), vol. 2.

[49] Herbert Grundmann, "Die Papstprophetien des Mittelalters", *Archiv für Kulturgeschichte,* XIX (1928), pp. 77–138.

[50] Marvin B. Becker, "Florentine Politics and the Diffusion of Heresy in the Trecento: A Socio-Economic Inquiry," *Speculum,* XXXIV.1 (1959), p. 73.

to millenarian thought in Florence. For example, in a group of prophecies dated 1359 but obviously pertaining to the events of 1378 and after, the hope of social and political reforms at home is blended with the expectation of imminent religious reform and Florentine leadership in Italy: in Florence a *picciolo cittadino* will rule and a peaceful communal government will prevail, under which the city will live in liberty; in the Church the schism will be healed through the efforts of the kings of Norman birth, the Church will lose her political power and will experience a revolution (*novità*) in 1380; Florence the "new great city," the daughter of Rome, will be helped to freedom by the French and will extend her hegemony over her neighbors; the *bella città* will bring happiness to those who oppose the Lombards; amid the tribulations of Antichrist, Florence appears, pregnant with the hope of a new era (*nuovo tempo*).[51]

The passing of 1380 without *novità* did not put an end to the conviction that Florence had a peculiar political and spiritual destiny. Again and again, for more than a century afterwards, these beliefs and hopes were restated in new prophecies and in old ones brought "up to date." Since many of the purveyors and copyists of the prophecies were friars we can assume that these ideas were kept alive and broadcast in popular preaching as well as in written form, and that, therefore, they had a wider circulation than we would suppose from textual remains alone.[52] Thus, by Savonarola's time there existed in Florence a tradition, written and oral, of what might be called civic millenarian ideas which were supposed to derive from Joachim of Fiore and other authoritative interpreters of Biblical prophecy. As Savonarola changed his own ideas about the future of Florence, so he changed his mind about this civic tradition. At the outset, in his sermons on the Apocalypse in 1490, he took issue with the "simple people" who cited *diversas prophetias Ioachin, Sancti Vincentii etc.* as evidence that "the times are at hand." He himself, he said, preferred the evidence of his senses to that of visions: the wickedness that he saw all about him gave urgency to the message of the Apocalypse.[53] Thus at first Savonarola rejected the evidence of the modern prophets. He also seems to have ignored their millenarian aspects, for his sermons of 1490 offered no hope for a new future.

[51]  Biblioteca Nazionale di Firenze Ms. Magliabecchi XXX, 173 fol. 1.

[52]  For example the prophecy of Fra Antonio da Rieti, who claimed to have a vision upon his return from the Holy Land in 1468. The contents of the vision point to a later date, subsequent to the accession to the French throne of Charles VIII in 1483 and perhaps in the pontificate of Alexander VI. The success of the lily and the lion seems to stand for the eventual leadership of France and Florence. *Copia d'una rivelazione chè ebbe frate Antonio da Rieti dell'Ordine di Sancto Francescho de Frati Observanti* (Florence, n.d.).

[53]  The notes for Savonarola's *Lezioni sull'Apocalisse* are partly published in Pasquale Villari, *La storia di Girolamo Savonarola* 2 vols (Florence, 1859–61) I, append. xv. The full text is in *Sermones sive magis lectiones super Apocalypsim*, Biblioteca Nazionale di Firenze Ms. Conventi soppressi, I.VII 25 fols. 53–85.

Quite different was Savonarola's use of prophetic authorities in his so-called *Predica della rinovazione* of January 13, 1495 in which, in offering reasons for his belief in the coming renovation of the Church, he pointed out that "the abbot Joachim and many others predict and announce that the scourge must come at this time.[54] By then he had shifted his own focus from *flagello* to *rinovazione* and he was willing to use the additional corroboration of the modern prophets. Still, Savonarola was not willing to be identified too closely with these preachers of radical views. In his *Compendium of Revelations*, the apology which he wrote in the summer of 1495, he denied that he was an enthusiast of prophetic literature and said that he had never read the *Revelations* of St. Bridget and "never or only rarely" the prophecies of the Abbot Joachim.[55] How much he had read Joachim and the others, and how enthusiastically, we cannot know, but we cannot doubt that he was familiar with the prophecies circulating under the names of these authorities. Such themes in his sermons as the divine origin of Italy's tribulations, the invaders from the north who would come as servants of the Lord, the punishment of tyrants and of the clergy, Rome's loss of leadership, the appearance of a Holy Pastor who would reform the Church and unite the world, and, most especially, the prophecy of Florentine leadership in the new era, these can all be found in the Florentine prophetic literature. Even Savonarola's language – the *flagello*, or scourge, its rapid coming (*cito et velociter*),[56] the new Charlemagne, and the terms in which he described Florentine superiority and leadership – is familiar to the reader of the earlier prophecies. Such similarities are too many and too strong to be accidental. Savonarola's originality, some will say his inspiration, lay in his ability to unite these various civic traditions and aspirations, humanist and popular, spiritual and materialist, republican and imperialist, into a single millenarian vision that was also a program for action.

Judging by its enthusiastic response, this vision had great appeal. Savonarola's promise of civic harmony, power, and glory had the capacity to unite rather than to divide, while the program of religious and political reform made the millennium seem tangible and attainable, within the power of the Florentines to effect by their own actions. "I believed and I do believe," wrote Bartolommeo Redditi, "because his preaching made Florence a paradise on earth." [57] The synthetic character of the vision made it possible for men of widely differing views to find in it something for themselves, some cynically, perhaps, some ecstatically, as they saw the promise of fulfilling their hearts' desires. Much has been written about the religious enthusiasm

---

54   Savonarola, *Prediche italiane*, II, p. 40.
55   Savonarola, *Compendium Revelationum*, pp. 227–8.
56   Joshua 23.16; Joel 3.4.
57   Bartolommeo Redditi, *Breve compendio e sommario della verità e profetata dal R.P. fra Girolamo da Ferrara,* ed. Joseph Schnitzer (Munich, 1902), p. 49.

Savonarola aroused, the mass processions and burning of vanities, the sudden rise in the number of men and women who entered religious orders, many of them from patrician families and with humanist education,[58] in short, of the revival of the penitential and ascetic spirit in Florence. Little has been said, however, about the more extreme responses, as men saw in Savonarola's prophecy the revival and fulfilment of all the old millenarian dreams, or discovered new ones. Nor has anyone seriously investigated the persistence of Savonarolan influence into the sixteenth century.[59] The following examples indicate not only the continuation of such influence, but also the radical temper of sixteenth century Savonarolans.

Giorgio Benigno, a Franciscan theologian who had been tutor to Piero de' Medici, clearly linked the dream of Florentine glory to Joachimite anti-Roman millenarianism. Savonarola was a true prophet, he wrote, who correctly interpreted the prophecy of the fall of Babylon as he himself had first heard it expounded in England. Christianity would spread universally, Christ and his Church would become one and reign for a thousand years. God had chosen Florence because she was the heart and center of Italy and the ancient ally of France. Besides, the Florentines were the most intelligent and vivacious of peoples, and the most dedicated to religion.[60]

Girolamo Benivieni, the poet and former intimate of the Medici household who became the chief publicist of the Savonarolans, expressed similar convictions in the songs he wrote for the friar's religious processions. In one of them he wrote that the time would come when the odor of Florentine sanctity would spread throughout the world, when the people would be drawn to receive Florence's holy laws and learn the true mode of governing and living. The leaves of the gentle Florentine lily would be extended farther than ever over her neighbors because Florence was the city of the elect, the New Jerusalem, the City of God. All the people of the world would conform to her one true religion.[61] For Benivieni, the Savonarolan prophecy was the means of resolving personal spiritual and intellectual difficulties. A Neoplatonist, he had begun to doubt whether his writings on divine love were consonant with his faith as a Christian, and his philosophy seemed only to emphasize the tension between worldly pursuits and a life of the spirit. The sudden death of his dear friend and mentor, Giovanni Pico della Mirandola,

---

[58]  Schnitzer, *Savonarola* I, pp. 415–18. I cite the Italian translation (see above, note 1) which is expanded and revised.

[59]  But important contributions have been made by Schnitzer, *Ibid.*, II, pp. 427–603 and in his "Die Flügschriftenliteratur für und wider Girolamo Savonarola," *Festgabe Karl Theodor von Heigel* (Munich, 1903); Mario Ferrara, *Savonarola*, 2 vols (Florence, 1952), II, pp. 7–72 and his *Contributo allo studio della poesia savonaroliana* (Pisa, 1921).

[60]  Giorgio Benigno (Drachisich), *Propheticae solutiones* (Florence, 1497).

[61]  Girolamo Benivieni, *Commento sopra a più sue canzoni et sonetti dello amore e della bellezza divina* (Florence, 1500) fols. CXII-CXIIII.

on November 17, 1494 (the same day that King Charles VIII entered Florence), cast Benivieni into a still more acute depression; but under the influence of Savonarola he entered into the work for reform, his tension resolved by the promise of the realization of the beatific vision in Florence, God's chosen city.[62] He continued to write and work for the cause for almost half a century, interpreting the prophecies in the light of events until his death in 1542 at the age of eighty-nine.[63]

While Benivieni wrote his songs for a popular audience, other Florentine Neoplatonists expressed their enthusiasm for Savonarola in esoteric forms. Some of them had long dreamed of a regeneration of society through the recovery of the universal wisdom. Marsilio Ficino believed the keys to unlock this wisdom were the Neoplatonic writings and those works of late antiquity which in his day were attributed to Hermes Trismegistus, the Chaldaic Oracles, Zoroaster and others, as well as Plato's own writings.[64] Pico della Mirandola believed that Pythagorean number theory and the Cabala were the means to pass from diversity to the One.[65] Nothing could have been more alien to Savonarola, and in a discussion between him and Pico reported to us by the humanist Piero Crinito, Savonarola plainly rejected Pico's ideas on the relation between Christianity and pagan philosophy.[66] Still, it was an axiom of Pico's and Ficino's views that, given the correct approach, seemingly diverse systems of thought could be reconciled, and some of their disciples applied this notion to Savonarola's prophecy. Giovanni Nesi was one of these. His tract, *The Oracle of the New Era*, published in Florence in 1497, owes much to Pico and Ficino, to Savonarola, and to Florentine civic traditions of the kind we have been examining.[67] It is a metaphorical stew that must be read to be fully savored, and only a faint idea of its bizarre and radical quality can be given here. Nesi compounded Florentine republicanism, the more occult forms of Neoplatonism, Neopythagoreanism, and Christian millenarianism, all in the most recondite symbolism, to show that Florence would become the utopia sought by civic patriot, Platonist and Christian reformer alike. In it Savonarola appears to Nesi in a dream as a moon-based seer, likened to Thoth-Hermes, the god-man of the Hermetic teachings. With the wisdom of Plato, Plotinus and the Cabala he unlocks the secrets still hidden in Holy Scriptures. Those whom he regenerates with

[62]   See my dissertation, "Prophecy and Humanism in Late Fifteenth Century Florence," (Ph.D. thesis, State University of Iowa, 1957) pp. 227–37.
[63]   Caterina Re, *Girolamo Benivieni fiorentino* (Città di Castello, 1906) p. 57.
[64]   Marsilio Ficino, *Della religione cristiana* (Florence, 1568) pp. 96, 109–15.
[65]   Eugenio Garin, *L'umanesimo italiano* (Bari, 1952) pp. 138–39.
[66]   Piero Crinito, *De honesta disciplina*, ed. Carlo Angieleri (Rome, 1955) pp. 104–5. See also Savonarola, *Prediche sull'Esodo*, ed. Piero Giorgio Ricci, 2 vols. (Rome, 1956), II, pp. 290–1, cited by Eugenio Garin, "Ricerche sugli scritti filosofici di Girolamo Savonarola opere inedite e smarrite", *Bibliothèque d'Humanisme et Renaissance*, XXI (1959) p. 291.
[67]   Giovanni Nesi, *Oruculum de novo saeculo* (Florence, 1497).

this revelation will build the new Florence on the model of the Pythagorean oracles, Plato's Republic and the Celestial Jerusalem. The city will extend its imperium and become the center of the Three-Fold Good. With the entrance of the sun into the house of Aries, the astrological Great Year will begin, bringing with it the renovation of religion. Thoughtful men who participate in the religious revival will ascend to the upper circle where they will learn the meaning of the final mysteries, gain insight into the human condition, and learn the philosophy of portents and prophecies. A new race of men will arise in Florence, the eagle's nest, the City of the Sun.

Savonarola's downfall in 1498 did not extinguish such hopes. Among the followers of Pico and Ficino, Nesi and Pico's nephew, Gianfrancesco Pico della Mirandola, in addition to Benivieni, continued to write and work for the fulfilment of the dream.[68] At the more popular level, some of the more radical versions of Savonarolan millenarianism appeared only after the friar's death. In 1534 Bartolommeo Rinuccini had a vision of Savonarola, who showed him that a Holy Pastor would carry on the Lord's work in Florence, which was the city chosen for the renovation of religion because the regular leadership had failed.[69] Perhaps the most extreme of all was the version of a Florentine priest, Giovanni da Miglio. In 1512 he produced a prophecy which he attributed to a certain Albert of Trent, a Carthusian, indicating that Albert had made the prophecy in 1436.[70] Albert of Trent, or more likely, Giovanni da Miglio, "predicted" the coming of Charles VIII, the tribulations of Italy, and the mission of Savonarola in Florence. Savonarola would reveal certain secrets, among them the destruction of the Church.[71] Kings and priests in every part of the world would be punished by the people and by black and white dogs – presumably a reference to the Dominicans, the Domini cani – who would devour the Church and cause the keys to drop from the adulterous hand. After the death of Savonarola a new religion would arise, preached by a man of the people in Florence, in the year 1504 or thereabouts. In Florence also, the leaders of the Church would gather and there they would find a new book in which the whole law of Christ would be restored.[72]

---

[68] See Nesi's poems in Biblioteca Riccardiana (Florence) Mss. 2750 and 2123. On Gianfrancesco Pico see especially his De veris calamitatum nostrorum temporum ad Leonem X Pont. Max. (Mirandola, 1519) and his De reformandis moribus, which is included in Giovanni Pico della Mirandola, Opera omnia, 2 vols. (Basel, 1601) II, pp. 885–90.

[69] Bartolommeo Rinuccini, Visione d'un piagnone (1534) (Florence, 1868.)

[70] Biblioteca Nazionale di Firenze Ms. Capponi 121. "Dictante ipsomet Frate Alberto Cartusiensis ordinis die xiiª Septembris salutis 1490 Scripsi Paduae", fol. 1. At end: "Copiata per me Prete Joanni d'Agnolo di Miglio da Cetica Addi 18 di Settenbre 1512", fol. 10v.

[71] "et destructionem ecclesiae non tacebit . .", fol. 3.

[72] "liber habetur novus in quo renovabitur tota lex inreprehensibilis Jesu Benedicti . . .", fol. 9.

Giovanni da Miglio was a pious and unsophisticated priest,[73] who expressed in the language of the popular prophecies what the Neoplatonist Giovanni Nesi clothed in the language of theosophic mystery. Together their writings give us an idea of the continuing eschatological ferment in Florence at this time. It was a ferment, it should be emphasized, that cannot be explained as the result of immediate economic difficulties or lower class unrest. The theme of democratic aspirations had long since become a part of a more general civic millenarian tradition of republicanism and Florentine leadership. Savonarola tapped this tradition and appropriated its language and themes for his own revivalist movement, and, although a history of the Savonarolan movement in the sixteenth century is still to be written, the appearance of visionaries like Bartolommeo Rinuccini and Giovanni da Miglio, and the reemergence of such ideas in the republican revolt of 1527,[74] suggests the continuing inspiration of the Savonarolan vision.

DONALD WEINSTEIN
*Rutgers, the State University, N.J.*

[73] On Giovanni see the biographical comments by his brother Agostino da Miglio, *Nuovo dialogo delle devozioni del Sacro Monte della Verna* (Florence, 1568), pp. 268–9. I am indebted to Signor Ivaldo Baglioni of the Biblioteca Nazionale of Florence for this reference and for invaluable help in identifying Giovanni da Miglio. So far I have not been able to identify Albertus Cartusiensis.
[74] On the influence of Savonarola and his followers in the republican revolt of 1527 see Cecil Roth, *The Last Florentine Republic* (London, 1925), p. 60 and *passim*.

# IV

# APPENDIX

# THE MILLENNIAL DREAM AS POETRY

*Poetic appeal* must be a factor in millenarianism – defined as anticipation of the return of a hero or divinity who will establish by fiat or leadership a revolutionary polity for the benefit of a coterie. Though it is impossible to calculate the relative importance of poetic appeal, medieval western literature, where evidence is now fairly well controlled, may guide us.

The myth of the slumbering hero who will arise to institute a select earthly paradise (e.g., the Seven Sleepers, Charlemagne, Frederick Barbarossa) was widespread and constantly retold.[1] King Arthur, who sleeps in Avalon until he will return to establish an earthly heaven for the Welsh, is an instance. The myth seems to combine Celtic, Teutonic, and Christian elements. Geoffrey of Monmouth, the first author who might have employed the myth in literature, did not, either because he did not know it, or because he thought his readers disinterested, or because his very delicate time-serving authorship dictated that he pose no such threat against his Norman patrons, who were trying to conquer the Welsh. The last of these three possibilities seems most probable. His successor and paraphraser, Wace, was patronized by Henry II, who campaigned in Wales and had reason to fear just such intangibles as mythic Arthur. Writing *roman* explicitly for the expansionist Angevin court, Wace had every economic, social, political, religious, and ethnic reason for avoiding mention of the myth; yet he did not resist including it at the very end of his poem, the emphatic point, though he disclaimed personal belief in it. His successor Layamon, writing midland English from Worcestershire (we know the deadly Cambrian-Saxon antagonism), went further than Wace and had the dying Arthur promise, "I will come again to my kingdom and dwell with the Britons in supreme joy." Layamon expressed no scepticism. More than two centuries later, Malory, from Warwickshire, who also had every political reason to exclude the myth from his already overburdened tale, first gave us *Hic jacet Arthurus Rex, quondam Rex que futurus*. In short, of these four popular poets, all of whom show clear evidence of catering to the prejudices of their chosen audiences, three include a millenarian myth antagonistic to the purely social prejudices. The obvious explanation is that the myth was poetically satisfying.

[1] E. K. Chambers, *Arthur of Britain* (1927), pp. 217–232, names many examples, found among every western nationality.

Analogous instances beside the Arthurian myth are plentiful, for apocalypses were a standard genre in medieval literature. For comparison I cite only the DUX prophecy of Dante's *Purgatorio* xxxiii. In this instance unquestionably the author of *De Monarchia* and *Convivio* had a fanatic personal desire for reanimation of the Empire, and modern readers have no difficulty identifying the DUX as Henry of Luxembourg. Moreover, in line with his polysemous method, Dante asks his readers to attach a factual political meaning to his verses at almost every turn. Nevertheless, though he is most specific and unambiguous about Henry in *Paradiso* xvii, 82, xxx, 137 and elsewhere in his many works, he is so obscure about DUX in *Purgatorio* that his contemporary audience apparently did not visualize Henry, the Empire, or the hopes of that specific coterie. The whole apocalypse of *Purgatorio* xxix-xxxiii is clearly intended as *poetry* in the best medieval, that is, Virgilian, sense. The nascent babe of Virgil's Fourth Eclogue, which no critic has ever been able to explain in other than purely poetical terms, was equally Dante's model with the Scriptures. I, at least, believe that he included this element in his apocalypse primarily, if not solely, because it was poetically satisfying. I assume that the illiterate find the same kind of satisfaction in other millenarian myths.

CHARLES W. JONES
*University of California (Berkeley)*

# A NOTE ON RELATIVE DEPRIVATION THEORY AS APPLIED TO MILLENARIAN AND OTHER CULT MOVEMENTS

I will not attempt to review the history of theories of deprivation and relative deprivation, especially since they enter, explicitly or implicitly, into so many explanations of specific religious and political movements and so many general theories in this area. I will rather attempt to supply a statement of my own viewpoint, recognizing that many parts of it can be found in the works of others.

Relative deprivation is defined as a negative discrepancy between legitimate expectation and actuality. Where an individual or a group has a particular expectation and furthermore where this expectation is considered to be a proper state of affairs, and where something less than that expectation is fulfilled, we may speak of relative deprivation. It is important to stress that deprivation *is* relative and not absolute. To a hunting and gathering group with an expectation of going hungry one out of four days, failure to find game is not a relative deprivation, although it may produce marked discomfort. It is a truism that for a multi-millionnaire to lose all but his last million in a stock market crash *is* a major deprivation. The deprivation, then, is not a particular objective state of affairs, but a difference between an anticipated state of affairs and a less agreeable actuality. We must furthermore consider the expectations as *standards*, rather than merely as prophecies of what will happen tomorrow.

The discovery of what constitutes serious deprivation for particular groups or individuals is a difficult empirical problem. It requires careful attention to the reference points that people employ to judge their legitimate expectations, as well as to their actual circumstances. Among the obvious reference points that can be, and are used for such judgments are: (1) one's past versus one's present circumstances; (2) one's present versus one's future circumstances; (3) one's own versus some one else's present circumstances.

The first and third types of judgment are easily illustrated. Any one who worked among the Navaho Indians in the 1940's was obliged to notice that for many Navahos the Government livestock reduction of the 1930's had created a situation where they viewed themselves as worse off than they had been, and as worse off than they should have been. And the impression one derives from Margaret Mead's account of the Manus, in *New Lives for Old*, is that these people regard themselves as worse off than they should be, by comparison with full participants in Western material culture.

Perhaps the second type of judgment requires some elucidation. If, let us say, a group of elderly pensioners have a particular standard of living, and have reason to believe that the shrinking dollar value of their pensions will not long permit this, then, with only a little strain they may be regarded as relatively deprived: their *prospective actuality* is worse than their standard of legitimate expectation.

The critical feature of these and subsequent examples is that they involve not only relative deprivation, but a deprivation which stems from *change*, actual or anticipated. It is where conditions decline by comparison with the past, where it is expected that they will decline, in the future by comparison with the present, and where shifts in the relative conditions of two groups occur, that the deprivation experience becomes significant for efforts at remedial action. Indeed it is change itself that creates discrepancies between *legitimate* expectations and actuality, either by worsening the conditions of a group, or by exposing a group to new standards.

The previous examples are very much concerned with material goods. It is not necessary, however, to assume that all deprivation experiences are primarily concerned with such goods. I have attempted a rough classification of types of deprivation. They fall into four groups: possessions, status, behavior, and worth. They may furthermore be classified as *personal* and *group* or *category* experiences. A man whose house is destroyed by fire experiences a personal deprivation of possessions – since this is *not* an experience most of us plan on. An American Indian tribe expropriated from its land, experiences group deprivation of possessions. Allowing for this, we have, in fact, at least three measuring points for deprivation, and at least four areas of deprivation, classified in each case as personal versus group (e.g., tribe) or category (e.g., Negro). This provides a 24-cell table of deprivations, one too large to illustrate in detail.

We can, however, eliminate the purely personal deprivations. If the individual does not find that there are others in like circumstances, their significance for social movements, millenarian or other, political or religious, would appear to be trivial. I will attempt to illustrate the others, using Navaho examples and only one frame of reference for comparison: present (undesirable) versus past (desirable). Navahos who had large herds in the 1920's lost them through livestock reduction in the 1930's. Those with such herds constituted a category, and their loss of stock adversely affected other Navahos who had benefitted from their generosity, so that the Navahos as a group or set of groups experienced deprivation of possessions, with respect to diet, trade goods procured through sale of animal products, etc. In addition, the large owners suffered deprivation of status. The society was reduced to far more egalitarian relationships; the man who had had followers to herd for him, gratitude for generosity, and standing because of his wealth now was almost as badly off as any other Navaho. His comparison here was to his past status in *his* group, not vis-à-vis the outside world. These were among the key deprivations experienced by Navahos during this period.

With the decline in livestock holdings came a necessary decline in certain types of behavior viewed as desirable by Navahos. Kin did not fulfil their obligation to kin, neighbors to neighbors, "rich" to poor, because the where-withal for reciprocity and generosity was no longer there. There was a pervasive feeling that people did not *behave* as they should, or as they once did, and this I would call a deprivation in the area of behavior. This particular type of deprivation can be equally well illustrated by a shift to a different frame of reference for deprivation. With continued exposure to Americans, under circumstances which make Americans a model, some Navahos have come to feel that they do not behave as they should, by comparison with Americans: they are dirty, or superstitious, or eat "bad" foods (e.g., prairie dogs).

Finally, I come to worth, which is to some degree a residual category. It refers to a person's experience of others' estimation of him on grounds over and above his alterable characteristics – of possessions, status, and behavior. It is best illustrated again by those Navahos who use the outside world as a point of reference. Navahos with most contact have come to realize that to some degree neither wealth, occupational status, nor "proper" behavior can alter the fact that they are Navahos, and that they are therefore regarded as inferior and undesirable. Their total worth, then, is not what they feel it should be, and they experience a sense of deprivation in this regard. Many Navahos are still sufficiently insulated from the larger world not to have this experience.

Now I conceive of any of these types of deprivation, measured by any of these reference points, to be the possible basis for efforts at remedial action to overcome the discrepancy between actuality and legitimate aspiration. (They can also be the basis for apathy, disorganization, despair, or suicide.) Insofar as the actions are undertaken by individuals and not by groups they are not relevant for present considerations. But the fact of deprivation is clearly an insufficient basis for predicting whether remedial efforts will occur, and, if they occur, whether they will have as aims changing the world, transcending it, or withdrawing from it, whether the remedy will be sought in direct action or ritual, and whether it will be sought with the aid of supernatural powers or without. The Navahos, have, for example, attempted to influence the Indian Service, hide their sheep, form political organizations, and protest to Congress. They have, in isolated instances, had visions of the total destruction of the whites, and in groups, Navaho members of the peyote cult have used the ritual of that cult both to attempt to foresee further Government plans and to seek new wealth through God's help.

I take it that the interest of the conference in millenarian movements was primarily in those movements which seek supernatural help, or which, at any rate, see supernatural intervention in the affairs of men.

A sense of blockage – of the insufficiency of ordinary action – seems to me, as it has seemed to many others, the source of the more supernaturally based millenarian, nativistic, revitalistic, and cargo movements – to use terms applied to various types of movements which we somehow sense as belonging together in some respects. And, difficult as it may be to anticipate whether a group's aspiration will be to return to the past, achieve the standards of the outside world, or transcend earthly standards completely, there is usually no serious difficulty in deciding whether, at a particular time, a particular group faces obstacles which are empirically unsurmountable in short-run terms. No one knew whether the Navahos would become violent over stock reduction, but every one knew that in the 20th century the violence of a few tens of thousands of American Indians could be put down if it became necessary to do so. We then add to our focus on deprivation types, attention to the question whether direct action could be expected to solve the group's problems. If it could not, we expect a correspondingly large increment of religious and magical action, although we cannot outlaw the possibility that this may lead to violence.

If we now turn to types of deprivation, we can have some expectation that the ideology of the movement will be related to the type of deprivation – or at least that emphasis in the ideology will be so related. The Plains Ghost Dance, although it originated elsewhere, spread among the Plains when the buffalo were gone – and anticipated the marvelous removal of the white man and a life of abundant hunting and gathering. It was oriented to deprivation of possessions. The Handsome Lake cult, originating long after the conquest of the Iroquois, focussed vigorously on morality and thus had a strong component of reaction to deprivation in the behavioral area. Peyotism, one of the most viable of American Indian nativistic movements, contains in its beliefs and values: elements of magical aid, including assistance in gaining more wealth; certain compensations for loss of status; a code of morality vigorously opposing drunkenness, adultery, and shiftlessness, three plagues of Reservation life; and hundreds of items designed to restore the self-respect of the Indian as an Indian. It is no accident that peyotism can therefore appeal to the traditional, who have suffered material deprivation, the formerly well-to-do, who have suffered status deprivation, the disorganized sufferers from deprivation in the behavioral area, and the marginal men with their ambivalence about being Indian in a white world. No one peyotist need come to peyotism for all of these, but a variety of sufferers can be accommodated.

This framework seems to me to be a profitable one for the inspection of various cults, including millenarian movements. It is not limited to absolute deprivation, nor to the assumption that the deprived are always those at the bottom of the status hierarchy. By the same token, it has a certain excessive flexibility. It is always possible after the fact to find deprivations. What is important is to be able to predict either the types of deprivations that lead to certain ideological formations, or the degree of deprivation which crystallizes a cult movement. To date neither of these goals is achieved, although we are closer to the first than to the second. It is more appealing to me, however, to attempt to work within this formula than to assume randomness of social behavior or an indefinite plurality of causes. At a minimum, it is fair to say that millenarian, revitalistic, and cargo cult movements do not arise under circumstances where the members of a group think that the world is so nearly perfect that transformation or translation must be just around the corner. There is sufficient evidence of abundant distress in many instances to make this approach at least valuable for exploration.

Lastly, we come to the millenarian movement itself, rather than to the family of movements of which it is a part. My own experience has been largely with other than millenarian movements, and my exposure to the millenarian materials presented at the conference was a new experience.

The question is, what good is relative deprivation theory for the analysis of such movements? First, I will give to the adherents of the boredom theory of millenarian movements as many specific instances as they choose to claim, provided it is not maintained that *most* millenarian *movements* involving some active participation of believers are inspired by boredom. Second, I grant nothing to the utility of theories which are based on supposedly pan-human experiences, since constants cannot be used to explain variables. Third, the fact that a movement is *millenarian* is a totally insufficient basis for deciding what type of deprivation is important (in cases not involving boredom); both inspection of the ideology and of the condition of the adherents is necessary for this purpose, as Cohn's paper amply demonstrates. There is no reason why only the deprivations of peasants, and why only hunger and landlessness need be considered as bases for deprivation, or why the proof that it wasn't the peasants (or the disoriented new urbanites) that were involved is any reason not to look further for the deprivations of groups that did participate. Fourth – and this is prejudice – I am unwilling to admit that pure existential unease or concern with spiritual discomfort dissociated from the social conditions of participants forms a useful basis for explaining these movements.

This all adds up to the assumption that millenarian movements are susceptible to analysis in terms of deprivation theory, in the same way as cargo cults, the Handsome Lake cult, the peyote cult, and so on. Furthermore, the tense expectation of the millenium is not a sufficient basis for classifying these movements, since the things their ideologies react against are diverse. Hence there is one sense in which they should be parcelled out with their nearest non-millenarian cognates, and this we did not attempt. It is possible that the Tupi-Guarani movements, for example, belong in the family of ideologies of expansion, quite as much as in the family of millenarian movements. This position, however, also leaves something to be desired, since we have an uneasy sense that in one way or another the millenarian movements *do* share something besides tense expectation. I would suggest that many of them have one thing in common. The millenarian ideology often justifies the *removal* of the participants in the movement from the ordinary spheres of life. Indeed, this removal is frequently not only social but spatial, whether it takes the form of withdrawal or of wandering. I would suggest that the deprivations which form the background for the movement not only involve the sense of blockage to which I have referred earlier, which leads to resort to supernaturalism, but also the sense of a social order which cannot be reconstituted to yield the satisfactions desired. The millenarian ideology justifies the removal of the participants from that social order, by reassuring them that the order itself will not long continue, and frees them to indulge in phantasy about the ideal society, or to attempt to build it in isolation or through violent attempts against the existing order. Those who suffer from acute deprivation and cannot withdraw from the world can only constitute sects of the elect, or utilize devices to compensate for deprivation. The millenarian ideology justifies withdrawal, and that is its functional significance.

DAVID F. ABERLE
*Brandeis University*

# THE PROBLEM OF EXPLANATION

The report of the Conference's discussion, on p. 14, takes note of a "third interpretation" of milllennial movements and also notes, accurately, that this interpretation was not pursued by the Conference. I should now like to develop this interpretation a bit further.

The question at issue can be stated very sharply. We have a good deal of evidence about millennial movements – their ideologies, their actions, and their cycles of development. This evidence, like any other evidence, can be made meaningful only by being related to some larger whole, in this case the society in which the movement has its being. One way of establishing this relationship, the way pursued by the Conference, may be termed synthetic: one asks what caused the movement, what psychological factors impelled people to join it, etc. Another way, which I think would be more fruitful, could be termed analytic; it would take the evidence of the movement itself as grounds for inference about the relationship of the movement to society, and about the psychology of the members. The movement always subscribes to an ideology that empties the existing social order of all value; it also invariably takes the form of a physical movement – a withdrawal from the existing order. Thus on the one hand its ideology is arbitrary, extravagant, and fantastic; on the other hand its social structure is all but nonexistent: it is a perfectly plastic mass, without the solidity that comes from a practical, working relationship to reality. Obviously, then, the typical member is a person radically alienated from the existing order and, either inherently or temporarily, lacking in qualities of criticism, realism, and intellectual honesty. And equally obviously, the principle of self-preservation requires the movement to maintain its total separation from the existing order, by various forms of internal or external withdrawal, or by putting itself into a posture of violent nihilism vis-à-vis the establishment.

Now, still proceeding analytically, it would be in order to relate the movement to society by constructing typologies of alienation and withdrawal. Here the task is that of the social psychologist and sociologist; I shall offer only one or two illustrations. For example, one type of objectively alienated person would be the man whose social and economic position is so precarious that he lacks even the attachment to the existing order that may be presupposed for the ordinary lower classes. Another type would be the man so neurotic that he cannot find adequate pleasure in the ordinary sources of delight. Another might be the man belonging to a persecuted race or religion. A typology of this sort, properly refined and detailed, would, in my opinion, be capable of producing generally valid statements about which types of alienation are apt to be associated with millennial movements. Typologies of withdrawal and of societal crisis could produce valid statements about the development of millennial movements and their origin, respectively. Thus the movement would be explained.

Such explanation would, as I have said, have the virtue of being based solidly on the positive evidence; since, as the Conference has shown, the evidence shows striking uniformities from movement to movement, there is no reason why the whole phenomenon of socially-active millennialism could not be comprehended within a single, complex analytical structure. On the other hand, it must be conceded that analysis of movements cannot by itself tell us why particular movements erupt into being (or who, specifically, will join them), except in circular terms: the movement includes or presupposes X; therefore when we find a movement we can be sure of the presence of X. But this circularity is equally present in the synthetic explanations. If we bear in mind the kind of causative factors that were considered at the Conference – anxiety, sense of deprivation, social suffering, etc. – we must admit that in no single case is it even remotely possible to deduce the movement from any single factor, any group of factors, or any definable degree of intensity of such factors. All such efforts lead directly to the circle: X is alleged to be necessary for the movement, but the only way we know that X is present is that a movement has come into being. Ideally a synthetic explanation based on precisely measurable causal factors would be possible; practically it is not, partly because so much evidence is irrevocably lost, partly because even precise measurement could not logically exclude non-causal correlations. And this last consideration is particularly to the point when such a crucial and controversial factor as the pattern of social recruitment is studied. Even if it could be proven that most people came into a movement from the lower classes, the fact might mean nothing more than that the lower classes were more numerous in the established society. Or, even if it could be proven that most people came into a movement from the middle classes, the meaning of that fact could hardly be determined within the framework given by the established society, which ordinarily does *not* produce movements. This hypothetical case would represent a supreme triumph of the synthetic approach to explanation, and yet even it would remain pointless unless picked up by an analytical explanation of the movement itself.

Finally, I should like to observe that explanation through typological analysis would unify the work of historians, sociologists, anthropologists, and social psychologists, in a highly desirable way. The historian who tries to produce a precise reconstruction of a particular case will be far better able to do so if he can make use of a well-developed body of abstractions. The synthetic explanation, however, lacks this unifying characteristic – within its framework, conceivably, the historian can contribute hard, positivistic lumps of fact to the sociologists, etc., but the latter can offer nothing at all to him, for the general theories of causation will never be worth much in a specific case.

HOWARD KAMINSKY
*University of Washington*

# A NOTE ON THE MILLENNIUM IN ISLAM

The medieval Islamic material, historically, is reasonably comparable to the medieval Western material. Both urban and peasant movements of both passive expectation and active revolt were nourished on a general Islamic assurance that a time of universal justice and well-being on earth was to come just before the End; this assurance is explicitly identifiable with the Christian millennialism (i.e., Jesus is to descend from the skies, etc.); but it did not ordinarily imply any set 1000 years.

The Mahdi, who was to usher in the ideal state, was commonly expected to rule seven (or five or nine) years. Jesus was sometimes expected to live for forty (or seventy) years after killing the Mahdi's opponent, the Anti-Christ. Both the Mahdi and Jesus were usually expected to die a natural death before the actual End of history, which, however, was to supervene shortly after their deaths (but in some versions, as much as 120 years after), and of which their careers were one of the Signs. In one version, the Mahdi is succeeded by his descendants in a forty-year age of justice.

Numerous predictions of how long Islâm would last involved calculations of a cosmic week of 1000-year days; Muhammad was often placed midway in the sixth 1000-year day, and the End at the end of it, till in fact five centuries of Islâm had passed; then expectations commonly focused on the end of the first millennium after Muhammad. In Ismâ'îlî circles, this sort of calculation was made into a full cyclicism, in which the seventh 1000-year day was sometimes to be introduced by the Mahdi (though not necessarily 7000-years after Muhammad); after the millennium had elapsed, however, instead of any Last Judgment, there would simply be a renewal of the historical 1000 year cycle. The Druzes may have started out with some such expectation, but at least later seem to have looked for Hâkim (their equivalent of the Mahdi) to return on earth permanently. The Nizârî Ismâ'îlîs (Assassins) at one time believed that the Mahdi had already come and triumphed, and that they were already living in the Millennium, which was interpreted in terms of a timeless state of mind.

For analysis of theories about the Mahdi, see Christiaan Snouck Hurgronje, *Der Mahdi,* in *Verspreide Geschriften* (Bonn, 1923) vol. I, 147–181, and 'Abd-al-Rahmân Ibn-Khaldûn, *The Muqaddima,* translated by Franz Rosenthal (New York, 1958), Vol. II, pp. 156–231. For an extensive treatment of social aspects of Mahdi expectations, see Emanuel Sarkisyanz, *Russland und der Messianismus des Orients* (Tübingen, 1955), chapters XVII-XXIII.

MARSHALL G. S. HODGSON
*University of Chicago*

## FURTHER BIBLIOGRAPHICAL NOTE

P. Casanova, *Mohammed et la fin du monde*. Paris, 1911.

D. M. Donaldson, *The Shi'ite Religion*. London, 1933.

I. Friedlaender, *The Heterodoxies of the Shiites according to Ibn Hazm*. New Haven, 1909 (originally in *JAOS*).

M. J. de Goeje, *Mémoire sur les Carmathes du Bahrain*. 2nd ed., Leiden, 1886.

Martin Sprengling, "The Berlin Druze Lexicon", *American Journal of Semitic Languages*, Vol. LVI (1939), pp. 388–414, and Vol. LVII (1940), pp. 75 ff.

M. G. S. Hodgson, "How did the Early Shī'a become Sectarian?", *JAOS*, 75 (1955), pp. 1–13.

M. G. S. Hodgson, *The Order of Assassins*. The Hague, 1955.

J. N. Hollister, *The Shi'a in India*. London, 1953.

B. Lewis, *The Origins of Isma'ilism*. Cambridge, 1940.

D. S. Margoliouth, *On Mahdis and Mahdism* (Proceedings of the British Academy, VII, 1916, 213–233).

# A NOTE ON THE DIGGERS

The hopes aroused by the revolutionary situation in mid-seventeenth-century England were probably the significant factor in the prominence of millenarian tendencies in left-wing English puritanism. There has been no doubt about the literal millenarianism of the Fifth Monarchy Men, the one sect openly unreconciled to the Restoration of 1660 and prepared to establish by violence the reign of "King Jesus." Concerning Gerrard Winstanley and the Diggers, however, there has been some question because of the apparently secular and class-conscious nature of their social utopianism. Marxian and other modern left-wing writers, beginning with Eduard Bernstein whose *Socialismus und Demokratie in der grossen Englischen Revolution* was published in 1895, have been responsible for the view that the religious terminology and symbolism of Winstanley cloaked an essentially economic, extraordinarily novel, and profoundly revolutionary plan for renovating English society – a plan which, for the Marxians, foreshadows modern, class-conscious, communism.

These writers have been mainly responsible for drawing attention to a previously neglected phase of the English puritan revolutionary movement, but their interpretation has been convincingly challenged by modern scholarship, particularly by A. S. P. Woodhouse in *Puritanism and Liberty* (London, 1938, Chicago, 1950), p. 99, n. 1 of Introduction; by George H. Sabine in *The Works of Gerrard Winstanley* (Ithaca, 1941), especially pp. 36–51; and by Winthrop S. Hudson in "Economic and Social Thought of Gerrard Winstanley: Was He a Seventeenth-century Marxist?". *Journal of Modern History,* XVIII (1946), 1–21. Since these scholars have fully and persuasively shown that Winstanley's thought was distinctly millenarian, only a brief summary of the case for this interpretation need be given here.

There is no question about the originality of Winstanley's communistic theory of society, but his adherence to a millenarian framework for his communism was basic to his way of thinking. Indeed had not Winstanley employed the familiar imagery of millenarianism he would not have experienced even the transient success he had. In no other millenarian movement had there been any initiating act comparable to the digging of the common waste land on St. George's Hill, Surrey, for the purpose of sowing it with parsnips, carrots, and beans. But Winstanley asserted that he had been summoned to this action by the Lord and the public declaration he then made was recognizably an eschatological sign. The digging was not the beginning of a worldly revolution but the outward manifestation of an inner confidence that the time had come for God's intervention. The millennium was to begin in England where at one time in the past, before the Norman usurpation, the land had presumably been a "common treasury." "I have Writ, I have Acted, I have Peace:" declared Winstanley, "and now I must wait to see the Spirit do his own work in the hearts of others, and whether England shall be the first Land, or some other, wherein Truth shall sit down in triumph." The eventual failure of the digging experiment naturally disillusioned Winstanley about the imminence of the millennium in England, but, instead of abandoning all hope, he retreated to a pre-millennial position. After Cromwell had won the battle of Worcester in 1651 Winstanley set forth in *The law of freedom in a platform* the Holy Commonwealth which Cromwell could, if he would, inaugurate preparatory to the millennium. What happened to Winstanley after this abortive attempt to influence Cromwell is not known.

WILLSON COATES
*University of Rochester*

# INDEX

## I. PERSONAL NAMES

## II. PLACE NAMES

## III. SUBJECT INDEX